George W. Liebmann is a lawyer and historian specialising in American and international history. His publications include *Diplomacy Between the Wars: Five Diplomats and the Shaping of the Modern World* and *The Last American Diplomat: John D. Negroponte and the Changing Face of US Diplomacy* (both I.B.Tauris)

THE FALL OF THE HOUSE OF

SPEYER

The Story of a Banking Dynasty

GEORGE W. LIEBMANN

I.B. TAURIS

LONDON · NEW YORK

Published in 2015 by
I.B.Tauris & Co. Ltd
London • New York
www.ibtauris.com

Copyright © 2015 George W. Liebmann

ISBN: 978 1 78453 176 8
eISBN: 978 0 85772 928 6

A full CIP record for this book is available from the British Library
A full CIP record is available from the Library of Congress

Library of Congress Catalog Card Number: available

Typeset by Freerange
Printed and bound in Sweden by ScandBook AB

Nobody in the nineteenth century or before (obviously) ever predicted that nationalism would be the strongest single force sweeping the world in the twentieth century. Other things were predicted – the military/industrial complex, the rise of Russia and America, German aggression, the revolt of the poor, the socialist revolution, enormous scientific and technological transformations, etc. etc. – but not that no movement, unless arm in arm with nationalism, had any chance of success in this moment of history.

Isaiah Berlin to Hamilton Fish Armstrong, 19 June 1972, in
H. Hardy and M. Pottle (eds), *Isaiah Berlin: Building, Letters
1960–1975* (London: Chatto and Windus, 2013), p. 496

CONTENTS

LIST OF ILLUSTRATIONS

ACKNOWLEDGEMENTS

The author is greatly indebted to three individuals: John Lukacs, who suggested to me that the subject was worth writing about; Antony Lentin, of Wolfson College, Cambridge, who has unselfishly shared with me much of the knowledge acquired in his preparation of *Banker Traitor Scapegoat Spy?*; and Hugo Beit, of New York City, grand-nephew of the Speyer brothers, who shared with me his recollections of James, documents about the last days of the German firm, Eduard's travel diary and the Speyer code book.

I am indebted to the President and Fellows of Wolfson College, Cambridge, for the facilities made available on several visits there.

I am also indebted to Joseph W. Bennett, Librarian of the Library Company of the Baltimore Bar, for obtaining books on inter-library loan, and to the staffs of the Sheridan Library of the Johns Hopkins University; the McKeldin Library of the University of Maryland; the Enoch Pratt Free Library, Baltimore; the Friedheim Music Library of the Peabody Conservatory of Music, Baltimore; the Library of Congress; the Library of the London School of Economics; and the Cambridge University Library.

I also owe a debt to the manuscript librarians of the Scott Polar Research Institute (Robert Scott Papers); the London School of Economics (George Paish Papers); the New York Public Library (James Speyer Papers); the Princeton University Library (George McAneny Papers); the National Archives, Lanham, Maryland (OSS Papers); Harvard Art Museum Archives (Paul Sachs Papers); and the Georgetown University Library (Richard Helms Papers).

Several little-known books have been of special value. They include William McNeal's *American Money and the Weimar Republic* (New York: Columbia University Press, 1986); Theresa Collins's *Otto Kahn: Art, Money, and Modern Times* (Chapel Hill: University of North Carolina Press, 2002); Peter Panayi's *The Enemy in Our Midst: Germans in Britain During the First*

World War (Oxford: Berg, 1991); and Philip Hoare, *Wilde's Last Stand: Decadence, Conspiracy and the First World War* (London: Duckworth, 1997).

Antony Lentin and my elder son, George W. Liebmann, Jr, read the manuscript and made helpful suggestions.

No thanks are due to Director John O. Brennan and the FOIA staff of the US Central Intelligence Agency which over a three-year period repeatedly missed promised deadlines for production of documents relating to James Speyer Kronthal, including his suicide notes.

As always, my greatest debt is to my wife, Anne-Lise Liebmann, my law partner, Orbie R. Shively, and my legal assistant, Susan H. Tifft, for providing peace of mind while I was engaged in research and writing.

INTRODUCTION

This is the chronicle of the last half-century of a once-famed international banking house with offices in Frankfurt, London and New York. The New York office closed in 1939, bringing to an end a firm that had endured for 102 years. The causes of its demise ran in parallel: one institutional and one personal.

The institutional cause was the recrudescence of nationalism before, during and after World War I, which aggravated prejudices against international bankers (not merely Jewish ones) and free traders generally, while diminishing their role and importance. This was accompanied by 'increasing state control, high taxation and organized labour'. This triad first began in Great Britain and Germany and then, 15 years later, in the United States. The two brothers who presided over the London and New York offices, as well as the in-law who was head of the Frankfurt house, also had the embarrassment of having been decorated by the Kaiser.

The personal cause for the demise of the house derived from the prickliness and vanity of both James and Edgar Speyer. This led to Edgar's enforced departure from the United Kingdom and to James's increased isolation after World War I.

The legacy of the members of the firm endures less in finance than in their remarkably far-sighted philanthropy, extending to their spouses. Their favoured causes include the management, and not merely the financing, of the London tube and omnibus system, the preservation of the Proms concerts, the patronage of notable musicians, including Richard Strauss and Edvard Grieg, and the creation of the Museum of the City of New York, America's first privately financed municipal museum. Additionally, James founded the Speyer School for gifted and talented children within a public school system and helped found the Provident Loan Society in New York. Edgar founded the Poplar Hospital, the Whitechapel Art Gallery and the King Edward VII Hospital in London, in addition to providing support for the Scott Antarctic expeditions. Both brothers were at least on the periphery of efforts to forestall or mediate World War I. The German branch of the family, and James, generously supported the University of Frankfurt and Paul Ehrlich's sulfa drug research. Edgar's wife Leonora won the Pulitzer Prize for Poetry in 1927; James's wife, Ellin Prince Speyer, helped found a pioneering settlement house which antedated the more famous Hull House of Jane Addams and Henry Street Settlement of Lillian Wald, and was an imaginative leader of the movement to prevent cruelty to animals, sponsoring a colourful Work Horses' March in New York. She also founded what is now the world's largest animal hospital as well as clubs for working girls and the girls' division of the New York Police Athletic League.

The brothers, who were far from unostentatious, lived on a scale unlikely to be seen again. James's financial district office was a replica of a Florentine villa; his Fifth Avenue home, built in 1915 and demolished in the 1950s, had a port-cochere and occupied a large part of a square block; his 200-acre estate at Scarborough on the Hudson was constructed to a similar scale. Edgar's house near Grosvenor Square (46 Grosvenor Street), which was commenced in 1910 and was used for concerts and for dinners for up to 200 people, cost £150,000 leasehold, the equivalent of £11.4 million today. In 1960 it became the Japanese Embassy and is now the headquarters of a stock-broking firm and was said to have 'ostentatiously had a silver bath'. His summer home at Overstrand in Norfolk is now a 28-room hotel, and his house on Washington Square in New York is part of the New York University Law School. When James entertained the officers of the German High Seas Fleet at his country home in 1912, the guests were transported in one direction by yacht and, in the other, by private train. The German family, not to be outdone, built a house that is now the nucleus of the leading hotel in Frankfurt.

The implosion of Speyer and Co. in 1939, battered by British and American Germano-phobia and German anti-Semitism, had an almost inconceivably dramatic aftermath. An associate of the firm, James Speyer Kronthal, a cousin by marriage, named after James by a long-time partner, according to undocumented allegations by some former officials of the CIA was assigned in the declining years of the firm to assist in a distasteful (and still concealed) business: the ransoming of modern artworks from Hitler's Germany by their exiled Jewish owners. In that capacity, Kronthal supposedly negotiated with Goebbels and Goering. He later allegedly worked with the Dulles brothers at Sullivan and Cromwell and for Allen Dulles in the wartime Berne station of the Office of Strategic Services (OSS), becoming its station chief after the war. His role there is somewhat shrouded in mystery, but likely extended to efforts to recover artworks looted by the Nazis. He was not among the OSS personnel commended for participation in the famous negotiations involving agents of Himmler and General Wolff and Kesselring resulting in a premature German surrender on the Italian front. Literature generated in the half-world inhabited by estranged CIA agents and Holocaust deniers includes an alleged transcript (almost certainly a forgery) of a supposed interrogation conducted by him in Switzerland of Hermann Muller, the last head of the Gestapo, who some allege was later secretly brought to the United States by the CIA.

It is asserted in three undocumented books that Kronthal, allegedly a closet homosexual, was found in compromising circumstances by the Germans, and that the records of this may also have been exploited by the Russians. Kronthal died in 1953, after an interview with Allen Dulles, an apparent suicide. One version asserts that he was offered the Deputy Directorship of the CIA and, conscience-stricken, confessed all to Dulles. Another asserts that his vulnerability was revealed in the course of the positive vetting resulting from the Truman loyalty security order and the so-called 'Lavender Scare' and that, on being confronted by Dulles, he was invited (or perhaps also assisted) to 'do the right thing', leaving behind a cryptic note to his sister stating that he did not wish to wait for 1984, a possible reference to the consequences which might have ensued if treachery on his part had been revealed at the height of the McCarthy period. It is incontestable that he worked for Speyer and for the OSS and CIA, and that he committed suicide. The reflections on his character and that of the Speyer firm in its last days require better evidence than any that has yet emerged.

PROLOGUE

Early Days

'A patrician one-man banking house
[which] seemed downright exotic'

The Speyers were not untypical of the great German-Jewish banking dynasties. It was both the glory and the fate of Europe's Jews to have been driven into occupations from which Christians were excluded by the medieval proscription of usury, a fate similar to that of later Greek and Armenian minorities in Muslim countries. Similar exclusions from the military, state bureaucracies and, in some places, from the ownership of land drove them into professional occupations for which education was required – the law, medicine and journalism, to name three. These exclusions, as the historian Gotz Aly has recently shown, became advantages as society industrialized. In all countries of Europe and even in England, Jews were dominant in merchant banking and highly influential in the professions, and in international banking their relative rootlessness provided a competitive advantage.

The Speyers are said to have been involved in some form of banking since the mid-fourteenth century. A head of the family, Michael Speyer, died in Frankfurt in 1686. Joseph Speyer, a rabbi, died in 1729, bequeathing a foundation known as the Joseph Speyer Stiftung (charitable trust) based on a fund of 4,000 florins. Historically, the Speyers had been the richest Jewish family in Frankfurt. The American branch was established in 1837 and became Speyer and Co. in 1878. A branch was set up in England in 1861. In the period 1770–1800, the Speyers were said to be worth 604,050 florins as against 109,325 for the Frankfurt Rothschilds. Isaak Speyer was nominated as an Imperial Court banker, leaving the Isaac Speyer Stiftung, valued at $17,000 in 1905. After 1787, Isaak's business was carried on by his three sons, but was discontinued in 1841. In the meantime, Isaak

Speyer's younger brother's son, Joseph Speyer, took over his father-in-law's banking business, the Ellissen firm, founded in 1809 and renamed Lazard Speyer Ellissen in 1818. Joseph's brother, Philip Speyer, came to New York in 1837 and established the American branch of the firm, which functioned as a mercantile and foreign exchange establishment, the export-import business being discontinued in 1878; he died in Frankfurt in 1876. James and Edgar Speyer were his grandsons. Philip was the first banker to float Union bonds in Europe during the Civil War. (The triumph of the Union cause owed more to Central European financiers and immigrants, including many Union soldiers and generals, than has generally been recognized.) The brothers' father, Gustavus Speyer, came to New York in 1847 and returned to Frankfurt in 1863, where he died 20 years later.

The Speyer firm was so long-established that it gave both Jacob Schiff and Otto Kahn of Kuhn Loeb their initial contacts in New York: Schiff in 1865, Kahn in 1893. Kahn had been employed by Deutsche Bank in London before Edgar Speyer offered him a job as an arbitrage clerk at Speyer in New York.

James Speyer inherited his interest in the New York firm from his Uncle Philip. He was born in New York in July 1861, attended a gymnasium, the Wochler School, in Frankfurt and thereafter studied at Oxford, where he became a friend of Eduard Beit, who eventually became his brother-in-law. At Oxford, he contracted syphilis, which left him sterile. While at Oxford, James introduced Beit to his sister Lucie, who was then 11 years old, having been born in 1870. She married Beit 12 years later, in 1892.

James began his banking career in London and Paris, returning to New York in 1885. Edgar settled in London in 1886 and was naturalized in 1892. James was described throughout his career as 'small, dapper, starch-collared, and rather prickly'. He was the only Jew to be admitted to the New York Racquet Club, and it was said that he 'could never seem to decide – to his own satisfaction – just how Jewish he was'. This attribute he shared with his brother Edgar, with Otto Kahn of Kuhn Loeb (who was sometimes described as 'the missing leaf between the Old and New Testaments') and indeed with many if not most of New York's secularized German Jews. His social ambition was such that he included his wife's Gentile forbears in his *Who's Who* listing, while omitting his own parents, including his mother, Sophie Rubino. He also arranged for the construction of a 'high-ceilinged, Old World office in a three-story Pine Street building modelled after the Palazzo Pandolfini in Florence [designed by Raphael], from which he operated a patrician one-man banking house [which] seemed downright exotic'.

1. Pine Street

Once, while lunching with the Kaiser in the 1890s, James Speyer regretted that he had no sons who could preside over the Frankfurt firm, which was in the charge of an in-law, Eduard Beit. The Kaiser promptly offered to ennoble Beit as 'Eduard Beit von Speyer', declaring that 'There must always be a Speyer in Frankfurt,' an offer which was accepted. Sir Edgar Speyer, who had been born in the United States in September 1862, 14 months after James, took charge of the London office in 1887 from Leo Bonn. He then married the German-American violinist Leonora von Stosch in 1902 in the English Church in Hamburg, having become at least a nominal Anglican. He was educated at the realgymnasium in Frankfurt, and spent a year in the Prussian Dragoons while at university. He did not take a degree. His Anglicanism renders even more lamentable the later reaction of the Clerk of the Privy Council, Sir Alaric Fitzroy, who recorded that Speyer 'was apparently quite ready to take the oath on the Testament, so long as he could do it with the rest; but I kept him to the Pentateuch and thus saved the Gospels from outrage'.

Edgar, like James, was sometimes described as a prickly character who 'rubbed people the wrong way'. He was characterized by the journalist T. P. O'Connor as 'a small, well-shaped man, with a very striking face, brilliant black eyes, olive skin, regular features, a small black moustache, a very soft expression … [he] ought still to be an Oxford undergraduate, instead of one of the great financial forces of the age'.

James Speyer, born in New York in 1861, trained in Europe before returning to the United States in 1885, when he discovered that, as a Jew, he could not have a serious career in the German military, and became head of the New York firm in 1899, succeeding William Bonn, Leo Bonn's brother. The Bonns played similar custodial roles while James and Edgar came of age. It was said by an unfriendly competitor that 'within fifteen years James not only managed to irreconcilably alienate the most experienced partners in his firm, but he and Edgar lost their footing for cooperation with the leading bankers of Wall Street and London'. Jacob Schiff of Kuhn Loeb concluded that 'the decisions of Bonn and two other partners to eventually quit the house were due to "James Speyer's deficiencies of character".' William Salomon, who established an important firm of his own, withdrew from the Speyer firm in 1901.

Many years later, James recalled that after the Civil War 'our firm sold millions of dollars of American railroad securities in Germany, Holland, Switzerland and all over Europe … Whereas the British had initially been wary of the Western railroads, the Germans were less so.' In 1869, the firm served as broker for Jim Fisk in one of the 'railway wars' of the period.

James and Edgar's brother-in-law Eduard Beit undertook an around-the-world tour lasting for 15 months in 1888–89. A diary of more than 400 pages recording it survives. Beit inherited his father's interest in a Hamburg bank and also his mother's inheritance from the Langenburg banking family before marrying Lucie Speyer in 1892, thus linking three great fortunes. His father's brother, Sir Alfred Beit, made a fortune in South African mining and played a role in British politics as a supporter of Joseph Chamberlain – a bridge that links South Africa and Zimbabwe is named after him. Eduard was wounded in the Great War and suffered from Parkinson's disease from an early age, thus being denied the extraordinary energy of James and Edgar.

A reference book based on German tax returns published just before World War I estimated Eduard Beit's fortune at 88 million marks. Another tabulation of Jewish family fortunes listed the Rothschilds with 310 million, the Speyers with 121 million, the Mendelsohns with 105 million, Gans/ Weinberg with 71 million, and Bleichroder/Schwabach with 70 million. The largest individual fortunes, Jewish and Gentile, in 1910 were said to be those of Bertha Krupp with 187 million, Furst Henckel with 177 million, Christian Furst zu Hohenlohe with 151 million, Max von Goldschmidt-Rothschild with 107 million, Hans Heinrich Furst with 84 million, Hans Ulrich Schaffgotsch with 79 million, Mathilde von Rothschild with 76 million and Eduard Beit von Speyer with 76 million. Franziska Speyer, the widow of George Speyer, had the sixteenth largest fortune with 45 million.

2. Franciske Speyer

The Speyers were not *nouveaux riches* in Germany; they 'were linked directly or indirectly to the court Jews of the age of absolutism'. Eduard had become a Protestant by the time of his ennoblement in 1901. Another Speyer, Anna, married Arthur Gwinner of Deutsche Bank, an alliance which became important to the Speyer firms. While there were three separate houses before World War I, the American firm also did business in Paris and Frankfurt and the British firm in Berlin.

Eduard and Lucie built an enormous town house in Frankfurt in 1904, which Eduard's heirs were able to sell to the City of Frankfurt in 1934 before they fled Germany for Switzerland. Lucie, heartbroken at the death of her son Erwin in the war, died in 1918 at the age of 48. From 1959, the house was the headquarters of the Max Planck Society, a leading scientific research organization. In 2000, it was acquired by the Forte hotel organization and, after additional rooms were added, it became the Rocco Forte Villa Kennedy, today the leading hotel in Frankfurt. It was part of the Wilhelmine building boom of which the great cultural historian Jacob Burckhardt had written in 1875:

> Frankfort, furious building of palaces by Jews and other company promoters and, what is more, in German Renaissance. Clumsy ornamentation of every description naturally has been smuggled in under that rubric; people who are incapable of producing something beautiful are unable to do so whatever the style, and all the 'motives' and 'themes' in this would not help a man without fantasy.

3. Villa Speyer

The Frankfurt Jewish families had few associations with their counterparts in Berlin. They were more prone to marry outside the Jewish faith, as did both Edgar and James Speyer and their nephew, Herbert Beit von Speyer, a phenomenon perhaps explained by the 'relative absence of anti-Jewish prejudices in the Western provinces [of Germany] together with the relatively liberal attitudes and occasionally middle-class occupations of some of the local nobility'.

The Speyer brothers had a second sister, Henrietta, who made a less brilliant marriage to Felix Schwabach (1855–1928), who began his career in the German railroads and was the co-author of a book on North American railroads published in 1906. He was a member of the Reichstag for Memel from 1907 to 1918 and of the Prussian parliament from 1908 to 1913 as a National Liberal. He was also a privy councillor.

The Speyer dynasty did not survive, partly because the brothers between them produced only Edgar's three daughters. While they were emancipated women for their time – one a racing car driver, one an American WAC during World War II – high finance was not a career then open to women. Had it been otherwise, the fate of the family banking houses would not have been much different. The great investment banking houses fell victim to nationalism and to the end, or at least eclipse, of the railway age.

ENGLAND

CHAPTER 1

The London Tube

'Perhaps the finest of its kind in the world'

The early relations of the Speyers with the Morgan firm were cordial. In 1880, the head of Morgan's London office, J. S. Morgan, wrote a colleague: '[W]e have the best opinion of them and have no doubt that they are possessed of large means and that their business is well conducted.' By 1902, possibly as a result of conflict over London tube issues, a less charitable view prevailed: '[W]e should dislike [to] see business largely in the hands of Speyer and Co and similar houses.' In 1901, Speyer had assisted the Chicago entrepreneur Charles Yerkes in purchasing the District Railway. In 1902, Speyer had founded an Underground Group, capitalized at 5 million, in return for 'strict control over the company, including the appointment of directors, solicitors and consulting engineers, as well as the equivalent of $625,000 in contingent certificates'. The Controller of the London County Council testified in 1903 that:

> It seems to me that the public were invited to take up these shares in a very roundabout sort of way ... First of all, the shares were allotted at par to the Underground Company, they in turn sell them to the Messrs Speyer brothers at a price which is not mentioned; then the latter firm sell them to the public at par, and Messrs Speyer Brothers get a 6 per cent commission – 1 per cent in cash and 5 per cent in shares – and out of that commission which they receive from the Underground Company, they have, I suppose, to pay certain commissions to other people. As far as I know, the public only subscribed about half the £2 million and the underwriters were left with the remaining £1 million, but of course, as far as Messrs Speyer Brothers are concerned, they would have unloaded the whole £2 million and the underwriters would have the whole £1 million left on their hands.

In 1902–3 the London office, in cooperation with Yerkes, raised £18 million (the equivalent of £1.43 billion in 2012) for the construction of three underground railways in London (now the central sections of the Northern, Piccadilly and Bakerloo lines) and the electrification of a fourth, and had also provided capital of £5 million from its own resources. Most of the money was raised overseas, $27 million in the United States in 1903–4. The Speyer firm had won out over Morgan for management of the issue, a fact that caused subsequent resentment. It was predicted that the three new lines would have 145 million passengers in the first year of operation; the actual number achieved was 71.5 million.

The line being improved was projected to have 100 million passengers. Instead, it achieved 55 million. By the time the three tube lines had opened, the value of the £100 notes had fallen to a third of their sale price and Speyer had to bail out the company with his bank's money by paying off shareholders who were threatening to launch bankruptcy proceedings. He blamed the state of the money markets, bus and tram competition, delays in completion, low fares and the burden of rates and taxes. The underground lines, to this day, have never been seriously profitable. Though indispensable parts of London's infrastructure, they were, in financial terms, casualties of the motor age and became a public corporation in 1933 before being nationalized in 1948.

Speyer became chairman of the combined company in December 1905 and remained as chairman until 1915. The company engaged in prolonged litigation with the Yerkes estate, ultimately recovering more than half its claim after Yerkes' art collection was sold for $2.2 million. A. Moreton Mandeville, in a pamphlet sharply critical of the House of Speyer, published in 1915 during the war, acknowledged, 'We give Edgar Speyer all credit for the admirable transportation system with which London is equipped and which is perhaps the finest of its kind in the world.' It probably required a sharp practitioner with enormous drive like Yerkes and an 'outsider' banker like Speyer to carry into effect the Tube's major innovations: an end to 'cut and cover' construction and the replacement of steam by electric engines.

Between 1903 and 1905, Speyer had raised huge sums for the London Underground, half of them from 'profit sharing notes' offered to existing shareholders. This was 'an amazing achievement when one takes into account the unsettled nature of the economy during those years'. Upon Yerkes' death in 1905, Edgar became chairman of the united company and its effective manager. 'As the redemption date in 1908 for the £100 "profit sharing" notes approached, their value fell to £35 and Speyer had to pay £175,000 from the bank's resources to appease the holders who

4. 'A Yet Wider Control'

were now threatening bankruptcy proceedings, there were instead technical liquidation proceedings in the High Court, bankruptcy being prevented by an injunction on July 21, 1908. Speyer and George Gibb, then the Tube's manager, produced a proposal to exchange the notes for a mixture of fixed interest bonds redeemable on 1 January 1933 and preference notes due on 1 January 1948. In the face of liquidation, 96 per cent of the shareholders accepted the scheme, as did the holders of profit sharing notes.' In 1976, Henry Morgan stated bluntly that 'we did not like the way James Speyer did business'. Morgan's son-in-law Herbert Satterfield wrote:

> The syndicate which [Morgan] organized to finance these new tubes was in competition with Speyer and Co. for the franchise. However it was found that the omnibus lines, which had the rights for the streets under which the tubes were to be built, controlled the situation. Apparently, under English law, the right to run vehicles on the surface of the ground extended downwards to an

indefinite depth. Mr. Morgan and his friends thereupon took the bus line into partnership in their enterprise, though this was not known publicly at the time. Not long afterwards, the Speyers quietly bought up the omnibus company stock, thus blocking the Morgan subway development ... [later a] House of Lords Committee rejected the bill to authorize the construction of the Charing Cross and Hammersmith Railway tubes. This was ... the main line, about fourteen miles in length, which passed through the centre of London beneath Piccadilly ... The rejection by the Committee showed the power of the Speyer group, which was financing Charles T. Yerkes, the American railroad builder, who already had put a circle around London and expected to absolutely control its underground transit and maintain the tariff of fares that was then in effect.

Yerkes, early in life, had served a sentence in a Pennsylvania state prison; he later developed inter-urban railways in Chicago, including the famous 'loop', but left Chicago amid controversy, 'one step ahead of the sheriff'. Three of Theodore Dreiser's novels, *The Titan, The Financier* and *The Stoic*, are thinly fictionalized versions of his extraordinary life.

5. Charles Yerkes

Morgan characterized Speyer's acquisition of the omnibus line stock as 'the greatest rascality and conspiracy I ever heard of'. James Speyer and Morgan's son had earlier said that 'no Morgan would have [any] connection with any enterprise of which Mr. Yerkes had the management', while a member of parliament expressed doubt 'whether for a long time, if ever, such a very dirty transaction was ever done by parties coming before Parliament'. The Morgan resentment was later expressed by a London partner, E. C. Greenfell, who wrote that Speyer was 'very prominent and successful about 1900' but 'entirely discredited' by 1911 due to mismanagement, and that its attempt to break into the underwriting of British bond issues was not successful for long.

Ultimately, the Speyer combine was successful in electrifying the Metropolitan (1908) and Circle (1905) lines and in constructing the Piccadilly, Bakerloo and Northern lines (1907). These projects were based on two innovations: deep tunnelling in place of the cut-and-cover method previously used, and electric traction in place of steam engines with their attendant soot. After Yerkes' death in 1905, Edgar Speyer became the effective manager of the project, designing the signage and the station layout. He was alarmed by Yerkes' death, since his firm had invested £400,000, a huge sum for the time, to salvage the Tube project. At the ensuing stockholders' meeting he brushed aside concerns about overcrowding on the Tube, minimizing safety concerns, which proved largely unfounded. He explained, in terms which will resonate with users of the New York and Tokyo subways, that 'Straphangers mean dividends!' The line, he said 'enabled the poorer classes more easily and pleasantly to reach that happy land where houses ceased and where fields, trees, and flowers begin'.

In 1907, Edgar vainly sought government assistance from Lloyd George who later claimed to have evaded 'some of the loveliest traps ever set for a minister'. Speyer declared that the London Underground was the only such system built without public support, and that it saved the state money that would otherwise have been spent on widening streets. He proposed that the London County Council lend £5 million at 4 per cent interest, with a right of purchase in 21 years. 'Such socialistic ideas from the mouth of a capitalist were not to be taken seriously.' In 1912, the finances of the combined tube company were stabilized by acquisition of the London General Omnibus Company. This concern had an effective bus monopoly and had been paying large dividends. In November 1912, Edgar Speyer negotiated the acquisition of London's two other Tube railways, the Central line and the City and South London railway, seeming 'to constitute himself and his directors as a de facto traffic board'. Profitability of the lines was undermined by the growth of private motoring. In January 1920, Speyer Brothers sold its remaining London tube holdings for about £1 million, the equivalent of about £30 million today.

In 1906, Edgar was made a baronet. The following year, he was appointed as a member of an official departmental committee on the 1907 Companies Act and in 1909, with the support of Winston Churchill, among others, was made a privy councillor, in recognition both of his work on the London tube and his philanthropic activities. Ernest Cassel, another German-Jewish banker, received a privy councillorship at about the same time. There were (and are) about 125 privy councillors.

Sir Edgar's railroad interests were not confined to the London tube. His critic Mandeville alleged that investors suffered losses of $45 million in Brazilian bonds and $60–$70 million in Argentine bonds floated by the London house before 1914. Then, as now, Argentina was an international scofflaw. For a brief period before World War I, it was deemed the richest nation in the world; the Baroque architecture of Buenos Aires, like that of St Petersburg and Odessa, is a monument to its past glories during the Belle Époque.

The British Speyer firm provided the financing for the Guayaquil–Quito Railway in Ecuador, which opened in 1908. The railway required ten years to construct and reaches a height of 11,841 feet. It was a major project of a liberal president, Eloy Alfaro. When it was finally finished, the celebrations lasted for several days. The line runs for 600 miles and has been described as 'the most difficult train in the world'. It unified the country and reduced to two days a journey that had previously taken several weeks. The railroad was never profitable. The Ecuadoran government had acquired a 49 per cent interest in it, and in 1925 acquired additional shares at a cost of $600,000 to give it a controlling interest. This action was in part precipitated by a long legal battle ending in a victory for Speyer in the Second Circuit Court of Appeals in New York in 1918 arising from Speyer's efforts to foreclose on Ecuador's customs duties. The railroad fell into disrepair after World War II, and service was interrupted during the 1990s as a result of storm damage. The present Correa government reopened the line in June 2013; hoardings on Washington, DC buses now advertise its attractions to potential tourists.

CHAPTER 2

English Philanthropy

'Preparing for emigration and colonial life'

Sir Edgar contributed £2,500 to the Whitechapel Art Gallery to bring beauty to the residents of London's depressed East End. It survives, and completed a $13 million expansion, doubling its size, in 2009. He was Chairman of the Nervous Diseases Research Fund, President of Poplar Hospital on London's East India Dock Road (closed in 1975, demolished in 1982) and a member of the board of the King Edward's Hospital Fund, to which he contributed £25,000 in 1902 (the equivalent of £2 million today). The hospital, favoured by the Royal Family and armed forces, still operates in London's West End.

He was the sponsor of an annual prize for the best essay on the efficient operation of voluntary hospitals. He is said to have made weekly visits to the accident ward of the Poplar Hospital, visiting the bedside of every patient. In December 1904 he bailed out a small penny savings bank at Needham Market, Suffolk, at a cost of £5,700 (about $400,000 in 2013), for which he had no financial responsibility, out of sympathy with its small depositors. It is pleasant to record that when Speyer died in 1932, the members of the bank sent a condolence letter to Lady Speyer.

A client entrusted him in 1905 with responsibility for distributing to charity the sum of £100,000 left in his estate, the so-called Bawden Fund, the equivalent of about $7 million today. Sir Edgar's distribution of it gave a hint of his charitable priorities, apart from music: £16,000 to complete the initial endowment of University College, London; £10,000 each to the East End Emigration Fund and for children's country holidays; £5,000 each for the King Edward VII Hospital and the London Hospital; £3,000 each for the Charity Organization Society, the City of London Hospital for Diseases of the Chest, the Poplar Hospital in the East End and the

National Hospital for the Paralysed and Epileptic; £2,500 each for the Royal Waterloo Hospital for Children and Women, the Cancer Hospital at Brompton, the German Hospital and the National Refuge for Homeless and Destitute Children; and £2,000 each for the Whitechapel Art Gallery in the East End, the United British Women's Emigration Association, Queen Charlotte's Lying In Hospital, the Royal Hospital for Incurables, the Factory Girls' Holiday Fund, Mrs Gladstone's Free Convalescent Home, St Mary's Home for Working Women, the Working Women's Holiday Fund, Dr Barnardo's Maternity Homes, the Invalid Childrens' Aid Association, the Metropolitan Convalescent Institution and the Haven for Homeless Little Ones. The sum of £1,000 each went to the Horticultural College, Swanley, for preparing women for emigration and colonial life, Clapham Maternity Hospital, Kellin Open Air Sanatorium, May Wardell's Home for Scarlet Fever, the Cripples' Home and Industrial School for Girls, the Home for the Aged Poor, the East Anglian Sanatorium and the National Industrial Home for Crippled Boys.

His emphasis, like that of James and Ellin in their philanthropies, was on small-scale rather than large-scale projects, on 'levelling up' rather than 'levelling down', on rehabilitation rather than relief. As the choice of charities shows, emigration was regarded as an important social safety valve in Britain during the Victorian and Edwardian periods. During the period 1881–90, nearly 2.5 million emigrants left the United Kingdom, from a population of about 35 million. In the period 1901–5, the number of emigrants was about 470,000, rising to about 900,000 for the ensuing five-year period, 1906–10. The overwhelming number of emigrants went to either the Empire or to the United States.

CHAPTER 3

The House of Music

'The greatest examples of Music and Art are world possessions
and unassailable even by the passions and prejudices of the hour'

Edward Speyer, a member of the preceding generation of the Speyer
family, was a noted patron of music. He died at the age of 95 within
a year or two of Edgar. He was referred to in England as 'the Elstree
Speyer' after the location of his estate; Sir Henry Wood observed that 'those
two [Edgar and Edward] did not quite hit it musically; Edgar was all out
for the modern in music; Edward for the strictly classical'. Edward's estate,
Ridgehurst, was also a gathering place for musicians. He had been brought
up with the Mendelssohn family and retired from banking in 1887 at the
early age of 47.

It has been observed that 'the last blaze of cultural creation had centred
largely in music, the most truly representative art-medium of European
culture, which found in its Wagnerian Twilight of the Gods the conclusion that
Greek art found in Pergamane sculpture ... cultural exhaustion was becoming
evident. Sculpture, painting and architecture were losing their inspiration'.

Edward Speyer, like Edgar, was an organizer of concerts in London and
collected Dutch masters. Owing to a series of financial reverses, he was
obliged to sell many pictures and in 1931 moved into a lodge on his former
estate. At his death he left £646,507 in securities of which £241,236 were
in Speyer Ellisen. The latter were presumably worthless due to the closing of
its business shortly after his death in 1934.

Edgar Speyer for many years contributed £2,000 per year (the equivalent
of $160,000 now) to cover the deficits of the promenade concerts of the
Queen's Hall orchestra. The subsidized tickets were 4d per night. Edgar
served on its board from 1902 to 1914. He had rescued the Queen's Hall
from bankruptcy in 1902. The concerts had been started in 1895.

'Whether by good luck or judgment, Henry Wood was singularly fortunate in his choice of Madame von Stosch as his first soloist of the century ... she played the *Rondo Capriccioso* by Saint Saens on the first night and was booked to appear another five times during the 1900 season. As a direct result, Wood and Newman came to know her husband well.'

His Grosvenor Square house was the venue for many concerts for society audiences of up to 200 people. When it became the American Women's Club in 1923, it was described in a contemporary newspaper article:

> It occupies three ordinary lots and is not only fitted up with superb carvings, panelings and frescoes, many brought from historic Italian palaces – but also possesses a delightful courtyard where the members may sit in warm weather by antique fountains, amid beds of flowers. The front door gives into a large hall extending the full width of the building. Carved pillars cut off the centre from the wings and the ceiling between these arcades is frescoes taken from the Doge's Palace. At either end of the hall, staircases with elaborately carved balustrades lead to the upper floors. One is in the Renaissance style, while the other which follows Gothic lines and runs up three stories nearly to the top of the house is a magnificent piece of work. In its original Italian habitation it must have been built around a central shaft and it has been so fitted as to delight the eye by a succession of graceful balustrades.
>
> Behind the hall is a dining room with walnut panelling and a beamed ceiling with carved cherubs and scrolls ... Opposite the main club building is a loggia of Italian design, unexpectedly picturesque for a London yard. It contains a comfortable library, and opening off it is a card room. The principal room on the second floor is a ballroom. It has great hanging cut-glass chandeliers, gilt regency furniture and a perfect dancing floor. At one end is a large electrically driven organ. There are more than 30 bedrooms, some of them magnificent, and one suite occupied by Miss Peggy O'Neill contains the famous silver bath that was built for Lady Speyer's use.

A more recent description declares that 'the whole of Speyer's house passes from exoticism to exoticism with dazzling rapidity ... a riot of flamboyant Gothic woodwork such as might be found in the Musée de Cluny climbing up one side and more modest Italian Renaissance styling on the other ... mixing features genuine and antique upon its path'. The silver bathtub was by the noted metalworker W. Bainbridge Reynolds; the interiors mostly by Fernand Billerey; the whole according to one critic 'the *ne plus ultra* of the exotic vulgarian'. According to an article in *The Sphere* of 10 June 1944, when the house was owned by the American Women's Club, the bathtub was still in place, and it was asserted that it scalded persons using warm water and froze them when the water was cold.

6. Grosvenor Street

As patron of the promenade concerts, Edgar Speyer stopped musicians from sending underprepared substitutes to perform in their places. Claude Debussy (1908–09) and Richard Strauss conducted their own works there; two of Elgar's major works had their first performances at the Queen's Hall in 1910 and 1911. In 1913, there were first performances of Sibelius's *Finlandia*, Debussy's *Iberia* and Stravinsky's *Firebird Suite*. Leonora Speyer gave the first private performance of Elgar's *Violin Concerto*, as well as the first performance of Faure's *Violin Sonata in A-major*, with Faure on the piano, in 1909 and the first performance of Richard Strauss's *Violin Sonata* with Strauss on the piano in the summer of 1914. The Grosvenor Street mansion contained a suite of rooms for visitors, of which Edvard Grieg wrote 'we live even more elegantly than kings and emperors. We wade among masterpieces of art.' A critic rather unfairly declared that his 'munificence has involved colossal losses to the

British investment public'. Speyer had suffered losses himself from the London tube and Brazilian railways.

Richard Strauss's *Salome* (1905) was dedicated to Edgar Speyer; it was initially regarded as a scandalous work. On his first appearance in London, Debussy received a hostile review in *The Times*: 'As long as actual sleep can be avoided, the listener can derive great pleasure from the strange sounds that enter his ears, if he will only put away all idea of definite construction or logical development.' Later, 'Debussy seemed delighted – almost like a child – because he thought we in England appreciated his music more than his countrymen – not even Strauss had received a warmer welcome.' This was so even though Speyer 'had not been able to promote the interests of Debussy on the lavish scale he reserved for Strauss. Nevertheless Speyer remained one of Debussy's principal supporters.' Debussy's seventh and last journey to England took place in the summer of 1914, when on 17 July he stayed at Grosvenor Street and took part in a private concert. Often pressed by his creditors, he described this engagement as 'a drop of water in the desert of the awful summer months'.

Speyer's relations with Elgar were more mixed. Elgar was closer to Edward Speyer than to Edgar; Edward had 'taken with panache to the life of an English country gentleman'. Elgar was annoyed at Edgar's favouritism to foreign composers: 'They pay any foreigner 4, 5, 6, 7, or even 8 times the amount given to me and lose largely over the visitor because they say it's good for art.' On the other hand, 'it was to Lady Speyer to whom Elgar turned for the earliest private performances of the slow movement of his violin concerto in early 1910', although 'her huge house was always full of guests interested in her husband's Queen's Hall syndicate and her own very feminine beauty might no longer be such a clear aid to working out the implications of the music'. In addition, 'Sir Edgar Speyer ... sent Elgar a cheque, the fruit of a speculation. Elgar, who was negotiating with Sir Edgar about the first performance of the *Second Symphony*, felt he could not possibly accept the money. Lady Elgar considered it a 'very human kind touching episode, Dear of Sir Edgar and of course perfect of Edward'. Elgar stood by Sir Edgar throughout his troubles during and after World War I. On 24 October 1914, Edgar wrote to say how much he and his wife had been 'touched by your kind letter and we appreciate the friendly greeting and mark of confidence at a time when sense of fairness and proportion and logic seem to have forsaken a section of the people'.

In Britain, the Lord Chamberlain required deletions from *Salome*; in the United States, J.P. Morgan and his daughter caused it to be banned in New York as sacrilegious. Other interpreters have alleged that it has anti-Semitic themes. None contest the importance of the music. Works by Arnold Schoenberg (*Five Orchestral Pieces*, 1912) and Hugo Becker (*Three Pieces for Cello, with Piano Accompaniment*, dedicated to Speyer) premiered at the Queen's Hall, and Speyer was also friendly with the Australian composer and pianist Percy Grainger. Grainger left England in 1915 at about the same time as the Speyers; a contemporary cartoon entitled 'The Flight into Egypt' depicted Sir Edgar as a horse and Lady Speyer as his driver, the horse being led by Grainger.

7. 'Flight Into Egypt'

On the occasion of a visit to the National Gallery with Strauss and Elgar, Speyer remarked, 'Here we have a revolutionary [Tintoretto] who broke ground at the very end of the glorious Venetian period. Shall we say that Tintoretto was to painting what our friend Richard Strauss is to music?' Edgar Speyer's house was 'a centre of musical and artistic society. Here [one] could [it was said] meet Henry James or Debussy, listen to Mme. Grieg sing her husband's songs and enjoy a sumptuous dinner in company with John Sargent.'

Grieg's diary recorded his visit to the Speyers in the year before his death. He found Sir Edgar to be 'a gracious and natural human being ... First I played various things, then they persuaded Nina [Mme Grieg] to sing, and she did so in such a way as to move Mr. Speyer to tears (!). That was something none of us had imagined. Then I played the *G major Sonata* with Mrs. Speyer, after which she performed Bach's *Chaconne*. To be sure, one notes now and then evidences of amateurism, but otherwise I have deep respect for her musicianship, rhythmic, energetic and musical.'

Eight days later, Grieg recorded, 'In the afternoon, big reception at the home of Mr. and Mrs. Speyer in honor of Mr. and Mrs. Grieg. Close to 200 people! Printed music program. Started at almost 11 p.m. The whole program was by Dr. Grieg, who had to play the G major Sonata with the hostess. She has a lot of talent and life – but she is too shallow. We go to bed at 2 a.m. I say once and never again. This was for our kind host and hostess as thanks for their hospitality. But polite society! To hell with it. Fortunately, there were a few artists.'

(a)

PROGRAMME.

SONATA in A minor for Violoncello and Pianoforte *Grieg*
  (a) Allegro agitato.
  (b) Andante molto tranquillo.
  (c) Allegro marcato.
Professor HUGO BECKER and Miss JOHANNA STOCKMARR.

SONGS   ...   .   *Grieg*
  Madame and Dr. EDVARD GRIEG.

SONATA in G major for Violin and Pianoforte...   *Grieg*
  (a) Lento doloroso.
      Allegro vivace.
  (b) Allegretto tranquillo.
  (c) Allegro animato.
Mrs. EDGAR SPEYER and Dr. EDVARD GRIEG.

SONGS   ...   .   *Grieg*
  Madame and Dr. EDVARD GRIEG.

Two SLÂTTER (Norwegian Peasant Dances)...   *Grieg*
  (1) Gibõens Bruremarsch.
  (2) " Rötnaesknut "; Halling.
  Mr. PERCY GRAINGER.

(b)

8. Grieg

One of the guests, who performed with Grieg and Lady Speyer, was Grainger, whom Grieg had asked to meet. He became fast friends with Grieg during the remaining year of Grieg's life, visiting him in Norway. Grainger's 'circle of friends, combined with his eccentric off-stage behaviour, set him apart from the Speyers' social circle'. 'Lady Speyer was known to have remarked: "Every town has its village idiot, Percy, and you're London's!"' Grieg was a difficult guest on his visit in 1910, since according to Lady Speyer 'he would simply sit in the hall with his hat and coat on, rarely speaking to anyone'. He also suffered a minor misadventure by tripping over the head of one of the Speyers' less than modest tiger-skin rugs.

Sibelius was eager to meet Speyer, exclaiming, 'Sir Speyer has three hundred million francs!' Speyer proposed a concert to take place on 26 May 1913, but in the final event, Sibelius did not perform at the Queen's Hall until 1920.

The Edgar Speyers had become important public figures. A portrait of Edgar by William Orpen was exhibited at the Royal Academy in 1914 and one of his wife by John Singer Sargent was painted in 1907 at a cost of 1,500 guineas, Sargent also composing a pencil sketch of him. He is said to have protested to Sargent about his wife's portrait, '[M]y wife's neck is not green.'

9. *Sir Edgar Speyer* by Sir William Orpen

Speyer made a major contribution to music appreciation in England. 'Banality and mediocrity reigned supreme in the social establishment as England's greatest musical genius for two centuries, Elgar, found his audience mainly in Germany. Although his greatest works embodied so much the spirit of his age – its ebullience, its colour, its sense of space and freedom. His spirit darkened and his work lost ebullience but gained in poignancy. Other composers of merit, Delius, Holst, Bancroft brought to the Edwardian age an achievement as in painting which was to prove remarkable and lasting.' Edgar was described as 'a lover of art willing to spend any amount of money to advance the cause of good music'. When he subsidized the Proms Concerts at the Queen's Hall from 1902 to 1915, he did not stint in sponsoring rehearsals; some concerts had as many as 17 rehearsals, including rehearsals in sections. When he left England, Sir Henry Wood, the director of the Proms, observed that 'he left it richer in music than he found it, at a cost of more than £30,000 [about $2.5 million today] to himself'. Wood recalled that when his wife was ill (dying in fact), 'the kindness of the Speyers during the next few weeks I cannot recall without a lump in my throat. They left me at perfect freedom to take meals in their house at any hour.'

In 1914, with the outbreak of war, an episode took place two weeks later that was a tribute to Edgar Speyer's liberality of spirit, described in a notice issued by the manager of the Proms:

The Directors of the Queen's Hall Orchestra think that some explanation of the change of programme on Monday evening August 17, is due to their Subscribers and to all who have so loyally supported the Promenade concerts in the past. The substitution of a mixed programme in place of a wholly Wagnerian one was not dictated by any narrow-minded intolerant policy but was the result of outside pressure brought to bear upon them at the eleventh hour by the Lessees of the Queen's Hall. With regard to the future, the Directors hope – with the broadminded cooperation of their audience – to carry through as nearly as possible the original scheme of the Concerts as set forth in their Prospectus. They take this opportunity of emphatically contradicting the statements that German music will be boycotted during the present season. The greatest examples of Music and Art are world possessions and unassailable even by the prejudices and passions of the hour.

For the Directors of the Queen's Hall Orchestra.
Robert Newman, Manager

By contrast, the Royal Philharmonic, save for a single performance of a Wagner overture, totally abstained from German music for a four-year period

When the Proms were again in financial danger during the 1924 season, Wood appealed to Edward Speyer, who had remained in England. He was a conservative in both politics and music, and he recommended old-fashioned works to Wood – 30 by Bach, 35 by Mozart and 13 by Haydn. He had originally come to England in 1859, 30 years ahead of Sir Edgar.

The memoirs of Chappell's chauvinistic manager at the Queen's Hall, William Boosey, who had displaced Speyer during the World War I hysteria, asserted in 1931 that 'Sir Edgar Speyer's programmes were aggressively German – in fact contained nothing but German music.' This called forth an angry reply from Sibelius's friend and patron Rosa Newmarch, which appeared in the *Monthly Musical Review* in 1932: 'In the scheme for 1914, there will be found side by side with these "German" geniuses the names of Elgar, Bantock, Vaughan Williams, Ruthur Boughton, Walford Davies, Goossens, O'Neill. Continental music was represented by Cesar Franck, Bruneau, Saint-Saens, Debussy, Dukas and Ravel, Dvořák, Sibelius, Moussorgsky and all the Russian school.' A tabulation of the Queen's Hall performances in the Speyer era, 1895–1914, showed that Wagner led the list with 2,383, followed by Beethoven (681), Tchaikovsky (611), Sullivan (508), Gounod (487) and Mozart (390). There were more than 200 performances of works by Saint-Saiens and Berlioz and more than 100 of those by Verdi, Bizet, Rossini, Grieg and Dvořák.

Edgar served as Richard Strauss's banker. This proved to be a misfortune for Strauss, as the amounts he deposited, 'the savings of thirty years', variously estimated at from £50,000 to £150,000, were sequestered by the British government and were never returned after World War I. 'For a week,' Strauss wrote, 'I was depressed; then I started again from the beginning to earn money by the sweat of my brow just when I had entertained hopes of devoting myself exclusively to composition from my fiftieth year onward.' Richard Strauss's popularity was widely credited to Speyer.

Notwithstanding the nationalism of Chappell and Boosey, the Proms concerts live on. Few realize that they were sustained and nurtured to maturity by a man de-naturalized by an ungrateful England.

CHAPTER 4

The Scott Expeditions

'The most interesting little sketch of our mountain'

Sir Edgar Speyer was the largest single contributor (of £5,000, the current equivalent of $400,000) to the Scott Antarctic Discovery expedition of 1901–4. A later American writer, unaware of the 80-fold multiplication necessary to convert 1913 pounds into the dollars of a century later observed that 'No other single contributor in Britain matched even this not very munificent sum.' The government finally granted £20,000 in 1902; there were £22,600 in contributions, including £5,000 from Llewellyn Longstaff and £1,000 from the New Zealand government. At the time Speyer made his contribution, only £9,500 had been raised. He donated £1,000 to the last 1910–12 expedition, for which Scott had to embark on an onerous begging tour, raising £2,000 in Manchester, £1,387 in Cardiff, and £740 in Bristol, together with £500 from the Royal Geographical Society and £500 from the Royal Society. Lloyd George, the Chancellor of the Exchequer, refused to contribute a government grant. Speyer also agreed to assume responsibility for any remaining liabilities: 'Thanks to his sound advice the finance of the Expedition was used to the best advantage ... The Treasurer, with his characteristic generosity, gave him to understand that he would do much to see the venture through.' In the final event, because of public subscriptions following the tragic outcome, there was no need for further help from Speyer. In March 1912, when it became evident that the last Scott Terra Nova expedition would be fatal to its members, Scott addressed a final pencilled letter to Speyer that was found at his base camp after his death:

> My dear Sir Edgar: I hope this may reach you – I fear I must go and that leaves
> the expedition in a bad muddle – but we have been to the Pole and we shall die

like gentlemen – I regret only for the women we leave behind – I thank you a thousand times for your help and support and your generous kindness – If this diary is found it will show how we stuck by dying companions and fought the thing out until the end – I think this will show that the spirit of pluck and the power to endure has not passed out of our race – If recognition of this fact can be given by people will you please do your best to have our people look after those dependent upon us – I have my wife and child to think of – The wife is a very independent person, but the country ought not to let my boy want an education and a future … I am quite sure you will do your best to see this provision made and will strike while the iron is hot. Wilson, the best fellow that ever stepped, who has sacrificed himself again and again to the sick men of the party, leaves a widow entirely destitute. Surely something ought to be done for him and for the humbler wife of Edgar Evans …

[At that point the writing became fainter]

I write to many friends, hoping the letters will reach them sometime after we are found next year. We very nearly came through, and it's a pity to have missed it, but lately I have felt that we have overshot our mark. No one is to blame and I hope no attempt will be made to suggest that we have lacked support. Goodbye to you and your dear kind wife. Yours ever sincerely, R. Scott

Publication of the letter evoked an overwhelming public response to the appeals for annuity funds contained in it, a surplus being used to finance the Scott Polar Research Institute at Cambridge. In the final event, £75,509 was received, enough to pay off £30,000 in expedition debt and to generate a surplus of £12,000 which was used for the Scott Polar Institute. Mount

10. Scott Polar Institute

Speyer in Antarctica at 78 degrees 52 South, 160 degrees 42 East was named in Edgar's honour. It stands at the head of the Kehle Glacier at a height of almost 7,500 feet (2,430 metres). Leonora wrote Captain Scott in 1906 to thank him for forwarding 'the most interesting little sketch of our mountain. As it is so doubtful our ever seeing it, we prize the portrait all the more.'

Through the efforts of Professor Antony Lentin, a chronicler of Sir Edgar Speyer's denaturalization trial, a plaque in Sir Edgar's memory was belatedly erected at the Scott Polar Institute in 2014.

CHAPTER 5

Leonora

'She would dominate any room she entered'

Leonora Speyer, daughter of a German aristocrat who had emigrated to America, was born in 1872. Neither Speyer's cultural accomplishments nor the tactlessness leading to his exile from England can be understood without reference to his strong-willed and equally remarkable wife.

Leonora had been a performer at the Queen's Hall in 1900 after studying in London, Paris and Leipzig; she won a first prize at the Brussels Conservatory at the age of 16 in 1888. She had been a musical prodigy, as a pianist and composer, and from the age of 11 as such gave concerts in Washington and Baltimore. She studied under Professor Joseph Kaspar of Washington, who encouraged her to study at the Brussels Conservatory of Music, where she remained for two years, being awarded second prize at the end of the first year and first honours at the end of her course. She performed in Berlin before Joachim and at the Monnaie Theatre. In 1891 she studied under Marsick in Paris, and returned to the United States, where she performed with the Seidel's Orchestra in New York and at private musicales; an article about her appeared in *The Illustrated American* when she was 20 years old, describing her as 'tall and symmetrical, having a charming face lit with vivacious intelligence, and with manners a happy mixture of dignity and warmth'. She performed with the Boston Symphony at the age of 17, and later with the New York Philharmonic.

At the time of her marriage to Edgar, though of German descent, Leonora did not speak German. Although some accounts say that the marriage took place at the English [Anglican] Church in Hamburg, an official list of marriages records a marriage taking place at St George's in Hanover Square in London in early 1902. At their marriage, she was 30 and he was 40. She had previously married Louis Meredith Howland in 1894;

they were divorced, an unusual phenomenon in that period, in Paris in 1902. Howland was a member of a socially prominent New York shipping family associated with President Franklin Roosevelt's forbears; Howland was later a law client of Roosevelt in the 1920s. Edgar met Leonora 'when she performed at a concert organized by composer Maude Valerie White in the Cotswold village of Broadway'.

Leonora was awarded the Pulitzer Prize for poetry in 1927, and died in 1956 at the age of 84. Each year during their joint lives, the family performed on her birthday a short verse-drama composed by Edgar, who issued a printed tribute to her, published in Munich, on the occasion of their 25th wedding anniversary in 1927. Edgar, like Ernest Cassel and the

11. *Leonora Speyer* by Sargent

German banker Alfred Ballin and unlike his brother James and his own wife Leonora, was broken by the war, and lived for only 13 years thereafter in a sort of luxurious retirement. He was one of those who 'lost their sense of a future of manifold possibilities'.

Lady Speyer, who was descended from a Silesian Count, also did not escape criticism during World War I. Though she was American-born, and her mother was English by birth, the *Sydney Bulletin* declared of Edgar: 'He married Fraulein von Stosch, so he can't even talk about his dear English wife and children.' In October 1914, the British journalist Leo Maxse wrote of Speyer, 'your millionaire alien walks abroad with his society wife, who may be a common spy'. Her unhappiness with her persecution and that of their daughters contributed to Sir Edgar's imprudent later letter to Prime Minister Asquith. Despite Leonora's extraordinary gifts, one of her grand-daughters, Gabrielle Thorp, said that she could be 'egocentric, difficult, would be either hot or cold, never consistent. She had charisma and would dominate any room she entered.' It did not help that on seeing young Englishmen drilling in the early stages of the war, she said to an English friend, Sir Henry Wood of the Proms concerts, 'My dear Henry: How can these young untrained boys hope to conquer our armies of trained soldiers. It is so dreadful!'

A British journalist, Claud Cockburn, described the atmosphere at the Speyers' house on Washington Place in New York on the day of the great crash in 1929:

Since becoming a journalist I had often heard the advice to 'believe nothing until it has been officially denied.' But despite this, even the ominous blandness of Mr. Lamont did not shake me into full awareness of what was going on. The shake came a little later at lunch with the Edgar Speyers.

'Edwardian' was the adjective which inevitably occurred to you in the presence of Edgar Speyer, and equally inevitably he recalled to me the Rothschilds as I had seen them in my boyhood days at Tring. He was an American now, had been an American for years, and he and his brother were not only millionaires but had made themselves powerful figures in the cut and thrust of Wall Street, but the aroma of Edwardianism still hung about him like the scent of a good cigar. This was natural enough since it was in Edwardian England that this originally German Jew had risen to wealth and prominence. He had been Sir Edgar Speyer then, and a Privy Counsellor. Then he was caught in the storm of indignation against Germans in high places in England which at the beginning of World War 1 swept even Prince Louis of Battenberg out of the Admiralty. He could afford to recall what for many people might have been a disaster with an amiable shrug.

His enforced good-bye to all that had by no means been disastrous for him. He just got on a boat and went to Boston and made a couple of million dollars. Later he advanced triumphantly on New York and, at the time I knew him, lived in one of the lovely rose-colored houses on the north side of Washington Square. It housed, not in any special gallery but as part of its furnishings, a small but luminously beautiful art collection composed chiefly of Chinese paintings and porcelain. The atmosphere was one of elegant calm, in which the rich odor emanating from pots and pots of money was naturally, but not disagreeably, perceptible. It was at that time one of the few houses I visited in New York where you did not have to talk about the stock market or any other form of business, and the food and wine were so good that nobody thought it odd if at lunch or dinner you were perfectly silent for minutes on end.

There were a middle-aged English butler and a youthful English footman, but, except for their age, one might have supposed that they had been trained in Edwardian England and come over with Speyer on the boat to Boston in 1914. Their only departure from an older tradition was that they, both of them, left the room as soon as each course had been served by the footman under the butler's supervision.

Leonora Speyer was a writer. She had, as I recall, recently published a volume of poems, and on this October 24 of 1929, the Speyers and their four guests were talking about modern American poetry. I was eating pompano and listening to somebody telling something about some poet I had not yet heard of, when I perceived to my astonishment that some kind of disturbance was going on at the other side of the dining-room door, which faced me as I sat at the table. Something had certainly bumped against the door. I heard a very faint thump, and I saw the door shiver slightly. The idea of anything, as it were, untoward occurring in the Speyer household was nearly inconceivable. I concluded that they must be the owners of some large dog, which I had never seen, and that this dog had escaped and was probably at this moment being hauled off to its proper place by the footman. And then, just as I was about to give full attention again to the conversation, something else happened.

The handle of the door turned very, very slowly; the door shuddered again and moved an inch or so inward. Then it closed again, and again the handle very, very slowly turned in the direction opposite to its direction before. There was no longer any doubt about it. Either somebody in an ecstasy of indecision was trying to make up his mind to come into the room, or else, as seemed more likely, two people were struggling over the handle of the door, one of them trying to open it and the other to keep it closed.

In any other house, there might have been a dozen explanations for this – children loose in the passage, for instance; perhaps children playing with a big dog. But in the Speyer household things were so ordered that a disturbance of this kind was as startling as it would have been to find the dining room too hot or too cold, or to have a draft blowing down one's neck. Fascinated by the mysterious struggle behind the door, I found myself gazing at the man who was talking intelligently about this poet with an expression, as I could see from the surprised look he gave me, of absolutely idiotic vacancy. I was so placed that I was the only one at the table who, when the door opened, could see right down the corridor outside, and what I saw, when the two menservants came in to put a saddle of lamb in front of Speyer, was that at the end of the corridor either four or five maidservants of various ages were grouped together in what seemed to be an excited attitude, and one of them – unless I was under some kind of hallucination – had actually shaken her fist at the footman as he came through the door. Within a few minutes the butler and footman had again withdrawn, but we had swallowed no more than a mouthful or two of lamb when the noise in the passage became so loud that nobody in the dining room could even pretend to ignore it. A woman shouted, 'Go on – or else!' and then the door was burst open, and the butler, very red in the face, nearly bounced into the room as though he had been pushed violently from behind at the last moment.

He closed the door and as collectedly as possible marched across the room to Speyer and in low, apologetic tones begged him to come outside for a moment. Listening with an air of astonishment, Speyer, after a few seconds' amazed hesitation, left the room with him. Almost immediately Speyer came back again looking a little dismayed. He begged us to excuse him. The staff, he explained, had of course their own ticker tape in the kitchen premises, and of course they were all heavily engaged on the stock market. And now the ticker was recording incredible things. In point of fact the ticker was by that time running just over an hour and a half late, owing to the enormous volume of trading, so that the prices which the Speyer staff were reading with horror at a quarter to two were the prices at which stocks had changed hands at the very worst moment of the morning before the bankers had met and the formation of the bankers' pool had been announced. The staff saw their savings going down in chaos; since they were certainly operating on margin, they might at this moment already have been wiped out. Among the stock in which all of them had speculated was that of Montgomery Ward, and that had dropped from an opening price of 83 to around 50 before noon. And all this was going on before their eyes, while their employer – reputedly one of the shrewdest financiers in New York – was calmly sitting upstairs eating pompano and saddle of lamb. They absolutely insisted that he go at once with them to the kitchen, study the situation, make telephone calls if necessary, and advise them what to do for the best. Speyer left the rest of his lunch uneaten, and his wife and her guests finished the meal under conditions of confusion and makeshift, which probably had never been seen in the Speyer household before. I left as soon as I decently could and did not see Mr. Speyer to say good-bye. He was still in the kitchen.

In 1935, Leonora attended a banquet in honour of the American Arctic and Antarctic explorer Admiral Richard E. Byrd, and unexpectedly presented to him just before he took his place on the dais a Moroccan leather portfolio containing Scott's letter to her husband. The Admiral declared: 'I have here something that I shall cherish more than any of my possessions as long as I shall live. It was presented to me here tonight by Lady Speyer, the widow of Sir Edgar Speyer, to whom it was written by Captain Scott.'

For several seconds he studied the faded pencil marks in the handwriting of Scott before declaring that Scott 'left a heritage to England he never could have left if he had lived'. He then read aloud the letter. As he finished, a few persons rose to their feet, and then everyone in the room stood. There was no applause but simply a spontaneous tribute eloquent in the very silence in which it was made, to the memory of Captain Scott.

In 1938, Admiral Byrd wrote Leonora to say that the Scott letter was still his favourite possession. The letter was sold by Admiral Byrd's heirs for $34,000 in a Sotheby's auction in New York in 1988 and was again sold at Bonham's in London in 2012 for £163,250.

Leonora had inherited only about $300,000 from Sir Edgar in 1932, and in 1936 sought to develop apartments in a house adjacent to her residence in Washington Place. She was prevented from doing so by a lawsuit based on restrictions against sub-letting in a ground lease. The trial judge observed that 'the change both in [the] plaintiff's [Leonora's] situation and in the neighbourhood should prompt an amicable settlement of the case'. A sale of some of her furniture took place at the Parke-Bernet Galleries in New York in 1943, and a further sale of her Flemish and Dutch paintings at the Parke-Bernet in 1952, four years before her death in New York in 1956 at the age of 84.

Leonora was led into poetry by her friends Amy Lowell, Harriet Munroe and Robert Bridges. She published four books of poetry – *A Canopic Jar* (1921), *Fiddler's Farewell* (1926), *Naked Heel* (1931), and *Slow Wall* (1951) – and her work appeared in numerous magazines, including the *American Mercury*, *The Atlantic*, *Harper's*, *The New Republic*, *The New Yorker* and the *Saturday Review of Literature*. The poet and critic Glenway Wescott referred to *Canopic Jar* as 'the first book of a mature woman too intelligent to be content with gifts already fulfilled and creations accomplished', crediting her with 'these speculative adventures and flashes of interpretative insight which, when fixed in pattern or rhythmic utterance, we call art ... unpretentious beauty and clear thought, and no earmarks of vulgar success or sacrosanct largeness ... Who shall say that her fire in the rushes, which gives so fair a light, may not come to burn gold!'

The first poem in her *Fiddler's Farewell* (1926), which was awarded the Pulitzer Prize for poetry in 1927, was 'Ballad of a Lost House', which betrays some bitterness:

> Hungry Heart, come, make haste, make haste
> Out of the house of hopes laid waste
> Out of the town of teeth laid bare
> Under its smiling debonair
> Wait not, weep not, get you gone
> Better the stones to rest upon
> The wind and the rain for a roof secure
> Hyssop and tares for your nouriture:
> These shall endure. These shall endure.
> For out of that house went its soul with me
> Leaping and crying after me
> To bear me faithful company
> Over a clear and quickening sea.

Because of arthritis in her hands, she turned from the violin to poetry, as explained in the title poem:

> Let me find words
> With which to sing of silence
> Better than all this blurred half-sound
> Of tattered music trailing on the ground
> (That was a banner in the wind),
> Words
> And their pacing pride
> For the frustrated heart
> That stoic singer in the side,
> Unviolined!

In January 1944, having survived the passions of one war, she published a poem, 'Birthday Cake: A Refugee's Story', 'based on an incident told me by a friend from one of the occupied countries' about a German officer in another war:

There was a son, he too was five
He lived to be five, his hair as yellow
As Jackie's own, his eyes as blue
His son, his son, and Jackie who asked
'Was he a Nazi, too?'
Never shall I forget the cry
Of the Colonel – 'No' and again 'No, no'
The fire that blazed in the anguished eye
Flaring, fading to ash again;
The stumbling words: 'He was but five …
Of course, if he were now alive …
You see, there were no Nazis then'
And Jackie who asked him, 'Why?'
No answer to that. We spoke of the rain
The sodden fields, the flattened grain;
I asked, 'Was it wrong to save – for the cake?'
And I was aware of the ghost again
In the mirthless eye, as the Colonel said,
'The cake? What cake?' and rose from his chair
Cried Jackie, 'That means he won't tell!'
His face aglow. 'You know me so well.
Small sir?' was the answer, and bowing low
'Madame, my thanks!' and again 'My thanks'
Saluting old Anna who growled 'Good day'
A thundercloud to the last
And then a sound! A sound I knew
(Ah, who did not?)
Splitting the dark in two – a shot
A gun's sharp word – and I heard a call
Loud and alone: 'O Gott! O Gott!'
And the blow of a heavy body's fall
I only know the Colonel died
Thus, of a child's light questioning
And un-accusing, pure, clear-eyed
Foundering there in that guileless tide.

By the end of World War II, any Germanophilia had long since disappeared. This is from 'A German Woman Weeps':

> I only know I do not trust that weeping woman
> Nor the ashes in her heart
> I do not trust the very ashes of her town!
> Vengeance is mine, And forgiveness.
> And healing.
> Saith the Lord!
> And I would rather (very humbly) that it were His.
> I would rather.
> I will sleep, and my children will sleep,
> Better, If it be His.
> My country will sleep
> Better
> Let all the earth,
> Let Germany,
> Stand in awe of Him.

Leonora was invited to substitute for a friend, Joseph Auslander, in teaching poetry at Columbia in 1942. She taught there for more than a decade, preparing an essay *On the Teaching of Poetry* in which she observed: 'I urge a rewritten better written poem in preference to the newer one,' and noted that 'There is not much stitching and unstitching in some of the hasty and cocksure writing of today … Death to the adjective … and the adverb I insist.' She urged 'clarity, as opposed to the commonplace', and quoted an unremembered poet as declaring that 'Two words are not / As good as one.' 'The actual process of poetry-writing, the colour and harmony of words can be, surely must be, learned; the instrument must be mastered like any other instrument.' She delighted in her students' work: 'Swinging from my strap in the subway, returning from Columbia, books slithering from my grasp, I reflect: "What wondrous life is this I lead! Ripe apples drop about my head …'

It was a long way from the House of Music to the New York subway, notwithstanding her husband's appreciation of tubes, but Leonora Speyer had successfully re-invented herself.

Her three daughters by Speyer, who had been denaturalized along with her and her husband, ultimately all returned to England. 'It is a mark of splendid (if remote) rebuke to the Government of that day and age … That they were granted leave to remain in England is small recompense indeed.'

Her oldest daughter (from her first marriage), Enid Howland Hewitt, was a vocalist, who died in 1978. Pamela, the eldest of her children with Speyer, married Count Hugo Moy, a partner in the Speyer house in Berlin, who died shortly thereafter in a hunting accident. The wedding took place in the rectory of St Patrick's Cathedral in New York in 1926: 'Religious obstacles to the ceremony were removed when the Catholic authorities decided not to recognize Count Moy's first marriage to Lina Ansel, a Munich cabaret singer and a divorcee.' Pamela lived in Germany, but when her mother gave up her substantial house in Baden-Baden after the rise of Hitler and shortly before World War II, she returned to America with her and lived on the West Coast. The house later was the residence of the Nazi Gauleiter and French governor-general during the postwar occupation. Pamela owned a 1932 MG automobile and in her youth was a frequent participant in automobile rallies. Leonora ('Baba'), her second daughter with Speyer, was married for less than a year. Thereafter, she lived with the concert pianist Maria Donska. Leonora's youngest daughter, Vivien, who returned to England as an American WAAC in World War II, died in Norwalk, Connecticut, in 2001 at the age of 94.

Leonora was of a type, the cultivated woman of leisure who, both as producer and audience, sustained the arts and literature, which has almost vanished. Of such a person, Justice Holmes wrote in his 91st year: 'the civilized man creates a new atmosphere that is one of the greatest gifts to mankind … you are to me a civilized woman and so you make life better for the world. Part of the greatness of a great life I think consists in leaving it unadvertised. A woman with your gifts who does not let her cultivation decay and doesn't worry over the chances of displaying it, seems to me to be living nobly, and to have a right to be content.' Female participation in the workforce and the levelling of classes may have contributed to economic productivity. Its contribution to cultural flatness and mediocrity is less appreciated.

CHAPTER 6

Influence on the Liberal Party

'Capital to develop the good things which nature
has stored up for the use and benefit of mankind'

The era before World War I was not an era of economic nationalism. One could travel to and throughout Europe (except for Russia and Turkey) without a passport. Free trade, even after repeal of the Corn Laws, was never uncontroversial, but until the coming of the war British investments abroad and German investments in Britain were taken for granted, and there was increased freedom of expression, political and cultural. All these tendencies were put into sharp reverse by the war.

Sir Edgar Speyer was incontestably an Asquithian Liberal with a commitment to free trade, well-connected with the Liberal party. He was a friend of Prime Minister Henry Campbell-Bannerman. He had at one time leased a house to Asquith. Winston Churchill's mother, Lady Randolph Churchill, was a frequent visitor to Speyer's country residence, Sea Marge at Overstrand, near Cromer, on the Norfolk coast. Churchill was in residence in Pear Tree Cottage on its grounds at the time of the outbreak of World War I. Clementine Churchill used Speyer's telephone to stay in touch with her husband in London, Winston cautioned her, 'This is a very good plan of ours on the telephone. Ring me up at fixed times. But talk in parables – for they all listen.' This may have reflected the suspicion of the Speyers held by some of Churchill's associates, including the Secret Service agent Tupper and Admiral Lord Beatty.

In 1905, in a speech to the Institute of Bankers widely reported in both England and America, Speyer gave an early warning of Britain's relative decline. Central government expenditure in the previous ten years had increased by 30 per cent over the preceding decade even after allowing for the costs of the Boer War. Municipal expenditure had increased by 50

12. Overstrand

per cent. Annual foreign investment in the 1880s was £80 million, only £25 million in the 1890s, and was flat in the current decade. He urged increased taxes on luxuries like tobacco and spirits. He decried residential overbuilding, a position somewhat ironic in light of his enormous investment in his home on Grosvenor Square, although his 'House of Music' was almost a public institution. He urged an increase in the taxation of inhabited homes. Few in the Edwardian-Wilhelmine era, which saw an orgy of residential overbuilding in the United States and Germany as well as in England with neglect of other social needs, were thus self-conscious. Few in the United States recognize the phenomenon, fuelled by mortgage interest tax preferences, in our own time, when the British have abolished such preferences and the Germans foster sub-division of houses. The speech was credited by the economist Sir George Paish, whose help on it was acknowledged, with starting the Edwardian capital export boom: 'Sir Edgar incorporated my notes in a most successful speech he gave in the City. More than that, he himself prepared to make some new capital issues; his activities aroused other issuing houses to action.'

On 24 May 1911, Edgar delivered a published address to the Liberal Colonial Club on 'The Export of Capital', declaring:

In the ten years from 1894 to 1904, Great Britain raised an enormous sum for the government, the municipalities, the railways, the construction of houses, etc. It spent a great deal of money on unproductive purposes; a very large sum was spent on the Boer War. It did not provide during that period capital needed to increase the world's supply of food and raw materials as it had done in former years.

As soon as the rate of interest that rules at home gets near the foreign yield, the inducement to invest abroad goes. The matter settles itself. In a little over 60 years [Britain] has increased her population by nearly 60 percent, she has doubled her consuming powers per head, and has quadrupled her wealth.

We are fortunate here to conduct our business without government interference, such as the governments of France and Germany see fit to exercise ... its commerce is an immense and almost incredible thing. We may well recall Ovid's line: 'I am about to sing of facts' but some will say I have invented them. Think of it and ponder over this stupendous achievement, £3.5 billion of capital to develop the good things which nature has stored up for the use and benefit of mankind! In the year 1911 Great Britain will receive about £180 million for interest upon the great capital she has placed in other lands in past years. This income will come to her almost entirely in foodstuffs and raw materials, for it comes mainly from the agricultural and mineral countries of the world.

Given that the amounts in pounds must be multiplied by a factor of about 80 to yield 2014 dollars, and that the population of Great Britain was about one-sixth the current population of the United States, the magnitude of British foreign investment and the return upon it was indeed stupendous.

Speyer was the author of a pamphlet opposing Joseph Chamberlain's policies of Imperial Preference published by the Liberal League (Pamphlet 128; see also the responses published as Pamphlet 202). He was definitely seen as a partisan of the Liberals.

James Speyer in May 1911 composed an essay entitled *International Finance: A Power for Peace* expressing similar views:

Should not the few really great World Powers also make an effort in their own interest to encourage their citizens to invest their savings in the enterprises and securities of other first-rate nations? ... do away with the artificial discrimination against 'foreign' investments, such as higher stamp and other taxes imposed thereon [and] arbitrary exclusion of foreign securities from the list of funds in which savings banks and trustees may lawfully invest.

He also urged that issuers of securities 'adapt their form, as regards denominations and currencies, to the customs of the people who are to buy them'.

James prophetically observed that 'very few nations in modern times can carry on any prolonged foreign war with their own resources only' and urged that neutrals deny credit to nations not arbitrating differences at The Hague. The first insight was shared by the American diplomat Lewis Einstein in his *A Prophecy of War* (1912) but by very few others. On the outbreak of the war, both the American *Army-Navy Times* and the Austro-Hungarian vice-consul joined in published prophecies that its duration would be short; this was also Asquith's view.

Sir Edgar Speyer was one of 249 names on Asquith's list of persons to be appointed to 'pack' the House of Lords in the event that it rejected the Parliament Act. He had been appointed to a committee to revise the Companies Act and advised Lloyd George on creation of a Port of London Authority. Sir Ernest Cassel, something of a protectionist, was not on the list. Speyer, like Ernest Cassel, had been accorded a baronetcy (hereditary knighthood) and raised to the Privy Council by the Asquith government; they were among the few bankers who refused to sign a City manifesto opposing Lloyd George's 1909 budget.

Sir Edgar's service on the committee to revise the Companies Act was not merely honorific. Though joining the principal recommendations of the majority report (there were three dissenters), he appended a separate statement with resonance today in which he urged increased liability for negligent directors:

> Having had twenty years of experience of business life in the City of London, during which I have had every opportunity of watching the development of joint stock enterprise in this country, I am more than ever impressed with the following defects and abuses: a) the growth of pluralist or 'guinea-pig' directors, particularly among men in public life; b) the fact that such ornamental directors are sought after obviously in many cases as decoys on the front page of a prospectus; c) the enormous increase in the number of companies that have gone into liquidation and consequent losses to the shareholders and creditors; d) cases of company frauds; e) the impossibility of making directors personally liable for negligence in the discharge of their duties as directors.
>
> The suggestion that men will not so easily accept directorships under more stringent conditions is, it is submitted, no answer. There is small moral sanction for the position of a man who has ten or more directorships whose companies go into liquidation through mismanagement, and who, apart from what he may have paid for his qualification shares, loses nothing, not even his market value

as director, for he is free to reap an income by joining other boards. A trader who is negligent in the management of his business and ends in bankruptcy has to bear the stigma and the disabilities of the status of a bankrupt. I submit that a director ought not to and need not be in any better position than an ordinary trader. As the number of directorships which a director could accept must necessarily be diminished should the above suggestions be accepted, the remuneration of a director ought then, in my opinion, to be increased.

In 1909, Edgar Speyer wrote to Chancellor of the Exchequer Lloyd George suggesting that the economic analyses of the orthodox free trader Sir George Paish would be useful to him. Speyer had been associated with Paish since 1904. Lloyd George took this advice and in the middle of 1909 Paish began advising him on economic matters, a service he rendered to him for the following six years, which [Paish] called his 'happy association with that great statesman'.

13. Sir George Paish

Paish had published pioneering articles in the *Journal of the Royal Institute of Statistics* on the stimulative effect of foreign investments and their relation to world peace. He asserted that 'England was always prosperous when she was making issues of new capital freely for colonial and foreign countries.' Unlike orthodox economists, he did not foresee a recession in 1909, and his optimistic forecasts were welcomed by Lloyd George in preparing his 1909 budget with its expanded welfare state and its new expenditures on unemployment and health insurance and old age pensions. Previous revenue estimates had ignored capital exports. Paish met frequently with Lloyd George from 1912 onwards. He was an advocate of a strong navy, and his association of international investments with peace was persuasive to anti-imperialists like J. A. Hobhouse and Sir Norman Angell. It was said of Speyer and Paish that 'Two unorthodox individuals sustained the doctrine of export-led recovery and under-wrote Lloyd George's defiance of the City.'

The Asquith government also enjoyed the support of another German-Jewish financier, Samuel Montagu, first Baron Swaythling, the father of one postwar Liberal Cabinet minister, Edwin Montagu, and the uncle of another, Herbert Samuel. Paish foresaw a recession in 1914 and urged an early election before it occurred, a suggestion vitiated by the outbreak of war. The emphasis on capital exports he fostered had a deflationary effect on the domestic economy and on government expenditures, particularly on housing and education. On the other hand, the foreign investment he fostered helped to finance the war, and the investments in foreign agriculture led to cheap food during and after it. Of this, an historian observed, 'Then as now, it was easier to invest in the bounty of natural resources than to embark upon painful reforms of mentalities and institutions.'

The Speyers were indirectly responsible for another of Lloyd George's associates. Edgar and his manager, George Gibb, had hired from the United States, on James's recommendation, a manager of transit systems in Hoboken and Detroit, Albert Stanley (born Knattriess) who became general manager of the underground in 1907 and its chairman in 1910. On Lloyd George's initiative, he became member of parliament for Ashton-under-Lyme in December 1916. Max Aitken, Lord Beaverbrook, surrendered his safe seat to him in exchange for his peerage, and Stanley was promptly made President of the Board of Trade in Lloyd George's government. In May 1919, he was dropped from the Cabinet, Lloyd George having become disillusioned with his handling of labour questions: 'he has all the glibness of Runciman and that is apt to take in innocent persons like you and me'. (Lloyd George's prejudice against Runciman was amply vindicated at the time of the Munich Agreement.) Lloyd George wrote to his Coalition partner Andrew Bonar Law, who later was Prime Minister: 'Stanley, to put it quite bluntly, is a funk, and there is no room for funks in the modern world.' Stanley negotiated for creation of a public corporation for the Tube, instead of full nationalization, in 1933. He remained as general manager until the Tube's full nationalization by the Attlee government in 1948, having been raised to the peerage as Lord Ashfield in 1920, serving as manager of the Tube for more than 40 years in all.

14. Albert Stanley, Lord Ashfield

Lloyd George at one point had considered establishing a Cabinet of businessmen to broaden his support: 'They are very simple people, these captains of industry. I can do what I like with them.' He created new ministries headed by businessmen after the war.

In October 1914, when many of Asquith's friends were withdrawing investments from the Speyer firm after the declaration of war, the Asquiths invited the Speyers to dinner. The editors of Asquith's letters to

Venetia Stanley, commenting on this episode, observe: '[Sir Edgar] was a cosmopolitan financier who meant to keep his international links intact if he could. It was brave to invite him to 10 Downing Street, but he was not suitable to be a wartime prime minister's guest.' Similar views were expressed by Lord Bertie of Thame, whose diaries alluded to 'Speyer continuing to be a guest at Asquith's and matters which ought not to be divulged being discussed before him'.

Rudyard Kipling demanded to know how many times Asquith had entertained Cassel and Speyer; it is not clear what he was told, but Max Aitken (later Lord Beaverbrook) informed Kipling that his poem 'If', with its celebration of men who defy received opinion, occupied a prominent place on the wall in the Speyer office.

INTRODUCTION.

AT a time like the present, when the wholesale depreciation of securities has become a matter of serious moment to the investor, details of the record of Companies, the securities of which have been " vigorously placed " on the British public by a firm whose policy has been if not dictated by, at least interwoven with, German connections, should be most useful and interesting.

There is no' doubt for many years past the Teutonic influence on both the Trade and Finance of the British Empire has reached enormous proportions. It is merely begging the question to say the unremitting and often unscrupulous enterprise of the German commercial firms has eaten into the very vitals of British trade at home and abroad, with the result many manufacturers have been forced out of markets in which they hitherto enjoyed, if not a monopoly, at least the bulk of the business transacted. To go into the details of how and why this has happened is not within the scope of this introduction. That it *has* happened is a melancholy fact; and, unfortunately, this Teutonic influence has not stopped at trade only, but has permeated the most in-timate financial transactions of the Empire. It is not too much to say for years past the Stock and Share business of this Country has been to a very great extent controlled by the German element in the Stock Exchange, and, if the war had not occurred, there is no knowing how far this pernicious influence would have carried, For many months now (in fact, ever since this journal was founded in 1913) the " Financial Mail " has investigated and given details of many Companies which have been promoted by various firms, including Speyer Brothers. English investors have heavily invested in the securities of these concerns; in nearly every case with disastrous results. It is only necessary to peruse the details given herein to realise the enormous loss the British public has suffered by participation in these promotions—losses which would have been avoided had the advice of my journal been followed. I trust one result of this book will be to prove the methods adopted, and the means employed, have been in many instances ruinous, and to point the moral that in future British Capital should be employed in Companies, the promotion and subsequent working of which are entirely and solely British.

A. MORETON MANDEVILLE,
Editor.

15. Mandeville Preface

16. Mandeville Cartoon

On 29 October 1914, Asquith wrote Venetia Stanley and observed: 'I can't describe my disgust at the conduct of Ruby Peto [nee Lindsay, a relative of neighbours of Asquith] in withdrawing at a moment's notice all her investments from Speyer to whom she and her rotten husband owe everything in the world in order to place them in the hands of an English man of business. Ingratitude and baseness could hardly go further.'

Asquith was perceived by his nationalist opponents as being unduly influenced by German bankers. The firm's severest critic, Moreton Mandeville, observed that 'Schuster, Speyer and Schroeder are names to conjure with in a Liberal Government.' Max Aitken asserted in a letter to Leo Maxse that the New York Speyer house 'was undoubtedly financed from London in the early days of the War. Undoubtedly his money is supporting Germany.' Michael Hicks Beach, who later died in the war, charged Speyer with failing to donate payments which he had received when a squadron of the Royal Gloucester Hussars had been billeted on his property.

A biographer of the Unionist advocate Edward Carson was to write after the war that:

[Carson] stood at the head of a formidable Opposition of men, of interests, and of ideas. Mr. Asquith fought the war, as his biographer claims, without forgetting the adage – to behave as if your enemy might again be your friend. He was, besides, the head of a Free Trade party under whose administration before the war the hostile and aggressive economic system of Germany had spread its roots and its branches under and over the British Empire. In certain great trades, as for example in iron and steel, in the base metals, in chemicals, in the electrical industry, in sugar her domination had become so strong that the war left it unbroken. International capitalists like Sir Edgar Speyer and Sir Ernest Cassel, who were thought to support these connections, remained influential in the counsels of the country. Speyer, whose sentiments if not whose activities were known to be at least invidious, was thought to have the ear of the Prime Minister. The British manufacturer, the British producer, and those British merchants whose interests lay in the export trade, to make an end of this common servitude, brought their grievances to Sir Edward Carson.

Carson, despite this apparent super-patriotism, had been guilty of what amounted to sedition in the Ulster Crisis before the war. He was memorably described by H. G. Wells:

> In spite of his Dublin origin, he set up to be a leader of the Ulster Protestants, and he brought to the conflict that contempt for law which is all too common a characteristic of the successful barrister, and those gifts of persistent, unqualified, and uncompromising hostility which distinguished a certain type of Irishman. He was the most 'un-English' of men, dark, romantic, and violent; and from the opening of the struggle he talked with gusto of armed resistance to this freer reunion of the English and Irish which the Third Home Rule Bill contemplated.

Remarkably enough, Carson was later made Attorney General in the coalition Cabinet forced on Asquith, and was a law lord in the postwar period.

A wartime committee led by Carson demanded the removal of naturalized Britons from the Privy Council. King George V's rejoinder to demands for internment of naturalized Germans was 'Intern them all indeed! Then let them take me first! All my blood is German, my relations are German. Let me be interned before Cassel or Speyer.' The hostility toward international bankers in Britain, unlike that on the Continent, was a product of nationalism more than anti-Semitism. 'Germano-phobia almost saturated Britain in a way that anti-Semitism never had done. It was a fear created by the prospect of a possible defeat by Germany.' There were anti-

German riots in dozens of British cities, in which the shop windows of innocent German grocers and butchers were smashed and looted; one riot in London lasted for several days and produced nearly a thousand arrests.

Party politics had more than a little to do with the assault on Sir Edgar Speyer. Edward Speyer had a different experience: 'I had been a member of the Conservative Club since 1886 and one day some six months after the outbreak of war saw a notice at the hall requesting members of enemy origin to resign. Immediately I sent in my resignation, but the committee asked me to withdraw it, which I naturally did.'

Nationalism, of course, was not the sole cause of the downfall of the Liberals (and, ultimately, of the international bankers). As Churchill said, 'The great victories had been won. All sorts of lumbering tyrannies had been toppled over. Authority was everywhere broken. Slaves were free. Conscience was free. Trade was free. But hunger and squalor and cold were also free; and the people demanded something more than liberty. The old watchwords still rang true; but they were not enough. And how to fill the void was the riddle that split the Liberal party.'

The inconsistent Lloyd George, who alternately exploited and sought to dampen war hysteria, at one point mused, 'I'm not sure that I'm not the only survivor on the Treasury Bench who is not of alien origin.' On the other hand, a contemporary cartoon showed Lloyd George shooting down a Zeppelin whose passengers were Asquith, Grey and Speyer.

Though anti-Semitism was a subordinate theme, from some quarters it was a persistent one in the vituperation directed against Edgar Speyer. 'Actual international connections,' the political philosopher Hannah Arendt was to later write, 'naturally stimulated the general popular delusions concerning Jewish political power all over the world.' In Britain, however, that power was not inconsiderable: the period from 1870 to 1914 was a golden age for Britain's Jews, most of them of German origin. Though representing a fraction of 1 per cent of the population, they accounted for 23 per cent of non-landed millionaires, as well as supplying a Chancellor of the Exchequer (Goschen, 1887–92), a Lord Chancellor (Herschell, 1887, 1892–95), two Solicitors General (Jessel, 1871–3; Isaacs, 1910), an Attorney General (Isaacs, 1913), a Lord Chief Justice (Isaacs, 1913) and a Postmaster General (Samuel, 1914). 'Among the 31 millionaire merchant bankers between 1815 and 1939 no fewer than 24 were Jews, 4 Anglicans, while one each belonged to the Church of Scotland, Greek Orthodoxy, and Lutheranism.'

Similarly, in Germany, 'the tax returns [in Prussia] for 1908 show that 'of the 29 families with aggregate fortunes of 50 or more million marks, 9

(31 per cent) were Jewish or of Jewish origin. Of the six names at the top of the table, two were Jews.' The historian Fritz Stern has noted that in 1881 in Berlin, Jews, who were 4.8 per cent of the population, accounted for 8.6 per cent of journalists, 25.8 per cent of those engaged in the money markets, and 40 per cent of wholesalers, retailers and shippers. In 1887, 20.4 per cent of Prussian lawyers were Jews, who were in almost complete control of private banking.

Jakob Wassermann provided similar figures for turn-of-the century Vienna: 71 per cent of financiers, 65 per cent of lawyers, 59 per cent of doctors, half of journalists. Jonathan Steinberg noted Disraeli's vivid description of the extravagant private home of the court banker Gerson Bleichroeder, observing: 'This kind of extravagance gives rise to ill feeling in any society but the public do not worry about it until things begin to go wrong.' Bernard de Jouvenel has observed that 'the wealth of the rich merchant has been resented far more than the pomp of rulers'. The houses of parvenus were perceived as too perfect: 'In great old houses there is a muddle where hideous new furniture stands carelessly alongside magnificent old inherited pieces. In the rooms belonging to the ostentatious nouveaux riches, everything is too defined.' The jaundiced view of many Jewish upstarts, not without some elements of truth, as to some, but not Edgar, was that of the journalist Wickham Steed: 'trained to conjure with the law and skilled in intrigue ... unknown and therefore unchecked by public opinion, without any "stake in the country" and therefore reckless'.

As early as 1903, James Speyer's antennae were sensitive to a possible reaction against this good fortune; he then observed that 'a promise of great prosperity invariably carries with it certain excesses and that when the change comes the sins if such there may have been will be visited upon those who have committed them or their successors. [The] tariff argument appealing to patriotic feelings is taking some root in the English people.'

But as Europe plunged into the abyss, Sir Edgar Speyer had become more confident: 'The world nowadays is so inextricably united by common interests and bonds of sentiment that each country is necessary to all and all to each ... It is inconceivable that the nations who are in the van of the progress of humanity and whose activity has brought such advancement to the world should recklessly destroy their great and civilizing work by war.' It was said of Edward VII that his 'circle was, of course, at once aristocratic and rich, but also cosmopolitan, and what is so rare for monarchy, in no way anti-Semitic, for both the Rothschilds and the Cassels were close friends. Indeed, earlier they had rescued him financially, and helped to create the circumstances in which he could enjoy untrammelled his extravagant life.' His 'court', however, was criticized by some in right-wing circles.

Franz Joseph in Austria had proclaimed: 'I am fully persuaded of the fidelity and loyalty of the Israelites and they can always count on my protection.' Of the collapse of the empires, the Viennese-Jewish writer Joseph Roth was to prophetically observe: 'All the peoples will set up their own dirty little state-lets, and even the Jews will proclaim a king in Palestine.' The historian Carlton Hayes, former American ambassador to Spain, found that 'integral nationalism', 'placing country above everything … was a response to the industrialism and materialism of the age and to the pseudo-scientific propaganda which was spread nationally through the new mass movements, the new mass education, and the new mass journalism'.

The War Minister, Lord Haldane, who had once declared that Germany was his 'spiritual home', and his naval counterpart the First Lord of the Admiralty, Prince Louis of Battenberg, had both been raised to high places by the Asquith government. After they came under attack during the war, the King saw to it that they received the Order of Merit and Battenberg an appointment to the Privy Council. Neither was Jewish; the obloquy poured upon them in the early stages of the war was a function of their national origin and party affiliation. At one point Haldane received 2,500 abusive letters in one day. Unbroken, though dropped from the Cabinet by Asquith, he survived the war to become Lord Chancellor in the first Labour government. Under the impact of wartime hysteria, the Battenbergs became the Mountbattens as the British reigning house of Saxe-Coburg-Gotha became the house of Windsor.

On looking at twentieth-century history one must conclude that social resentment by the less privileged was not a sufficient condition for anti-Semitism in its more virulent forms. That also requires two other conditions: complicity of a governing class and defeat in war, conditions met in France after 1871, Russia after 1905 and Germany after 1918.

Such conditions never existed in Britain or the United States. The British had also been vaccinated against the disease by Disraeli and Lord Rothschild, who, unlike most of their continental counterparts, were identified with the establishment, not the rising middle class. The United States was a mercantile republic without landholding, military or ecclesiastical establishments. The fortunes of its bankers were dwarfed by those of its industrialists (though this may not still be true in today's age of tax preferences for the 'carried equity' of fund managers), and the Morgans were the greatest of its bankers. The Anglo-Saxon nations are not immune to bigotry, but the disease to be feared is nationalism, not anti-Semitism. This was also the conclusion of

Judge Learned Hand, who observed, 'If I were to lay my finger on the rotten spot, I would say it was the sense of nationality.' For him, Americans were 'a self-sufficient aggressive people who have never known and do not believe that this is a world of misery and terrors'.

The quintessential expression of the connection between extreme nationalism and anti-Semitism was that of G. K. Chesterton, which gave him a deserved historical reputation as an anti-Semite: 'I literally fail to understand anybody who does believe in patriotism thinking that this state of affairs can be consistent with it. It is in its nature intolerable from a national standpoint that a man admittedly powerful in one nation should be bound to a man admittedly powerful in another nation by ties more private and personal even than nationality ... the very position is a kind of treason.' Carlton Hayes thought that, 'In the United States, nationalism is invoked and pressed into service as creator and assurer of a novel and unifying American nationality.'

In the *Encyclopedia Brittanica* in 1910, Lucien Wolf, then vice-president of the Jewish Historical Society and later an important London newspaper editor, contributed an article which remains, at a distance of more than a century, one of the more penetrating analyses of the social roots of modern anti-Semitism:

> Its origin is to be found in the social conditions resulting from the emancipation of the Jews in the middle of the 19th century ... It was an advanced development of the main attributes of civilized life, to which Christendom in its transition from feudalism had as yet only imperfectly adapted itself ... the pastoral Semite ... was steadily trained, through centuries, to become an urban European, with all the parasitic activities of urban economics, and all the democratic tendencies of occidental industrialists. Excluded from the army, the land, the trade corporations and the artisan guilds, this quondam oriental peasant was gradually transformed into a commercial middleman and a practiced dealer in money ... When the mid-century revolutions made the bourgeoisie the ruling power in Europe, the semblance of a Hebrew domination presented itself. It was the exaggeration of this apparent domination ... by its enemies among the vanquished reactionaries on the one hand and by the extreme Radicals on the other, which created modern anti-Semitism as a political force.

Wolf closed with the ironic reflection that Zionism 'is a kind of Jewish nationalism and is vitiated by the same errors that distinguish its anti-Semitic analogue', and with an all too accurate prophecy: 'Though anti-Semitism has been unmasked and discredited, it is to be feared that its history is not yet at an end. While there remain in Russia and Romania over six million Jews who are being systematically degraded, and who periodically overflow the western frontier, there must continue to be a Jewish question in Europe; and while there are weak governments, and ignorant and superstitious elements in the enfranchised classes of the countries affected, that question will seek to play a part in politics.'

The psychoanalyst Franz Alexander from his patients' conversations similarly found Nazism to be '[a] rebellion gainst the growing cosmopolitan, levelling, super-national trend … a neurotic defense against loss of identity on a national scale'.

The Speyers, unlike most of those who were cosmopolitan in tastes and economic philosophy were also distinguished for their local patriotism, one of the possible antidotes to such crises of identity. Wolf's reflections on Zionism were similar, but failed to take into account the anti-Semitism that irredentist policies in Palestine have awakened:

> Modern Zionism is vitiated by its erroneous premises. It is based on the idea that anti-Semitism is unconquerable, and thus the whole movement is artificial. Under the influence of religious toleration and the naturalization laws, nationalities are daily losing more of their racial character. The coming nationality will be essentially a matter of education and economics and this will not exclude the Jews as such. With the passing away of anti-Semitism, Jewish nationalism will disappear. If the Jewish people disappear with it, it will only be because either their religious mission in the world has been accomplished or they have proved themselves unworthy of it.

It was the fate of the 'six million' that the optimist Wolf failed to fully foresee. Like many German Jews, but unlike Felix Frankfurter and Ambassador Horace Rumbold, 'they simply didn't see why others needed another Zion'. (In extolling Zionism, Frankfurter had written Judge Learned Hand in 1920 to explain 'having seen something of eastern and western Europe, I am convinced that there is no other solution to the so-called Jewish problem and the continuance of millions of people').

As Vice-Chairman of the Peel Commission in 1937, Rumbold had urged a Jewish state in Galilee, a project warmly supported by Chaim Weizmann but vitiated by the territorial ambitions of the Jewish fascist Immanuel Jabotinsky (the effective founder of the Likud party), aided and abetted by David Ben Gurion, Golda Meir, Lords Reading and Samuel, Winston Churchill, David Lloyd George and the Grand Mufti of Jerusalem.

The passions aroused by Jewish expansionism in Palestine have ensured that neither anti-Semitism nor Jewish nationalism have disappeared. Indeed, the latter has helped inflame nationalism in the United States: the America of 1945, which envisaged a world of 'five policemen' and which supported European unification and the Universal Declaration of Human Rights, now has factions which, in addition to limiting the effect of the Geneva and Torture conventions, repudiate the principles of Magna Carta, the Treaty of Westphalia and the United Nations Charter.

CHAPTER 7

Anti-Germanism and its Consequences

'It will be a terrible thing if we English go to war with us Germans'

Upon the outbreak of World War I, there was pressure on prominent British residents of German origin originated by Sir Arthur Pintero (himself of Jewish origin) to write so-called 'loyalty letters' to the newspapers, demonstrating their patriotism. Sir Ernest Cassel did so, relating that his nephew was serving in the forces and that he had enlisted in the London Regiment and become Judge Advocate General. Edgar Speyer, believing that his public services were enough evidence, refused to do so. He had arrived in London in 1886 and had been naturalized in 1892.

He was born in the United States before the Civil War. He was certainly not an enthusiast for the Great War, and was quoted by Sir Almeric Fitzroy, the Clerk to the Privy Council, as having declared in 1912, 'It will be a terrible thing if we English go to war with us Germans.'

There was more than a small amount of irony in this. Barbara Tuchman erroneously noted of Edgar Speyer that on

> returning to his birthplace in Frankfurt-an-Main in 1886 after 27 years in England [he] found that three victorious wars and the establishment of Empire had created a changed atmosphere in Germany that was 'intolerable' to him. German nationalism had replaced German liberalism. Great prosperity and self-satisfaction acted, it seemed to him, like a narcotic on the people, leaving them content to forego their liberty under a rampant militarism and a servility to Army and Kaiser that were 'unbelievable.' University professors who in his youth had been leaders of liberalism 'now kowtowed to the authorities in the most servile manner.' Oppressed, Speyer gave up after five years and returned to England.

This view, attributed to Edgar Speyer, was in fact expressed by Edward Speyer, a member of the previous generation in the family. Wild rumours were spread about Edgar Speyer. It was alleged that he was signalling to submarines from his house at Overstrand, and that he had been arrested as a German spy. This suspicion was prompted by the fact that the Speyers' house on the cliffs could be seen for miles out to sea and its lights continued to shine each night until the early hours. Local gossip connected the Speyers with a wireless receiver found behind a winnowing machine in a barn.

Overstrand was referred to by Lord Cromer, the former Controller-General of Egypt, as 'Jerusalem-on-Sea'; a similar reference appears in a biography of the Liberal classicist Gilbert Murray. Demonstrators appeared outside Sir Edgar's London house, requiring a police guard. Many withdrew funds from his bank; others threatened to withdraw their children from a school unless his children were withdrawn. Some announced that they would cease their contributions to a hospital until he left its board. The landlord of Queen's Hall refused to renew his lease for the Proms concerts, sponsorship of which was taken over by the landlord, Chappell and Co., in 1914. In the midst of this obloquy, Speyer received supportive letters from Edward Elgar and George Bernard Shaw, and one from Prime Minister Asquith declaring 'I am not a little ashamed of the readiness of my fellow-countrymen to suspect and believe evil.' He thought this would disappear 'once this quarrel has been completely and definitely settled'. On this, Lady Speyer later noted, 'It still hasn't been settled.' It was manifest that in its early stages, Asquith thought that the war would be short. The Speyers also received a letter from Margot Asquith, saying that, unlike civilians, British troops were not bitter at the Germans. Shaw's letter said 'the conduct of so many of us exposes all the rest to suspicion of going half mad with indignant war fever'. In 1923, Shaw wrote Sir Edgar again, urging him to return to England and predicting that America would be allied with Germany and Britain with Japan in the next war.

In this period, 20,000 Anglo-Germans were deported and 30,000 were interned, virtually eliminating an identifiable German community in Britain. The German population of Britain declined from 57,500 in 1914 to 22,250 in 1919. Of 37,500 German men in 1914, only 8,476 remained in 1919 after wartime internees were deported.

Finally, goaded by Lady Speyer, Sir Edgar wrote to Prime Minister Asquith asking him to revoke his baronetcy and Privy Council membership:

Nothing is harder to bear than a sense of injustice that finds no vent in expression. Charges and suggestions have now been repeated by public men who have not scrupled to use their position to inflame the overstrained feelings of the people. I am not a man who can be driven or drummed by threats of abuse into an attitude of justification but I consider it due to my honour as a loyal British subject and my personal dignity as a man to retire from all public positions.

This action may have been prompted by an editorial in the chauvinistic *Morning Post* suggesting that 'we should advise Sir Edgar and all in a similar position for their own good to leave the country during the continuance of the War or to live in such a way as to give no ground for the complaints that they exert any influence upon others, either personal, political, or financial'. Speyer's letter was written on 17 May 1915, a day before the *Globe* newspaper demanded that Anglo-Germans publish 'loyalty letters' and three days before Cassel did so. Asquith, with the concurrence of King George V, refused to let Sir Edgar resign from the Privy Council: 'I have known you long, and well enough to estimate at their true value these baseless and malignant imputations upon your loyalty to the British Crown. The King is not prepared to take any steps as you suggest in regard to the marks of distinction which you have received in recognition of public services and philanthropic munificence.'

The criticism by public men to which Speyer alluded included that by a Conservative MP, Pemberton Billing; by another MP, Henry Page Croft (later Lord Croft), whose National Party at its peak had seven seats in the Commons and three times that many in the Lords (and who became a junior war minister in Churchill's 1940 Cabinet); by Admiral Charles Beresford, who declared that 'naturalization does not change the nature of a man'; and by the editor of the *National Review*, Leo Maxse, whose denunciation of German bankers had an anti-Semitic tinge and started well before the war, though it significantly exempted Disraeli's banker, Lord Rothschild. In his later memoirs, Croft made no mention of his vendetta of 30 years earlier against Speyer and Cassel.

It was said of Billing, who also was a violent critic of Oscar Wilde (and also a pioneering aircraft designer), 'Billing represented the voice of the outraged British middle class, the defining voice of our era, the voice that calls for punitive measures against anything that threatens its own status quo. In the history of the Billing affair is reflected the swing of middle class sensibility and all the safety, reason and stability it represents.'

Billing's vituperation was boundless, alleging the existence of a list of 47,000 Britons with sexual perversions who were subject to blackmail by the Germans including the Prime Minister and his wife and the trial judge at a libel trial at which he was acquitted. He further denounced 'the German

Jew called Edgar Speyer who is now working out the damnation of this country in America'. *The Times*, remarkably enough, in its eagerness to do down the Liberals, was an apologist for Billing: 'In the days before the War there was growing in London, beyond any sort of question, that passion for excitement and for the latest novelty which is always the familiar beginning of a corrupt society. If one of the consequences of the Billing case is to give new value to the ancient virtues, then there may be some compensation after all for the work of a scandalous week.'

Maxse had written as early as 1909 that 'the cosmopolitan financier of London, who is rarely an Englishman, can be relied upon to deal a deadly blow to British credit at the right moment'. Alluding to a Speyer proposal for British participation in a Baghdad railway, which Speyer thought would ensure for Britain the friendship of Turkey, Maxse wrote: '[H]owever eager the Speyers, the Meyers & c. may be for the pickup of a great flotation, let us hope that not one shilling of English money will ever be invested in the razor to be used for the cutting of our own throats.'

The German–Turkish agreement had been negotiated by the Berlin banker Arthur Gwinner, Edgar Speyer's cousin by marriage. (In fact, in February and June 1914, Germany negotiated agreements with France and Britain providing for British control of the link from Basra to the Persian Gulf.) It has been said that 'Dr. Von Gwinner and his syndicate of German businessmen in fact did all they could to "internationalize" their railway.' The Marconi scandal caused Maxse to allude to 'the Hebrew clutch upon the Radical Party and the spread of Hebrew power and Hebrew ideals in Parliament, in the Press, finance, and society'. This was followed by an even more vituperative 'Warning to German Jews' in October 1913.

The root of this prejudice was similar to that of the prejudice against international bankers exploited by Hitler, as described by the British ambassador to Berlin in early 1933, Sir Horace Rumbold: 'The ostentatious mode of life of Jewish bankers and financiers – a tradition from the days when the ex-Emperor ennobled Jews who built ocean-going yachts or set up large racing stables – inevitably aroused envy when unemployment became general. The best elements in the Jewish community will now have to suffer for the sins of the worst.' 'The nouveaux riches found in the entourage of the Prince of Wales [later Edward VII],' one writer asserted 'could not fail to arouse the indignation of the old aristocracy.'

But in both wars, to the extent that German Jews were victimized in England, as by the temporary detention of tens of thousands of refugees on the Isle of Man in 1940 against the initial wish of the government, it was because they were Germans, not because they were Jews. The depictions of English anti-Semitism by the English barrister Anthony Julius and of British philo-Semitism by the American historian Gertrude Himmelfarb are both overdone; the position of Jews as such played only a limited part in British political discourse, as distinct from that of Germany and France. 'The Jewish origins of both men [Cassel and Speyer] seem to have been of less importance to their enemies than their German birth.'

Similarly, the anti-Semitism of the Ku Klux Klan in 1920s America was part of an indiscriminate assault against a resented wave of recent immigrants from Eastern and Southern Europe, as nativist in its inspiration as the Know Nothing party's campaign against German and Irish immigrants in the 1850s. Nationalism, or national socialism in its broadest meaning, is the gravest threat to racial or political minorities; as the historian John Lukacs has written, 'all the other isms are wasms'. The American and British anti-Zionist Jews of the 1930s, like Judge Joseph Proskauer and the British Cabinet minister Edwin Montagu, were acutely conscious of this, viewing the greatest threat to Jews as the perception that they had divided loyalties. Nonetheless, the predominant American Zionists decided to press for visas to Palestine rather than to the United States for the displaced persons in Europe. 'An unavoidable conclusion is that during the Holocaust the leadership of American Zionism concentrated its major force on the drive for a future Jewish state in Palestine. It consigned rescue to a distinctly secondary position.'

When Proskauer and the organizations he represented who had resisted this setting of priorities finally lent support to the state of Israel as an accomplished fact, it was on the agreed condition in the so-called 'Blaustein–Ben Gurion Agreement' that the new state would not proselytize for settlers in the United States or profess to speak for Jews in the diaspora. By then, the new state, and the wars and expulsions attendant on its creation, coupled with the expulsion of Jews from the nations of the Arab world, had created as many refugees as the new state relieved.

The Speyers' cosmopolitanism is to be greatly admired, but it flouted the nationalism that was the twentieth-century disease. They would have found unappetizing the posture of today's American neo-conservatives, of whom John Lukacs has written: '[T]here are fellow-travellers on the right as well as on the left ... who gain a sense of security from the company of nationalists and haters,' descendants of the post-World War II American Jewish apologists for Senator Joseph McCarthy united in George Sokolsky's American Jewish League Against Communism.

Speyer resigned from the boards of the Underground Electric Railway Company of London at the suggestion of its board, which he regarded as the unkindest cut of all. He also resigned from the boards of the Poplar

Hospital and the King Edward Hospital Fund. On 26 May 1915, he and his family left for America. Even the British committee that ultimately denaturalized him did not reproach him for this: 'No adverse inference should be drawn from his leaving this country. His life here for the time had become intolerable … due partly to his German name and race and partly to the pro-German and anti-British sentiments publicly expressed by his brother James Speyer in New York.' Sir Edgar declared, in a letter to George Bernard Shaw: 'I shall never forget nor forgive the treatment I received. This may not be a fine sentiment but it is the true one at any rate.'

A proceeding was brought on 15 June 1915 by an organization known as the Anti-German Union to oust Cassel and Speyer from the Privy Council on the basis of their German birth, citing the Act of Settlement of 1701. The suit was rejected in December 1915 by Lord Reading and two other judges in a divisional court on the basis that the section relied upon had been repealed by later legislation. It awarded costs in favour of Cassel but not Speyer, who was perceived as having 'told the King and Privy Council to go hang' by his letter to Asquith.

In another action, an Argentine debtor, a familiar phenomenon in those days as in ours, defended a suit brought by the Speyer Brothers partnership on the ground that Edward Beit von Speyer, an alien enemy, had been a partner in the plaintiff firm (which had been dissolved and reconstituted when he withdrew from it on the outbreak of war). The evidence revealed that Beit von Speyer held only a 2.5 per cent interest and owed £30,000 to the firm. A divided House of Lords held in 1919 that the Speyer firm could sue. A dissenting opinion by Lord Sumner repeatedly mentioned the unpopular Sir Edgar and referred to Beit von Speyer as 'Herr Speyer'.

In a memorandum dated 19 December 1915, Almeric Fitzroy, Clerk to the Privy Council, recorded a conversation he had with Lord Chief Justice Reading, who had just been named as an emissary to the US and later became Ambassador. Fitzroy asked him whether the fact of the American Speyer firm 'having become the depository of the huge sums placed by Germany in America for furnishing supplies to vessels engaged in the destruction of British commerce' was not grounds for Sir Edgar's removal from the Privy Council. Lord Reading is said to have agreed, noting that James Speyer had moved heaven and earth to gain an interview with him, but 'by dint of unremitting vigilance he had succeeded in baffling his efforts. He knew him to be the tool, if not the spy of Bernstorff and that was enough for him.' Sir Edgar Speyer did not lose his Privy Council seat, despite efforts to resign it, until he was denaturalized; even then, he retained his baronetage, since it was an inheritable position (though it became extinct when Sir Edgar died without male heirs).

After departing for the United States before Lord Reading's decision, Sir Edgar was considered (on slender evidence, as we shall see) to have consorted with the pro-German party, an embarrassment to Reading when he was named ambassador to Washington. Reading wanted to do nothing that would recall his involvement in the Marconi affair. On arriving in the United States in June 1915, Sir Edgar went to stay temporarily with his brother at Waldheim, and 'declined to make any comment on European affairs and said that he had been suffering from too much publicity in England recently'.

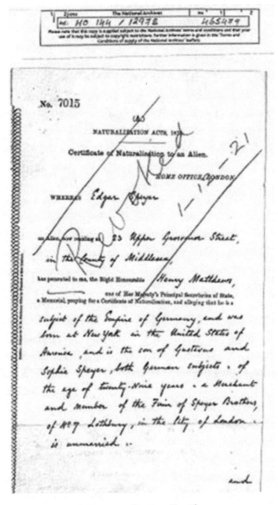

17. Denaturalization Certificate

Lord Alfred Douglas (famous for his vindictiveness in the Oscar Wilde tragedy) accused Cassel and Winston Churchill of issuing a false report of the Battle of Jutland in order to profit on the stock exchange, Cassel being alleged to have profited to the tune of £18 to £48 million and Churchill to the extent of £40,000. In the ensuing libel action, the plaintiffs were each awarded a farthing on the basis that there was no deliberate fabrication. Douglas was subsequently charged with criminally libelling Churchill and was sentenced to six months imprisonment. Churchill acknowledged having received a library from Cassel in 1905 and £500 as a wedding present in 1908, not insubstantial gifts. Cassel, though vindicated, was spiritually broken by the wartime questioning of his loyalty; he died in 1921, leaving a fortune of more than £ 7.5 million.

In August 1918, in a debate on the Denaturalization Bill in the House of Lords, Lord Lincolnshire reproached 'the brutal and insolent German manner in which Sir Edgar Speyer had resigned his dignity' on the Privy Council. Lord Curzon announced that the Home Office was examining his Privy Council membership. Speyer again tendered his resignation, but received no response from Prime Minister Lloyd George. The Conservative leader Andrew Bonar Law (who had himself been on the receiving end of a charge of trading with the enemy) had said of naturalized aliens:

> There are Germans who became British subjects purely for business reasons and who have not changed in their feelings of sympathy for Germany. These men are a danger to this country, and in my opinion the higher the position they occupy and the greater their wealth and influence, the more power they have to injure us. Therefore, there is no class that should be more carefully watched than this class.

Three of Lloyd George's slogans in the 'coupon election' of 1918 were 'Make Germany Pay', 'Hang the Kaiser' and 'Expulsion of the Enemy Alien'. The Denaturalization Act was tailored to the case of Edgar Speyer, penalizing in all-encompassing terms 'disloyalty by overt act or speech or communicating or trading with the enemy or [acts] not conducive to the public good'.

In 1921, over the initial objections of Prime Minister Lloyd George, denaturalization proceedings were brought against Sir Edgar and his family by the coalition government's law officers before the Home Office's Certificates of Naturalization (Revocation) Committee. After a hearing lasting 18 days, Speyer's naturalization was revoked on 1 December 1921 by a committee of three members all of whom had lost sons and otherwise suffered greatly from the war. On 13 December 1921, King George V signed an order removing him from the Privy Council, though declining to personally strike off Sir Edgar's name from its register, to avoid 'anything so personal, and, if may say so, theatrical'. On 7 January 1922, the committee's report was published. It considered nine issues, and a reader of it must conclude, contrary to the committee's conclusion, that the sum of nine zeroes is still zero, notwithstanding Edgar's amoral but eminently sane willingness to engage in innocuous communication with persons in enemy countries.

Speyer was reproached for being slow to resign from the board of the American bank of which his German brother-in-law remained a director. Edgar had declined a suggestion by James that he inquire of the War Office as to what it knew of the fate of Erwin Beit, a nephew fighting on the German side: 'Certainly, I have not worried the Government. Every day we see long lists of missing – and these are English soldiers.' James successfully made a similar inquiry of the State Department and learned of Erwin's death through the American Embassy in Paris: he had 'volunteered for a particularly dangerous reconnaissance [and was] surprised by an armoured motor car'. The Declaration of War occurred on 4 August; on 11 September a Royal Proclamation called on British subjects to sever links with companies doing business with Germany; Speyer sent a letter resigning his directorship on 22 September, backdated to 9 September, the New York Stock Exchange being notified on 5 October.

Speyer Brothers also did business with a Dutch firm with German connections in early 1915, profiting to the extent of £1,000. Edgar had continued to correspond with his German brother-in-law, using codes and intermediaries to do so; the evidence of Sir Edgar's disregard of the British censorship was incontrovertible, but no secrets were transmitted.

Letters from Eduard Beit (but not from Speyer himself) were said to show that Speyer planned to live in Germany after the war. His sister Lucie, who had festooned her house with bunting after the British defeat at Gallipoli, wrote him to exalt in German victories, a fanaticism possibly inspired by her son Erwin's death on the German side in the early days of the war.

While in America, Speyer remained friendly with the conductor of the Boston Symphony Orchestra, who was suspected of being a German agent and was later interned as such. Edgar funded a visit to Europe in 1916 by an American statistician who represented the United States on the International Prisons Commission and who met Speyer's sister while in Germany. The committee drew no inference of disloyalty from this. Speyer was reproached for lending money to keep a Boston newspaper which had printed some pro-German articles from going out of business. This was said to be imprudent but not disloyal, as was the payment by the Frankfurt bank of sums on deposit at the London bank, the committee noting that this was a breach of regulations but that leniency had been shown to others.

Edgar's offences were cumulative. From this it was concluded that Speyer had 'shown himself by act and speech to be, disaffected and disloyal to His Majesty and ... associated with a business which was to his knowledge carried on in such manner as to assist the enemy'. Speyer, responding to the report, declared that 'the whole thing is neither more nor less than the culmination of years of political persecution. The Home Secretary simply dared not give me the vindication to which I was entitled.' There was not in his view 'a strip of material evidence that would induce any fair-minded man to support the monstrous conclusions of this report'.

It is pleasant to record that when Speyer was naturalized in the United States in 1925, according to his friend Suzanne La Follette, 'the judge who officiated [Henry W. Goddard, much later in his career the judge at the second Alger Hiss trial] declared that this country was honoured on granting citizenship to such a man'.

On 1 April 1922, Speyer Brothers was dissolved. The Grosvenor Street house with its splendid music room was sold to the American Women's Club in early 1923 and was retained by it until at least 1944 and later (in 1960) became the Japanese Embassy and subsequently the headquarters of a brokerage firm, Killik and Co. Speyer rejoined the boards of the American and German banks and continued to live in New York. It is said that the characters of Sir Hermann and Lady Aline Gurtner in E. F. Benson's novel *Robin Linnet* were based on the Speyers, as well as that of Appleton, a villainous stockbroker, in John Buchan's *The Thirty-Nine Steps*, and the English Speyer firm makes a cameo appearance in Theodore Dreiser's posthumously published *The Stoic* (1947), the third in a cycle of novels based on the life of Charles Yerkes. It was likewise said of a similarly circumstanced Franco-Austrian family that 'The dislike of the Ephrussi keeps turning up in novels.'

Sir Edgar devoted his subsequent life in the United States to music, charitable activities, and travel. Edgar's house on Washington Square was not a modest establishment; his neighbour Rose O'Neill related that 'He had bought No. 22 on the north side of the square and had filled it with famous paintings, tapestries, works of art and eleven servants.' O'Neill had been introduced to the Speyers by the poet Witter Bynner; she described Leonora as having 'shining gold-brown hair, a strong face, and blue eyes' and as being 'tall, slender, handsome, and exceedingly well dressed'. The Syrian writer and artist Kahlil Gibran sketched three views of her face.

18. Washington Square

Edgar's relations with his brother were strained. After he withdrew from membership in the American firm after the declaration of war in 1914, there was an agreement in 1916 settling the accounts of the English and American Speyer firms. Allegedly, there was a 1914 verbal agreement that Edgar would rejoin the American firm after the war. In 1922, following the conclusion of an American treaty of peace with Germany, Samuel Untermeyer as Edgar's attorney presented to James when he was vacationing at Carlsbad a demand for $1.5 million, representing profits allegedly due to Edgar for his share of the profits of the American firm from America's entry into the war until the treaty of peace between Germany and the United States. This claim was ultimately settled for personal payments from James to Edgar (in which the other American partners did not share) of $750,000 over a period of years. A claim for taxes by the state of New York against

James based on disallowance of the payments as a business expense was subsequently litigated in the New York courts.

Edgar's attorney, Samuel Untermeyer (who had been counsel to the Pujo 'money trust' investigation, and who had represented Sir Edgar in connection with the British denaturalization investigation), noted that Edgar did some writing: 'the product of his pen [including a pamphlet in tribute to his wife including the text of plays annually performed by their children and written by him] is published privately and circulated only among the most intimate friends, the Speyers and their relatives'. Among other writings, he is said to have produced German translations of Shakespeare's *Hamlet* and Keats' poems.

Sir Edgar died in Berlin in February 1932; he had gone there to have an operation on his nose. (German doctors were held in high esteem in Britain and America both before and after World War I). According to a report by an American vice consul, he died at 4 Paulsbornerstrasse of 'blood disease' on 16 February, and was buried in the Dahlem cemetery in Berlin; two of his daughters, Leonora ('Baba') (von Wolff) and Pamela (Countess Moy) were present at the burial. His wife Leonora received the news of his death while on a liner en route to join him.

A report of his death in the Manchester *Guardian* saying that his body was cremated appears to have been in error. His not enormous estate amounted to $787,864, with debts of $479,761, including $119,000 due to his wife. On his death, poems in his honour were published by Padriac Colum and Rose O'Neill. The estate included 51 worthless holdings and a $25,599 claim against the Alien Property Custodian later rendered valueless by the German default.

Leonora retained the Washington Square house. At some point in the 1920s she had also acquired a house in Baden-Baden at 23 Maria-Viktoria Strasse. She left the house in 1937, presumably for political reasons; it was appropriated by a Nazi Gauleiter in 1939 and by the French occupation authorities after World War II but survived intact. It represented the Speyers's last connection with Germany.

AMERICA

CHAPTER 8

Mediation Efforts

'The side which was temporarily elated became
increasingly attached to the fetish of total victory'

The Speyers, like almost all international bankers, sought to foster international understanding. In 1905, Sir Edgar Speyer, together with Sir Alfred Beit, to whom he was related through his brother-in-law Eduard Beit, along with Sir Ernest Cassel, Baron Perclyde Worms and Baron Bruno Schroder founded the Anglo German Union Club.

In 1906, Edgar Speyer warned the German Ambassador in London, Prince Metternich, of Britain's determination to support France in the first Moroccan crisis. In 1909, his protégé, George Paish, met with Theodore Roosevelt and President William Howard Taft to promote international arbitration; an arbitration treaty between Great Britain and the United States narrowly failed to attain ratification in the Senate.

In 1911, Edgar Speyer met with the German Chancellor Bethmann-Hellweg on the Baghdad Railway project, and urged the British Foreign Secretary, Sir Edward Grey, to meet with Bethmann-Hellweg.

In April 1911, James Speyer gave a dinner for Ambassador Bernstorff at his then home, 257 Madison Avenue. Those present included George F. Baker, Andrew Carnegie, Elbert H. Gary and Mayor Gaynor of New York City.

In the same year, Ernest Cassel, together with Lord Haldane, the War Secretary, and Winston Churchill, First Lord of the Admiralty, participated in negotiations with Germany looking toward a limitation of the naval arms race between Germany and Britain. The German industrialist Albert Ballin of the Hamburg-America line, a Speyer client, facilitated the conversations. It is not clear whether Sir Edgar Speyer influenced Cassel's efforts, though Edgar Speyer's protégé George Paish met with both Tirpitz and Bethmann-

Hellweg in 1912. Although progress was made in initial discussions with Chancellor Bethmann-Hellweg, the negotiations foundered on the obstinacy of the German military, particularly Admiral Tirpitz: '[T]he one price at which substantial concessions could be obtained was a pledge of neutrality in the event of Germany being involved in war; in other words, we were to abandon France.' The requested neutrality pledge, to be sure, was not to apply where Germany was the aggressor and was not to impair pre-existing British agreements, but given Britain's naval superiority, it appeared to some in Britain including Foreign Secretary Grey, Sir Arthur Nicholson, Sir Francis Bertie, Sir Edward Goschen, and the British ambassadors in Paris and Berlin, as a demand of something for nothing.

The *National Review* in Britain (virtually all of which was written by Leo Maxse) condemned the negotiations: 'Germans doubtless approve the intervention of financiers in international affairs and know well how to make use of them in German interests, but Englishmen prefer that their Government should keep clear of the Cosmopolitans of *la haute* finance.'

Paish's emphasis on a strong navy as the best guarantee of international investments and peace may have given rise to Lloyd George's unfortunately overblown and inflammatory rhetoric in his Mansion House speech in July 1911: 'It is essential in the highest interest not merely of this country but of the world that Britain should at all hazards maintain her place and her prestige among the great powers of the world.'

In the spring of 1912, George Paish visited Germany, armed with letters of introduction from Sir Edgar addressed to the Chancellor, Vice-Chancellor, the Foreign Minister and Admirals Tirpitz and Von Koster. As usual, Tirpitz was the stumbling block, frankly declaring to Paish, 'We want you [Britain] to hold the ropes so that we can take anything we want from anyone else in the world.'

The war was not good to either Cassel or Ballin; Cassel as noted emerged from its persecutions a broken man and died in 1921; Ballin committed suicide in 1918. Although Cassel was awarded his costs in the 1915 denaturalization proceeding and no further proceeding was brought against him, the vituperation against him was a poor reward for his role as the largest English individual subscriber to the British War Loan, to the tune of £2.5 million. Edgar Speyer subscribed £378,000 in November 1914, while hard-pressed by his firm's investors, and another £27,000 a month after his arrival in the United States.

In September 1914, J.P. Morgan Jr complained that '"peace" talk has been fomented and worked up in a large measure by the German Jew element, which is very close to the German Ambassador'. In December

1915, writing of the new British ambassador Lord Reading (Rufus Isaacs), Morgan observed, in a letter to Edward Grenfell of Morgan's British affiliate on 15 December that 'most of the Jews in this country are thoroughly pro-German and a very huge number of them are anti-J.P. Morgan and it would be desirable if he [Reading] had not so close affiliations with them'.

But any view of the German international bankers as holding monolithic views would be a mistaken one. The Speyers did not float loans for either side, though Edgar personally subscribed to the British War Loan, Jacob Schiff refused to float Allied loans until after Russia left the war in 1917. Mortimer Schiff and Otto Kahn of Kuhn Loeb were pro-Ally from the outset. The Speyers were Asquithian free traders in economic philosophy, while Ernest Cassel was a Conservative and Otto Kahn before the war nearly stood for Parliament as a Conservative and a champion of tariffs and imperial preference.

A dinner at James Speyer's Westchester County house on 5 September 1914, including Speyer, Ambassador Bernstorff and Oscar Straus, former secretary of commerce in the Theodore Roosevelt administration, was viewed by many as having resulted in the most serious of all American efforts to mediate the war. The initiative took place after the First Battle of the Marne, the point at which Bernstorff concluded that Germany could not win the war. Straus had met Bernstorff during diplomatic service in Constantinople. In indicating receptivity to the proposal, Bernstorff almost certainly was acting beyond his instructions.

Straus went to Washington that evening and laid the proposal before an enthusiastic Secretary of State William Jennings Bryan the next day. At Bryan's request, Straus went to the British Embassy and described the proposal to British ambassador Cecil Spring-Rice and French ambassador Jules Jusserand. They agreed that the suggestion was worth following up. Bryan inquired of Jusserand as to what France would think of a restoration of the status quo before the war, leading to Jusserand's famous reply that more than the status quo would be required, since any such restoration would require restoring life to the French dead. Bryan, after interviewing Bernstorff, then informed American ambassadors Page, Herrick and Girard in London, Paris and Berlin of the overture, which was compromised by a detailed leak of the proposal which appeared in the *Chicago Herald* on 8 September 1914, following which Herrick did not pursue the proposal at all in Paris, and Page did little to do so in London.

Ambassador Girard was told by Chancellor Bethmann-Hellweg that 'The United States ought to get proposals of peace from the Allies.' When no response was received from either the British or French by 18 September,

Bryan concluded that nothing would come of the initiative and on 19 September addressed a letter to President Wilson citing the failure of private mediation and urging the president to call an international conference.

Wilson did not welcome Bryan's suggestion for a conference, but his adviser Colonel House pursued the Straus initiative, ascertaining that Bernstorff was willing to meet secretly with Spring-Rice to discuss peace terms. Spring-Rice thought that peace was possible on the basis of a restored Belgium but declined to meet Bernstorff for fear that the conversation would be exposed by the 'unreliable and unmoral Germans'. He urged Grey to start negotiations through Wilson on the basis of an end to militarism and restoration of Belgium. Grey replied on 26 September that if Bernstorff were given authority to approach Wilson, the British and French could be summoned to hear what Bernstorff had to say. Bethmann-Hellweg at almost the same time declared that 'if we accepted America's offer of mediation now our enemies would interpret it as a sign of weakness'.

'Thus it was,' Kent Forster observed, 'that each side reluctantly left open the door to a move by its enemies, but refused to take any positive step itself.' On 22 October the United States acquiesced in the British blockade of Germany, thereby surrendering a possible source of pressure on the British. House's efforts to promote a peace were damaged by his pro-British reputation, as well as by the egregious bias of the American ambassador to Britain, Walter Hines Page, who declared, 'At present, I can't for the life of me see a way to peace, for the one reason I have told you. The Germans wish to whip England, to invade England.' Grey had not even taken up House's inquiry of 4 December with the Cabinet or entente representatives as late as the twentieth of that month because he was as wary of inter-Allied peace discussions as he was suspicious of German peace-feelers. Kent Forster has observed that 'The antagonism between Colonel House and Secretary Bryan certainly did not facilitate the development of the Straus affair in September 1914.'

In July 1916, James Speyer was involved in organizing an American Neutral Conference Committee which urged a conference of all neutral nations to offer mediation in the war. President Wilson is said to have expressed sympathy with its objectives. Its members included Jacob Schiff, Irving Fisher, Oswald Garrison Villard, Jane Addams and Rabbi Stephen Wise. In November 1916, Jacob Schiff and Speyer were assailed by the Northcliffe press in England for their work for the committee. The *Daily Mail* expressed doubt that Viscount Grey would be able to defeat 'the manoeuvres of such clever men as Jacob H. Schiff and James Speyer ... two of the clearest and ablest brains in the United States'. A cartoon entitled 'A

Hyphenated Proposition', which appeared in the December 1916 edition of Punch, showed Uncle Sam looking at a peace kite in the shop window of Schiff, Speyer, Huebsch and Co. The caption read: 'Guess I'm Not Taking Any. I've been neutral about war and I'm going to be neutral about peace.'

In the United States, James Speyer also became involved in controversy arising both from wartime hysteria and his own stubborness. Edgar was annoyed at his pro-German statements at the start of the war: 'the obvious and considerate and wise thing to do would have been not to have allowed yourself to be interviewed, and not to say, as the papers reported, that Germany was acting in self-defense, etc. That was soon known here and showed that you were taking sides.' James Speyer had to scramble to leave Europe upon the outbreak of war. The new nationalism and its costs to the Speyers was dramatized by a *New York Times* story: 'The [American] Embassy has done a land-office business in issuing passports this week. Tourists who never before felt the necessity of such documents, investing $2 each in engraved papers which bespeak the protection and assistance of foreign governments for U.S. wayfarers. James Speyer of New York was one of the applicants for passports.' On disembarking from a ship on 8 August 1914, James Speyer was quoted as saying: 'I talked with many people on the train [from Berlin] and found that they did not want to make war but that they believed that Russia was determined to attack Germany and that they would have to fight. The people were with the Kaiser and believed that he was making every effort to obtain peace.'

Three days later, on 11 August 1914, *The New York Times* published a short article under the heading 'James Speyer Misquoted':

> James Speyer the banker denied yesterday that he made any reference to any of the belligerents in a conversation with a reporter at the Ritz Carlton on Saturday while calling upon Count von Bernstorff, the German Ambassador. Yesterday's newspapers contained a news agency story quoting Mr. Speyer as having said that England was 'the enemy of peace in the current crisis.' The news agency reporter who talked with Mr. Speyer supported yesterday his disclaimer of this utterance and attributed the misquotation to a misunderstanding over the telephone in reporting the interview to the news agency office.

In light of James's earlier gangplank comments, this retraction was not found to be convincing in England.

Before the war, in March 1910, James had given $125,000 to the Berlin American Institute for exchange scholarships. In May 1911 at the time of one of the Moroccan crises he had published an article exhorting bankers to withdraw money from nations displaying a desire to engage in war, leading to a critical *New York Times* editorial inquiring as to the effects of such a proposal on alliances and on investment in railroads. In June 1912, he entertained a visiting delegation of German naval officers. At the outbreak of war, he narrowly avoided being cut off from the world in Carlsbad upon the closing of the Austro-Hungarian frontiers.

In the early years of the war, the belligerents all sought to sell bonds in the United States, the initial British issue being one of $500 million. Germany sold only about $35 million in bonds in the United States; Speyer does not appear to have had a role in these offerings, both floated by Chandler and Co., though alone among major investment houses it took no role in the syndicates led by J.P. Morgan and Co. floating enormous loans for the British and French governments. The small German offerings did not fully sell, some bonds being left with the underwriters. Kuhn Loeb, whose partners were divided in their sympathies, had abstained from Allied offerings except for a single offering of the city of Paris for non-military purposes. As late as September 1916, Kuhn Loeb had considered making similar loans to German municipalities. Schiff's reluctance with respect to Allied loans was due not only to German sympathies, but to the hostility to Czarist Russia that had led him to make loans to Japan during the Russo-Japanese War. Since the British blockade precluded American shipments to Germany, the bond purchases were largely symbolic gestures by German-Americans. The Commerce Department *Handbook on American Underwriting of Foreign Securities* (1930) lists only two German bond issues of $10 million each in April 1915 and May 1916.

In January 1917, before American entry into the war, James had given support to a fund for German orphans. In April of the same year, his wife agreed to give a league for US servicemen free use of a house she owned, an action applauded by former President Theodore Roosevelt. Her agreement had a stipulation: that only the American flag be flown from it. This stipulation became controversial after the United States entered the war on the side of the Allies.

As noted by Ambassador Bernstorff's biographer, 'Even into the war years, he kept in close contact with the banker James Speyer.' Bernstorff's ne'er-do-well son, Christian Gunther von Bernstorff, was temporarily employed by Speyer at his bank, and was later reportedly wounded while fighting on the German side during the war. A writer in *The Times* observed, 'I think nobody in America is in any doubt where Mr. James Speyer's war sympathies are. There will be very few of my countrymen prepared to believe that Mr. Speyer's activity on behalf of a peace is disinterested or "neutral."'

Some of the $2 million spent on sabotage by the German Captain Boy-Ed allegedly passed through the Speyer bank. In a letter to Chancellor Bethmann-Hellweg in October 1915, Bernstorff alluded to his 'old friendship' with Speyer; as has been seen, that friendship had its fruit in a proposal to mediate in the war. Both Theodore Roosevelt and his friend, the British ambassador in Washington, Cecil Spring-Rice, took the view that the Jewish banking houses were on the German side, a phenomenon due to their German background and their aversion to the officially sponsored anti-Semitism prevalent in Czarist Russia from 1880 onward. In January 1914, Spring-Rice had expressed the view that 'Speyer, the brother of your friend [Sir Edgar] has lost his influence [among American Jews] by marrying a Christian. Bernstorff has sent his son into Speyer's office. The principal Jew is now Schiff.'

After his initial missteps in making pro-German statements, and notwithstanding his abstention from the making of Allied loans, Speyer undertook to retrieve his position: 'During the War he worked exceedingly hard to escape the wrath that was visited upon the German community throughout the country. He retreated to his country house, where he immersed himself in war preparedness efforts, allowing the local army reserve to use his house as a training camp – after he had taken down the sign bearing the name of his estate – Waldheim.' His wife organized a women's auxiliary which entertained members of the New York Aqueduct Guard. He also participated in a Plattsburg encampment in 1915 and a Preparedness parade in 1916. In October 1918, he issued a statement in support of a Liberty Loan: 'an oversubscription may even be a factor in bringing about an earlier end to the war … permanent proof of individual patriotism and of our combined financial strength'. By the end of 1919, he had only one American partner, Jesse Hirschman, a German partner, Richard Schuster, having withdrawn from the American firm when the US entered the war; revival of his firm began when Louis Grumbach, De Witt Millhauser and Leon Kronthal were admitted as partners in January 1920.

The mediation efforts failed for the reasons given by Carroll Quigley:

[A]ny negotiated peace requires a willingness on both sides to make those concessions which will permit the continued survival of the enemy. In 1914–18, however, in order to win public support for total mobilization, each country's propaganda had been directed to a total victory for itself and total defeat for the enemy. In time, both sides became so enmeshed in their own propaganda that it became impossible to admit publicly one's readiness to accept such lesser aims as any negotiated peace would require. Moreover, as the tide of battle waxed and waned, giving alternate periods of elation and discouragement to both sides, the side which was temporarily elated became increasingly attached to the fetish of total victory and unwilling to accept the lesser aim of a negotiated peace.

After the war, Speyer was a member of the small board of directors of the American Association for International Conciliation, an affiliate of the Carnegie Endowment for International Peace, serving with George Blumenthal (a former Speyer partner who was then head of the Metropolitan Museum), Thomas Lamont of the Morgan firm, and Columbia University president Nicholas Murray Butler.

CHAPTER 9

Ellin

'The qualities of essential womanhood as it was understood
in the days before feminism became synonymous with unrest'

In 1897, James married Ellin Prince Lowery, who was eight years his senior, at a ceremony in the bride's home presided over by Bishop Henry Potter of the Protestant Episcopal Church. Edgar came from England to be best man for his brother; the bride's nephew, John Dynely Prince, then an academic and later Minister to Yugoslavia, gave away the bride. Although only 40 people were in attendance, 'doorways and walls were festooned with curtains of smilax and clusters of delicate ferns. Magnificent palms were used in all available corners. There was a strikingly attractive canopy of smilax studded with white flowers.' The bride wore a girdle with a double row of diamonds, a gift from Sir Edgar. The Hungarian Band performed. After a wedding trip, the couple took up residence at 251 Madison Avenue. She was the daughter of John Dyneley Prince and the niece of the noted lawyer William Travers, by whom she was raised, having been orphaned at an early age. The aunt who raised her was the daughter of Maryland Senator Reverdy Johnson. 'Her background, enhanced by great charm and popularity, caused the Speyers to be much sought after by social New York.' She had been widowed in 1892 after a marriage of 21 years to James Lowery, a lawyer. According to one historian, 'she had been left so badly off as a result of her first husband's death that she had taken a decidedly un-ladylike step. Putting baking skills to good use, she opened a group of popular tea shops. Since her fashionable friends had not failed her then, she'd been a success.'

Before marrying James Speyer, she had shrewdly taken counsel of the arbiter of New York's 'four hundred', Mrs William Astor:

When it came to social taboos, Mrs. Astor proved … pragmatic. Ellin Prince was reportedly one of the earliest women in society to go into trade, opening a tea room in the Knickerbocker Building. Mrs. Astor did not hesitate to bring a party to enjoy the Elizabethan-style decorations and waitresses in period costume. When the Jewish banker James Speyer proposed to Ellin Prince, she turned to Mrs. Astor for advice … when directly asked by Ellin Prince whether anyone in society would receive a Jew or a Jew's wife, Mrs. Astor confronted the issue with modulated sympathy. 'I don't think we have any alternative, for we are all so fond of you. Marry him, my dear, if you want to. I for one will invite you both to my parties, and I think that everyone else will do the same.' Which is precisely what they did. For many years, Speyer was the only Jewish member of the New York Racquet Club.

A secretary of Speyer, Algernon Blackwood, noted that 'Social amenities were not always easy, for the position of a Jew in New York Society was delicate, but I never once knew James Speyer's taste or judgment at fault – he was intelligent all over.'

19. Ellin

20. James and Ellin

During the period of her prior marriage, Ellin was a founder of the United Hospital Fund in 1881 and of the New York Skin and Cancer Hospital in 1886, and was a co-founder and treasurer of the Irene Club, a club for working girls which she had founded with Miss Grace Dodge and Mrs Richard Irvin in 1884. In 1919, it was noted that 'Mrs. Speyer, whose wit is known by all in society, spends most of her time helping working girls. She herself was a self-supporting woman.' She had also organized a Red Cross society for the maintenance of trained nurses that raised at least $109,000 and put at least 55 nurses and five doctors in the field at various locations in connection with the Spanish-American War, some of whom accompanied wounded Spanish soldiers on their voyage to Spain. On 11 April 1899, President McKinley sent her a letter of commendation for her work. Her early charitable endeavours in this and other connections owed nothing to Speyer's wealth.

She had also supported a number of charities for black women and children, including St Mary's Free Hospital for Children, the Nursery for Coloured Children, and the National League on Urban Conditions Among Negroes. She was Chair of a Subcommittee on Unemployment Among Women appointed by Mayor John Purroy Mitchel of New York in 1915, which organized workshops for hundreds of women. A profile of her in 1908 described her as 'one of the cheeriest and best-liked little women in society', and said that she 'never gives large or costly entertainments' and that her homes were 'charming and comfortable, in no sense palatial but thoroughly homelike'. In 1906, she founded the Women's Auxiliary of the Association for the Prevention of Cruelty to Animals, which staged its first Workhorse Parade of 1,200 horses in 1907, rising to 2,500 in 1908, an annual event until 1914, and which in 1910 separated from the parent organization to become the Women's League for Animals.

Ellin Prince Speyer Hospital for Animals.
During the last quarter of a century, over a hundred thousand of man's anima friends of all kinds have been treated at this hospital at 350 Lafayette Street, whic was started as a clinic in a small way in an old building, but which has been enlarge . . . . . proportions to accommodate increasing numbers of patients. Sto

21. Speyer Animal Hospital

This organization in 1913 established the Ellin Prince Speyer Hospital for Animals; upon her death in 1921, the League issued a memorial magazine in her honour. Her concern was with the beating of workhorses and its brutalizing effects on their drivers and bystanders, not with the welfare of miniature poodles, although the hospital she founded is now largely a pet hospital.

The costs of the Workhorse Parade, about $6,500 a year, were defrayed by Mrs Speyer for its first two years, contributions being successfully sought thereafter. Lame, sick, thin or galled horses and those whose tails had been docked were excluded from the parade, as were those with blinders and dangling head ornaments. Use of a new bit-less bridle was promoted. Prizes were given to the best kept horses in various age and work categories, and to senior drivers, whose prizes of up to $25 ($500 now) were presented in gold. A luncheon was given for the drivers each year.

A $4 million building was erected for the hospital at a new location at 62nd Street and the East River in 1962. It is now known as the Animal Medical Center of New York, and is the world's largest hospital for small animals, with more than 70 veterinarians on staff. The large earlier facility at 350 Lafayette Street, which included an outdoor paddock, was a block long and was described in 1934 as 'a Noah's ark with its wide variety of patients. In 1934, the list included, besides dogs, cats, horses and birds, chimpanzees, a raccoon, owl, fox, turtle, parrot, and lemur.'

Ellin Prince Speyer died in 1921 after an illness of two years; Handel's *Largo* was played by a tearful Fritz Kreisler at her funeral. She was credited with 'helping many a young and struggling musician', and helped sponsor subsidized People's Concerts at Carnegie Hall and the Cooper Union. James gave a $35,000 organ to the Town Hall in Ellin's memory in 1924. Her monument in Sleepy Hollow Cemetery depicts Faith, Hope and Charity and was designed by the sculptor Adolph Weinman. One of her obituaries credited her with 'the qualities of essential womanhood as it was understood in the days before feminism became synonymous with unrest'. She had been greatly upset by the hostility visited on her husband during the war.

In 1885, Ellin had helped establish the first settlement house in the United States, University Settlement. In 1937, there was a ceremony upon its fiftieth anniversary. It had been inspired by Stanton Coit, who was in turn inspired by Canon Barnett's Toynbee Hall in England, but the Speyers were said to be 'largely responsible for the growth of the settlement house to its present eminence'. James noted his disagreement with 'those who feel the need had been lessened by reduced immigration ... In my opinion, it

22. University Settlement

is more important, if, as it sometimes seems, our class feeling is growing, to make good, tolerant citizens out of native-born youth of today than it is to Americanize foreigners. The making of true American men and women – that is the settlement's task.' He also noted that attitudes had changed in 50 years: when he first sought money among his friends on Wall Street, he was labelled a 'Socialist'.

In his view, settlement houses were agencies which benefitted more than the poor. In 1911, he gained public attention when he declared:

> I wonder whether some of those sociologists and we, who support them, could not also do very good work by establishing a Settlement near Central Park and study the conditions among the well to do and rich. Perhaps they would find that while the east side families are too large the uptown families are too small for real happiness and that while the east side boy and girl get into trouble because they do not have enough opportunity for play and amusement, the uptown boy and girl get into trouble because they have too much of such

opportunity … the uptown boy is not enough in the street and does not learn to appreciate other boys and the others' point of view … The law must be obeyed and enforced against all. I cannot understand how some people are constantly clamouring for our government to prosecute trusts and the rich, the same people that will not themselves lift a finger to help a policeman to arrest a thief or assist him against law-breaking strikers … what we all regard as a disgrace nowadays is to die, whether you are rich or whether you are poor, after having led a purely selfish life, without having tried to help your fellow-men in some way.

A commemorative ceremony was also held at 189 Eldridge Street in 1945. There was a staff of 150 in 1937. Among other benefactions to the settlement house, the Speyers had given a gymnasium to it in 1907. It currently has 550 staff members at 21 locations.

In 1905, Ellin Speyer established the Girls' Branch of the New York Public School Athletic League, which survives as the oldest organization of its type in the country. It began with 15 teachers and 200 children. By the time of Ellin's death in 1921, it involved 900 teachers and 20,000 children. In 1915, she initiated a drive which collected half a million bundles of clothing for New York City's poor, an effort commemorated in a newspaper article 25 years later, which also noted that Mrs Vincent Astor's participation was 'her first work for charity'. Upon her death, an editorial noted that 'Her works of beneficence were so many and covered so wide a field that, despite her own distaste for publicity, Mrs. Speyer grew into a great public character. Her devotion to a splendid ideal of citizenship inspired her to the accomplishment of tasks of such magnitude that her power of endurance became a subject of amazement to her intimates.' She was credited with 'executive skill', 'diligence', and 'enthusiasm'. 'This was a New York woman, the creditor of all of us.' The third verse of a memorial poem by Frederick L. Hoffman declared:

Not man alone: even the brutes
Feel somehow vaguely they have lost
A champion of their lesser rights
Who stood for what they needed most.
In peace and war she never failed,
Her country first: praise to her work!
God rest the soul of her who was
The best-loved woman of New York.

23. Newspaper clipping

Though today largely unremembered, Ellin was part of a generation of women reformers, including Mary Ellen Richmond, Jane Addams, Josephine Butler, Lillian Wald, Belle Moscowitz, Beatrice Webb, Grace and Edith Abbott and Sophinisba Breckinridge, not all from privileged backgrounds. Separately, and in combination, they had a transformative effect on both British and American society during the Edwardian era, before the energies of accomplished women had begun to be diverted by what one of them, the British housing and landscape reformer Octavia Hill, thought to be the false promise of women's suffrage.

CHAPTER 10

Carlotta

'A woman who greatly needed to be the wife and muse of genius'

After Ellin's death, beginning in 1921, James had an affair with the actress Carlotta Monterey, which ended in 1927 when she became the third wife of the playwright Eugene O'Neill. The affair outlasted her short marriage in 1923 to the caricaturist Ralph Barton, which ended in a rapid divorce. She had previously been married twice, first to a Scottish lawyer and then to a law student. She was born as Hazel Neilson Taasinge in 1888 and was orphaned at an early age. Her stage career, which owed more to her beauty than her acting talent, lasted from 1915 to 1924.

Speyer never lived with her, but provided her with an apartment during the affair. 'For all his generosity, he was displeased when Carlotta, who had a passion for shoes, spent fifteen hundred dollars for a pair of sandals inlaid with precious stones.'

Upon her marriage to O'Neill, she then became one of Speyer's philanthropies; he secretly gave her a trust fund, which yielded $14,000 per year. Such an arrangement was then not uncommon. The historian of the Cravath law firm has noted that 'Back in the lush 1920s, before heavy income taxes impeded such luxuries, uptown love nests were the source of many law problems ... often the liaisons were unknown even to the client's intimates until death revealed a contract to provide for the lady during her life.' 'Carlotta said years later that a friendly affection existed between her and Speyer, who was many years her senior, and that Speyer had in fact asked her to marry him. But when she told him she was in love with O'Neill, Speyer graciously surrendered the field.'

Speyer taught her how to invest money, knowledge that she passed on to O'Neill, to their mutual benefit; 'she had as much money as he did, or more'. After Carlotta married O'Neill, she and O'Neill remained friendly with

24. James Speyer, inscribed to Carlotta Monterey

James Speyer, and frequently saw Speyer at his estate, where they had long conversations with him about investments and finance. She occasionally referred to Speyer as 'poppa', leading O'Neill to think that Speyer looked upon her as the daughter he never had. Speyer got them through the 1929 crash in relatively undamaged condition. 'On the several occasions when O'Neill and Carlotta dined at Speyer's Fifth Avenue mansion, the two men were favourably impressed with one another.' O'Neill gave the Museum of the City of New York theatre memorabilia, including his father's acting script of *Monte Cristo*. Carlotta represented to O'Neill that her trust fund came from a legacy from an aunt.

Carlotta was a quarter of a century younger than Speyer. She had studied acting in London at Sir Herbert Beerbohm Tree's Academy of Dramatic Arts. She had a face of exceptional beauty and a long neck, though a harsh and unmelodious voice. After her marriage to O'Neill, she was

once compared … to Alma Mahler and Cosima Wagner, each of whom was a woman who greatly needed to be the wife and muse of genius. Carlotta needed

25. Carlotta Monterey and Eugene O'Neill

to make a home for a man who she could and did call 'the master' – pronounced 'mah-ster' – in which 'masterworks' could be created, and so play her part in the work of creativity. She believed she had found her life's calling in being Mrs. Eugene O'Neill. She had seen O'Neill at his worst and had lived daily with a man as pre-occupied and self-absorbed as only a writer can be. While the two made their peace with their differences and their demons, she found great satisfaction in the work of making their various homes, and in helping O'Neill fulfil his gifts.

Between their marriage in 1927 and O'Neill's death at the age of 65 in 1953, O'Neill composed some of his best-known works: *Mourning Becomes Electra, Days Without End, Ah Wilderness, More Stately Mansions, The Iceman Cometh, Hughie, A Moon for the Misbegotten, Long Day's Journey Into Night* and *A Touch of the Poet*. While O'Neill wanted *Long Day's Journey* to be withheld from publication until 25 years after his death, Carlotta arranged for its publication in 1957, when it was awarded the Pulitzer Prize and became O'Neill's best-known work. O'Neill was afflicted throughout the marriage by a rare neurological disease which made it difficult for him to use his hand to write. He had a variety of other disorders, some resulting from misprescribed drugs. Carlotta throughout the marriage bore half of the household's expenses, thereby relieving O'Neill of most financial worries and providing him with a series of attractive homes at Sea Island, Georgia, the California coast, and Marblehead, Massachusetts. Speyer thus did more than support a former mistress; he was a patron of O'Neill's art.

When Speyer died in 1941, his heirs, nephews and nieces threatened court action to abolish the secret trust fund. This alarmed Carlotta, not only for financial reasons but because a suit would reveal to O'Neill that Speyer had been more than a friend to Carlotta. 'The heirs decided against a suit that, unavoidably, would have tarnished the old banker's name. A few more years were to pass before O'Neill learned somehow that Speyer had been his wife's benefactor and one-time lover.' O'Neill reacted to this discovery with some bitterness. In the course of a quarrel with Carlotta, he told one of their friends that 'if a millionaire came along who wanted her [Carlotta] would drop me in a minute'. The fund ultimately passed to the Speyer heirs on Carlotta's death in 1970. Hers was a traditional model of female accomplishment, that of indispensable helpmate to a great man.

CHAPTER 11

US Railway Promotions

'Diminishing waste and giving spectacular
evidence of the productivity of modern labours'

Apart from the London tube, the Speyers' most important accomplishment as bankers was their contribution to railroad finance in the United States and Latin America. The London Speyer firm was responsible for several US railroad promotions, and a restructuring of the Baltimore and Ohio Railroad in 1896–8. 'Buying the securities at virtually any price [for sale in Berlin] [Edgar] Speyer seemed to ignore many unresolved business issues at the B and O.' The London house was credited with devising a reorganization plan for the railroad which was unusual in that the receivers did not merely adjust finances but spent $1 million on urgent physical improvements immediately after their appointment. Speyer Brothers presented the plan on behalf of large interests including the New York and London Morgan and Brown banks and Barings. The London *Economist* observed:

> [S]o far as we can judge, the plan has been devised on fair and equitable terms, and though Speyer Brothers are mainly responsible for its presentation, it is published with the full approval of the whole of the issuing houses connected with the company, as representing the various classes of bondholders ... by the creation of four new securities eighteen existing issues of bonds and stocks will be converted, thus greatly simplifying the present unwieldy capital account of the company ... the bondholders will be compensated ... for the loss of interest by the improved value of their securities in the market.

The plan provided for auditors of established reputations; for a saving of about $1.5 million annually in fixed charges; and for avoidance of foreclosure, which saved the company's Maryland charter which contained valuable tax exemptions. A large block of stock was bought by James Speyer's friend James J. Hill. 'The reorganization was completed just when an unparalleled era of prosperity was fairly under way … the receivership did much to enable the road to take advantage of the later prosperity [though it] increased its nominal capitalization and reduced its fixed charges less than any of the seven other reorganizations of the era … except the Erie.' The reorganization became effective in August 1898; the bankers surrendered control in July 1899 and the 'security holders were tenderly treated'. At one point in the reorganization, Edgar Speyer, after the B and O's default in 1896, offered to buy back all the coupons his house had sold. The reorganization is said to have 'meant, primarily, the end of the Baltimore and Ohio as a "hometown" private Baltimore enterprise and its emergence into the national field of railroad finance'.

In 1888, the English Speyer firm sold Chesapeake and Ohio Railroad bonds in London, probably because of James Speyer's ties to Collis Huntington. In 1896, the New York office reorganized the Lake Shore, Rock Island and Baltimore and Ohio railroads. Speyer acted for both Huntington and James J. Hill.

In 1911, £1.4 million in St Louis San Francisco Railway bonds were sold. Earlier, $10 million of its bonds had been sold in Paris by the Speyer firm. The railroad company went into liquidation shortly thereafter and its bonds sold for 50 cents on the dollar in 1915. The American Interstate Commerce Commission said that the sale 'invites and warrants condemnation of all who participated in it'; Speyer blamed the impairment of market confidence in the spring of 1913 and claimed that its profit on £105 million in transactions between 1905 and 1913 was only £1.3 million.

Speyer and Co. was the US bank to which Deutsche Bank was closest, particularly between 1896 and 1910. Marriage to Anna (nee Speyer) brought Arthur von Gwinner (of Deutsche Bank) into contact with many important private bankers, especially those from her family. Gwinner and Edgar Speyer were cousins by marriage. The Speyer group's position with Deutsche Bank started to weaken shortly before World War I. Although James Speyer, who took over as head of the New York office, was raised in Frankfurt, the group seemed to have lost a natural leader and familial contact with Deutsche Bank after the death of Edgar Speyer.

'The question seems to have arisen in early 1905 as to whether Deutsche Bank would do business exclusively with Speyer in the United States. Speyer also desired a seat on the Deutsche Bank supervisory board. James Speyer seems to have pushed the hardest to do more business and even on occasion using Deutsche Bank's name for transactions before discussing them with his larger "partner." Deutsche Bank, for its part, liked Speyer's good connections in Mexico and Cuba ... by avoiding a more exclusive arrangement, Deutsche Bank combined James Speyer's stirring and energetic presence with its own excellent representation and information sources in the person of [Edward D.] Adams ... During the 1896 gold bond negotiations ... Speyer was deliberately held at a distance ... Speyer's contacts with some German financial institutions aroused Deutsche Bank's jealousy ... like Dresdner Bank [in 1905].' 'James Speyer grated on many people, but he also had a loyal following. Although he served on many boards, Adams doubted that Speyer had much influence. Schiff, in contrast, was very popular because of his many charitable works.'

It was said of railroad receiverships that the

> formula was to consolidate bond issues at lower interest rates and thus reduce fixed charges upon the enterprise, exact from existing shareholders heavy assessments to discharge the floating debt and provide funds for improvement, and replace existing junior liens with an enlarged issue of new stock, common and preferred, entitled to make money only in contingencies. In this fashion, it was hoped, a new financial structure would correct the misjudgements and misdeeds of the past. Such readjustments certainly entailed less hypocrisy and proportionately no more litigation and loss than had attended the repudiation of their railroad bonds by the southern states and by the municipalities of the North ... the reorganizations of the nineties gave a new status to bankers in railroad management, further concentrated in the northeast the control of the railroad network, and through the imperial handling of leases, branches and connections hastened the trend toward large-scale railroading and consolidation.

The Harvard Business School began as the Harvard School of Railroad Management. Until World War II, the lion's share of American investment bankers' business concerned the financial problems of railroads.

In 1906, Speyer received a visit from two German privy councillors undertaking a study of North American railways for the German government. One of them was his brother-in-law Felix Schwabach, who was married to Speyer's sister Henrietta. The ensuing report noted that 'By virtue of personal relations we had an opportunity to discuss the plans for our inspections with a prominent German-American who as head of one of the most influential banking houses, is thoroughly familiar with the financial operations of the American railway corporations.'

Schwabach's ensuing report was kind to the bankers and their reorganizations which 'have mostly purified the bond issues, but seldom the common stock, either by merging the different issues and thus reducing the capital, or by adding new capital to the enterprise by actual assessments from the shareholders, or, finally, by reducing the high rate of interest'. He and his colleague took a more sombre view of the future of the United States. Some of their observations still resonate:

> A youthful and energetic people which is currently qualified, owing to its composition, for productive activity is called upon to exploit this wealth. What will happen when … the cream, so to speak, has been skimmed off; when the minor work begins; when the necessity arises to manage the balance economically because the abundance will soon be exhausted? The exploitation of wealth of the soil frequently approaching destructive waste, and the ruinous neglect of the forests amounting to devastation. The impulse toward the unlimited is hardly likely to prepare them in a proper manner for such conditions … In all work that requires handcraft, America is dependent, as before, on foreign countries … the labour conditions in the United States form in general one of the darkest spots in the economic life of the New World. The labour unions fetter the industries with an iron chain and do not permit rapid progress. A similar disadvantage arises from the short term of office of the President of the United States. This uncertainty as experience teaches begins to exert a general pressure on the entire business world about one year before any national election. Finally the difficulties must not be overlooked which continually arise for the economic life from the negro question, which is by no means definitely resolved.

James Speyer's involvement with the Reading Railroad was a less happy experience. In 1893 he took $10 million in trust bonds after other bankers including Drexel and Morgan declined to do so. Speyer claims to have thought that it was advancing money to the Reading's promoter, A. A. McLeod, for his personal account and not for what proved to be a reckless expansion in New England. A Speyer official testified at a court hearing that 'if Mr. McLeod had not assured me that the Reading was not liable for the stock purchases of Boston and Maine and New York and New England, the negotiations for the loans would never have gone through'.

The Reading adventure as much as the subsequent controversy over the London tube in one version is said to have given rise to the mistrust of the Speyers by the House of Morgan.

> After the eighties as a matter of custom clients were tied to certain banking houses and a breach of this practice led to retaliation. When the Philadelphia and Reading Railroad in its expansion sought to escape the Morgan suzerainty

by a resort to other bankers, a Morgan partner [Anthony J. Drexel] is said to have exploded, "That will be very bad for Speyers and the Reading;" and Morgan proceeded to regain control of the railroad from a president who once declared, "I would rather run a peanut stand than be dictated to by J.P. Morgan."

The Marxist historian Eric Hobsbawm was to write of the early part of this period that

> The 'romance of industry,' a phrase which generations of public orators and commercial self-congratulators were to drain of its original, and indeed of any, meaning surrounds even the bankers, the financiers, the stock-jobbers who merely found the money for railroad construction ... Their collapses have become landmarks in economic history ... It is hard to deny a grudging admiration even to the most obvious crooks among the great railway builders.

Hobsbawm later wrote:

> The bulk of [British foreign] investment (76 percent in 1913) took the form of public loans to railways and public utilities which certainly paid better than investment in the British government debt – an average of 5 percent as against an average of 3 percent – but were equally certainly less lucrative than the profits of industrial capital at home, except no doubt for the bankers organizing them. They were supposed to be secure rather than high-yield investments.

The early railroad activities of the American Speyer firm were even more impressive than those of its English counterpart. European capital had been important to American railroads as far back as the Civil War. Investment bankers played an important part in reorganizing railroads after the Panic of 1893. In 1899, James Speyer, 'thirty-eight years old and barely five feet tall, "with a brown moustache and a high collar" arrived by train in San Francisco'.

Speyer and Co. had been bankers for the Central Pacific and Southern Pacific since 1878, and was said to have 'stood by the company loyally in days of financial stress'. In 1878, Speyer had sold 50,000 shares of Central Pacific stock at $75 a share, as well as $10 million in 6 per cent bonds, followed by additional issues totalling 65,000 shares at higher prices in October 1880, October 1881 and May 1882. In 1893, Speyer granted a line of credit to Collis Huntington which saw the Southern Pacific through a depression in which the Union Pacific, Santa Fe and Northern Pacific went into receivership. In 1898, Speyer was brought into a national commission on Central Pacific debt; the ensuing settlement provided for 20 annual payments of $2.9 million each, Speyer advancing the money for the first four payments and sharing pro rata in the lien on railroad properties. 'This obligation of a reputable banking house to pay the substantial sum of $11,762,543.12 [at least a half billion dollars in today's terms] was a valuable thing in itself and materially increased the attractiveness of the whole plan from the government's point of view.'

'The importance of the final severance of all special relations between the Government and the Pacific railroads, which this settlement achieved, can hardly be overestimated … After more than thirty-five years of Government partnership, the Union Pacific and the Central Pacific were now completely separated from all relations to the government other than those occasioned by the Government's regulation of interstate commerce. For Congress, the executive branches of the government and even the judiciary, the removal of this constantly troublesome problem could not but be welcome.'

Known as Jimmie to his close associates, Speyer became Collis Huntington's personal banker and friend, a relationship that lasted close to 20 years: 'visionary railroad men in the late nineteenth century needed a close relationship with a banker to make their dreams viable … Edward H. Harriman had Jacob Schiff, Collis Huntington had James Speyer.' Speyer regarded Huntington as 'one of the most constructive Americans. He had vision.' Speyer had come to Huntington's attention as a result of Speyer's success in an early conflict with the financier Jay Gould over the St Louis South western (Cotton Belt) railroad.

By 1900, the Speyer firm, along with Morgan and Kuhn Loeb, was one of the three largest investment banks. James Speyer, however, had made some powerful enemies. J.P. Morgan refused to sit on boards with him, and Edward H. Harriman ousted him from the Southern Pacific board in 1906. Speyer was notorious for seeking first placement on any offering statement in which the firm participated, a traditional prerogative of the Morgan firm. In April 1900, Collis Huntington vigorously asserted his confidence in Speyer:

> For thirty years he has been my banker and has financed all my roads … 'you go on with your railroading and I will attend to banking.' I haven't sold a dollar's worth of Southern Pacific stock and I don't need to sell any. I have a few dollars saved up against the time I will be old and poor. All this talk of any quarrel or breach of faith between me and Speyer is rot. It makes me weary.

At an election in April 1901, Harriman gained control but Speyer remained on the Southern Pacific board. In 1906, Speyer, together with Kuhn Loeb representatives and James Hazen Hyde, was finally dropped from the board though his 'retirement had not been generally looked for on Wall Street.' Harriman attributed the changes to a 'desire to do away with all entangling alliances between banks and railroads'.

The Southern Pacific Railroad had been purchased in 1868 by the so-called 'Big Four' who owned the Central Pacific: Huntington, Charles Crocker, Leland Stanford and Mark Hopkins.

26. Collis Huntington

In 1899, Speyer and Huntington undertook to buy the remaining Crocker, Stanford and Hopkins Southern Pacific holdings; 705,000 shares in all (280,000 shares from Crocker heirs, 285,000 from Stanford and 140,000 from Hopkins). Huntington declared: 'I believe in snatching everything in sight.'

It was later related by the journalist B. C. Forbes that

[Mrs Leland Stanford] told me – and I like to tell the story for it is refreshing in days like these – that immediately upon her husband's death, she directed

Speyer and Co. of New York to sell her holdings in Southern Pacific. Speyer and Co. had been Governor Stanford's trusted agents both in this country and in London. Mr. Speyer told Mrs. Stanford that the market was depressed and stock prices were at a low ebb, Southern Pacific selling at $16 a share, but that he believed the market would recover later on. Mrs. Stanford insisted on the sale in order to get $1,000,000 to carry out one of the provisions of her husband's will relating to the plans for Stanford University. Mr. Speyer refused to sell the stock but instead advanced her $1,000,000 out of his own pocket. Subsequently, he sold the stock for her at $34 a share. The Speyers had presumably earned a large amount of money from Governor Stanford in handling securities and making loans. The gratitude of the firm to him and their way of showing it to his widow were charming.

When Huntington died in the following year, Speyer passed over his son, Henry Huntington, and in October 1900 caused Charles Hays of the Canadian Grand Trunk Railway to be elected President of the Southern Pacific. The younger Huntington then sold his stock to Edward H. Harriman, who then arranged to buy Speyer's stock as well, Speyer having lost control of the railroad. Harriman's purchase was said to be 'one of the largest in the railroad and financial history of the country', involving $66.4 million, the equivalent of over a billion dollars today. Thereafter, it was said, 'Anyone looking for a few real live enemies of Mr. Harriman and all he represents [could] find them in the white marble building on Pine Street which is the office of Speyer and Co.' Speyer's breach with Henry Huntington is said to have arisen from dividend policy, Huntington favouring reinvestment in the company and Speyer desiring to pay dividends 'to preserve the credit of the road in Europe ... Holders of stock are becoming impatient over the failure to receive any revenue from their stock.'

This breach between the interests of investors and managers was common. As Alfred Chandler, Jr has observed:

> The goals of these two groups were not always the same. The managers, who rarely owned large blocks of stock, looked to the long-term health and growth of the organization in which they worked and to which they had often devoted their whole careers. They were willing and indeed usually preferred to reduce dividends to assure long-term stability. The representatives of the owners, on the other hand, gave priority to maintaining dividends that would assure a reasonable continuing rate of return on their investment ... System-building proved costly to individual roads and to some extent to the national economy as well. The great growth of the individual enterprises often led to a redundancy

of facilities. During the 1880s more miles of track were built than in any other decade in American history and in the 1890s more mileage was in bankruptcy than in any decade before or since. The over-construction resulting from system-building was on a much greater scale than the overbuilding stimulated earlier by the optimism of promoters or the lure of land grants. In time, however, most of the new roads became fully used.

Where the initial costs of facilities was high, as was the case with the railroad, the telegraph, urban traction lines and other utilities, investment bankers ... continued to participate in decisions on the allocation of resources for the future ... by 1917, representatives of an entrepreneurial family or a banking house almost never took part in middle management decisions. Even in top management decisions concerning the allocation of resources, their power remained essentially negative. They could say no, but unless they themselves were trained managers with long experience in the same industry and even the same company, they had neither the information nor the experience to propose positive alternative courses of action.

Railroads required enormous amounts of capital and carried with them important economies of scale. As Charles Francis Adams saw at an early date, efforts to preserve inter-railroad competition were productive only of redundancy and higher rates. Insistence on this by Populists and Progressives gave rise to overcapacity and the incessant bankruptcies and reorganizations that followed World War I.

In tribute to the bankers, particularly Morgan, 'the chosen representative of the scattered votes of innumerable shareholders', Bertrand Russell was to observe, 'In fighting against the old anarchy these men were doing a useful and necessary work; they were diminishing waste, and by their vast fortunes they were giving spectacular evidence of the productivity of modern labour. In all that concerned the problem of production, they were in the right as against the devotees of competition. The problem of distribution they could not solve, but this problem was equally baffling to their opponents.'

John Maynard Keynes similarly observed that 'the immense accumulations of fixed capital which, to the great benefits of mankind, were built up during the half century before the war, could never have come about in a Society where wealth was divided equally'.

The historian Timothy Tzeng has said of Speyer:

[T]he success of his career was just beginning. After his long tenure with the Central and Southern Pacific railroads, Speyer transformed his firm into 'one of the strongest and cleanest of the American banking houses,' second only to J.P.

Morgan and Co. and Kuhn Loeb and Co., the firms that constituted the new term Wall Street.

Fittingly, Speyer and Co. was one of the 18 financial institutions that the Pujo committee charged as constituting the Money Trust. According to the committee, Speyer represented ten directorships, ten corporations and $2,443,000,000 of resources. During at least one point in the twentieth century, Speyer served as the primary fiscal agent for nine different railroad companies, a director of two trust companies and a trustee of a life insurance company. Adjusted with inflation, $2,443,000,000 in 1913 dollars is equivalent to approximately $52,000,000,000 in 2015 dollars. Speyer was financially invested in the Central Pacific, the Southern Pacific, the Rock Island, the St Louis and San Francisco, the Missouri, Kansas and Texas, the Missouri Pacific, the Lake Shore, the Mexican National and the Baltimore and Ohio Railroad. In 1888, the firm had also acquired $5.3 million in Chesapeake and Ohio railroad bonds and in July 1889 acquired 100,000 shares of C & O stock for $2.25 million.

At a 1932 congressional hearing investigating the sale of foreign bonds in the United States, Speyer reflected on his time as the Southern Pacific's primary banker. In a broad German accent, he told California Senator Hiram Johnson that

> it was my firm – my father [Philip Speyer] and I, myself, to some extent – who sold the Central and Southern Pacific Railroad bonds in Europe to enable the building of those lines, because this country at that time did not have the surplus capital … I would like to explain that the international banker, whom some people think of as having horns and hoofs, has performed some useful function in the world, and that this country would not have been built up after the Civil War without the international banker getting the money from Europe over here.

After his separation from control of the Southern Pacific, Speyer devoted himself to interests in the 'Third World': Mexican Railways, railways in Bolivia, Ecuador and the Philippines of which he was the primary financier, and a $35 million loan to the new republic of Cuba, in 1902.

In 1912, after the city of Los Angeles had failed to raise adequate funds to finance its aqueduct, Speyer agreed to do so on condition that 'the city shall not, prior to 1 January 1913, authorize [etc.] any other additional municipal bonds'. Speyer utilized this temporary monopoly over municipal financing, the grant of which had been opposed by two council members, to purchase $2.9 million in aqueduct bonds in addition to $3.5 million in Electric Plant bonds and $3 million in Harbour Improvement bonds, or a total of $9.4 million in Los Angeles infrastructure investments. Eastern capital ultimately financed $23.5 million of the $24 million cost of the aqueduct. 'To Speyer's mind, Los Angeles was no risk at all. His investments had built up the Southern Pacific Railroad decades earlier, and he had seen the city's trajectory all the way to the cusp of great emergence before E. H. Harriman had ousted him. Speyer's investment in the Los Angeles aqueduct was no less than the crowning touch on the young city that his – and his old friend Collis Huntington's – Southern Pacific Railroad first had created ... Except for James Speyer, every banker who invested in the Los Angeles aqueduct passed away before 1920. In a way, Los Angeles was the old guard's last joint venture, their final great act ... In post-aqueduct Los Angeles, eastern development of ... satellite nodes continued until Los Angeles' identity was quite literally cemented as a capital of urban sprawl, a city hostage to water from elsewhere and helplessly bound to the halls of Mammon.'

Speyer had rendered comparable service to the city of San Francisco, having floated $30 million in bonds for it in 1909, just after the earthquake there.

At the start of World War I, Edgar Speyer lost half his fortune with efforts to prop up the London tube and deal with the financial problems of the Frisco, the Missouri Kansas and Texas Railway, and the Brazilian, Manila and Mexican railways. In November 1915, trustees including James Speyer were appointed to control the Frisco railroad for five years. There were also $5.6 million in National Railways of Mexico notes offered on the American market in the first half of 1924. In 1890, Speyer had cooperated in a grandiose scheme for a North American Company to consolidate several western railroads including the Great Northern. Other participants included the Rockefellers, Deutsche Bank, Kuhn Loeb and Morgan. Speyer and Seligman were said to have gained full control of the Frisco in 1926. In its chequered financial career, it was in receivership in 1896, from 1913 to 1916, and from 1932 to 1936.

The American house was involved in $258 million of Rock Island issues and $82 million of Missouri Pacific issues, among others. Speyer became a member of the Rock Island board and finance committee in 1904, when he took $25.1 million of a refunding issue which 'transformed it from a moderate sized railroad with a clearly defined flow of trade into a great system sprawled over the Central West and handling at least three different currents of business'. '[T]he Rock Island had lost its former stability,' Stuart Daggett wrote in 1908, 'and must await a period of lesser earnings with serious apprehension.' It had grown from 3,819 miles in 1901 to 7,123 miles in 1903 and 14,270 miles in 1907. In 1912, Speyer sold an additional

$20 million in Rock Island bonds yielding 5 per cent. The Rock Island was a running sore for the Speyer firm. James Speyer voluntarily appeared without subpoena at an ICC hearing concerning its affairs in 1915: 'I am very sensitive. I care very much what the country thinks of the New York bankers. We have been very much abused.' He said he would not disclose his losses on Rock Island since 1912: 'my friends might think I am not a good banker' said the witness with a smile.

Jesse Hirschman of Speyer was a director of the Rock Island Railroad from 1917 to 1932 and was also a director of the St Louis and San Francisco Railroad. His membership of the Rock Island board was approved by the ICC in 1926. The purchase by the St Louis and San Francisco of Rock Island stock in 1926 was assailed before the ICC in 1938; an earlier proceeding had been dismissed by the ICC in 1932. Hirschman, who died in the next year, was too ill to testify.

In 1928, Speyer conducted a $100 million bond sale for the Frisco, the second largest railroad financing ever conducted in the United States, as well as a sale of 49 million shares of preferred stock, the proceeds being used to redeem $126 million in bonds. Earlier, in 1935, there had been an SEC investigation under the supervision of William O. Douglas, which featured an all-star cast: James Landis presiding and Abe Fortas conducting the examination.

Litigation was instituted with the approval of the court presiding over the receivership of the Frisco. It was dismissed by a New York trial court on legal grounds, was reinstated by the Appellate Division, and finally ended with the complete vindication of the Speyer firm, the trial judge declaring that he wanted to 'dispel any accusations which would stigmatize the [Speyer firm] as morally reprehensible by reason of over-reaching or sharp practice … the investment continued to be lucrative for a number of years afterward. [Losses resulted from] economic adversity which could not have been fairly foretold or envisaged at the time.'

In July 1941, Judge Samuel Rosenman of the New York Supreme Court denied a motion to depose Speyer in new Rock Island litigation on the ground that he had been sufficiently deposed in earlier lawsuits that had been lost. Speyer had participated in meetings concerning reorganization of the Rock Island in 1913 and 1916. The Rock Island, which never extended as far as the Pacific Coast though it had 7,500 miles of track, is said to have been strangled to death by ICC regulation: 'after waiting thirteen years for the cowardly ICC to make up its mind about the Union Pacific's offer of merger, [it] faded away like the Colorado River which, beset by users who take and give nothing back, dies without a whimper in the desert'. A critic of its management in the 1930s took the view that 'no railroad could survive Eastern banker management when those in control had no interest in the physical property, the territory or the people the railroad served – no interest whatever in anything except the dividends that could be derived from their holdings'. It had gone into bankruptcy in 1933 and lost its operating permit from the ICC in 1980, though all its creditors were ultimately paid in full. After the Staggers Act of 1980 deregulating the railroads, an act made possible by competition from the new Eisenhower-era interstate highway system, the Western railroads were allowed to freely merge, the Union Pacific with the Southern Pacific, and the Burlington-Northern Pacific with the Santa Fe, leaving the United States with two transcontinental railroad systems. Two of Amtrak's surviving trains, the Sunset Limited and the Southwest Chief, follow the lines of the Southern Pacific and Santa Fe respectively.

In 1919, before the return of the railroads to private ownership after World War I, Speyer urged the creation of an agency like the Federal Reserve Board to regulate railroad finance. Eighteen years later, in 1937, Senator Harry Truman would make similar suggestions, while denouncing the rewards that Speyer allegedly distributed to favoured railway officials and investors: 'The solution of the railroad problem does not lie in the government's pouring money into bankrupt systems but a wholesale overhauling of rates, finances, managements, coordination, and consolidation ... Lawyers and investment bankers sit around like vultures at the death of an elephant – they get all the flesh and the stockholders and the public get the bones.'

'Some of the so-called investment bankers had a gratuity list,' Truman declared. 'This consisted of high rail officials. One in particular was E. N. Brown, chairman of the board of Frisco. Speyer and Co, paid him a gratuity of $100,000 a year, and the poor old Frisco paid him as chairman of the board to help Speyer and Co. to loot it.' Speyer and Brown denied the allegation.

The Speyer firms' post-World War I railroad activities were derivative of its involvement with two of the giants of American railroading, Collis P. Huntington and James J. Hill. Speyer did no financings for Hill, but at congressional hearings in 1930 observed of his dealings with Huntington: 'the Southern Pacific and the Central Pacific did not fail because Mr. Huntington, perhaps to some extent with our help, stood by, but the Northern Pacific, the Atchison and others were all reorganized and the European investors lost their money'.

In December 1913, James met with President Wilson to unsuccessfully urge the appointment of his client James J. Hill of the Northern Pacific to the new Federal Reserve Board.

CHAPTER 12

Cuban Loans

'A good customer for our manufactured goods'

In 1904, the London house sold $35 million in Cuban government bonds due in 1944 which were selling above par in 1915, and which the Speyer firm's harshest critic acknowledged were 'really sound. But has not this government's business been subsequently transferred to the House of Morgan?' Speyer was the only bidder for the issue, the first loan after the Platt amendment. A condition of the loan were permanent Cuban taxes on tobacco, alcohol and sugar, which collectively became known as the 'Speyer taxes', together with a pledge as security of 15 per cent of customs duties. It was said that this American dollar loan together with a similar $40 million Speyer loan to Mexico 'set a precedent of financing needs of minor American nations here [which] will lessen the danger of friction over the Monroe Doctrine [and was] the first time an international loan ha[d] been arranged in American gold payable in New York'.

The loan was the first fruit of 'dollar diplomacy' after the Spanish-American War: 'The State Department informed the new Cuban government in 1902 that it would prevent extension of any loan until Cuba acceded to U.S. demands regarding lease of naval bases, trade reciprocity, and the protectorate treaty.' Speyer regarded the protectorate as adequate security in place of the usual customs receivership. At a later time, the Cuban government actually required the shipment of gold 'to see what gold dollars really looked like'. In addition, 'it was Speyer who provided the $16.5 million loan for the paving and sewerage concession awarded by [US General] Magoon [in Cuba]'. This loan was earmarked for the water and sewer system in Cienfuegos and paving and sewers in Havana and was secured by 10 per cent of Havana customs duties. The loan was for a 40-year term at 4.5 per cent at a discount of 12 per cent. Presidents Taft and

Roosevelt had ordered Governor Magoon to clear up long-standing disputes over these improvements.

Some Cubans professed to see evil in the loan because Franklin Steinhart, former U.S. Consul general and adviser to Taft and Magoon and Henry W. Taft, brother of Secretary Taft successfully negotiated the loan as the duly authorized agents of Speyer and Co. No evidence has been adduced to show that Steinhart, Taft or anyone else connected with the loan negotiations was guilty of any impropriety.

In 1922, James Speyer made a speech proposing a central bank like the Federal Reserve for Cuba, praising Cuba's avoidance of use of the printing press, and noting its timely payments of interest, and that no banknotes other than American dollars were in circulation there. Cubans, however, had not been taught to save, and were imperilled by extravagance and by the low price of sugar. He counselled a firm but generous policy toward Cuba, 'a good customer for our manufactured goods'.

In 1932, a commission to study the Cuban economy and tax system under Professor Edwin R. A. Seligman of Columbia University noted Cuba's almost exclusive reliance for revenue on the indirect 'Speyer taxes', and recommended increased reliance on direct taxation, including an imputed income tax based on home values of the sort in use in Greece and Belgium. In the following year, it was noted that the $35 million Speyer loan had been reduced by sinking fund payments to $11 million and the $16.5 million Speyer loan granted in 1909 had been reduced to $11 million, notwithstanding the low sugar prices that had prevailed since 1925. Some 15 per cent of the country's revenues were devoted to debt service on the Speyer loans of 1904 and 1909 and the subsequent Morgan loans of 1914, 1923 and 1927. The Speyer loans were eventually paid off in full in 1940. Cuba's subservience to American bankers was part of the narrative fuelling the ultimate triumph of Fidel Castro and his movement, which, however, did not produce greater economic progress than the orthodox finance that had preceded it, whatever its claims to social justice.

CHAPTER 13

Philippine Railroads

'Poor business propositions'

In February 1908 James had an interview with President Taft, the subject not being specified; he had also met with Taft in April 1905 to discuss the Philippine railways. The Philippine railways on Luzon, 800 miles in length, were financed in 1906, a syndicate led by Speyer agreeing to construct 428 miles of railroad and to operate the pre-existing railways established under the Spanish regime. A year was allowed for surveys, after which Speyer was to construct 150 miles in the first year and 75 miles in each year thereafter. Taxes were to be limited to half of 1 per cent of gross income for 50 years, and 1.5 per cent of gross income for the following 50 years, the franchise to be perpetual, though subject to government rate regulation.

Earlier demands by Speyer for guaranteed yields, freedom from rate regulation and from possible competition had been rejected in June 1905 and January 1906, before grant of the concession by the Philippine Commission Act 1510 on 7 July 1906. The railroads were acquired by the Philippine government in 1915. Following this nationalization, the American Speyer firm was involved in Manila Railway loans of $4 million in September 1916, $1.5 million in September 1919 and again in September 1922. It was later said that 'the new railroads proved to be poor business propositions and they did not, for various reasons, have a particularly dynamic impact on the Philippine economy'. As with the Cuban loan, Speyer made itself a beneficiary of the American colonies and protectorates resulting from the Spanish-American War.

The railways were severely damaged during World War II and by various typhoons afterward, but survive as commuter lines for the City of Manila, there also being an overnight passenger train to Southern Luzon.

CHAPTER 14

Mexican Railroads

'Failure to recognize the raw materials of a great social revolution'

In 1899, the Morgan firm solicited Speyer to participate in a Mexican loan. In 1901–3, both the American and English Speyer firms were involved in what was initially a financing amounting to more than $93 million for the National Railroad of Mexico, then one of several competing Mexican railroad lines. The line gained a competitive advantage by reason of being standard rather than narrow gauge, thus not requiring interchanging of cars at the Mexican border; it had the shortest route between Mexico City and the border towns of Piedras Negras, Laredo and Matamoros. 'All that the Ferrocaril National needed for its cup truly to run over was access to a Gulf Coast port near the centre of the country (Tampico or Veracruz) and it was the company's efforts to gain this access that eventually brought about its undoing.'

In 1904, the American firm made a $40 million loan to the Mexican government, followed by a second loan of $10 million in 1912. James Speyer was also involved with the Ferrocaril International, a competing Mexican railway controlled by Collis Huntington. The alliance of these two railroads in a stock and bond transaction in 1901–2 made possible through shipments from Mexico City via Huntington's Southern Pacific line to New Orleans and Eastern ports. In 1908–10, under pressure from the Mexican dictatorship of Porfirio Diaz (which lasted from 1875 to 1911), the English Speyer firm organized an elaborate transaction transferring 50 per cent stock control of the two lines and a third line, Ferrocaril Interoceanic, serving Gulf ports, to the Mexican government, which also received a large new $24 million loan for railroad development in return for not permitting a parallel line within 50 miles of the Gulf. The government's acquisition of control in the form of newly issued voting shares without dividend rights was facilitated by a fall in the price of silver, making possible the acquisition of outstanding shares, Mexico's currency being silver-based.

Edgar Speyer attributed the Diaz government's interest in unified government control to three causes: a desire to avoid friction between the railroads; fear that a unification of the Speyer and Huntington roads would be a vehicle for American absorption of the Mexican economy; and hopes for economies of scale. The unified Mexican railroad was not a sensationally good investment; the Mexican National declared 4 per cent dividends in the period 1906–8 and preferred stock dividends in the period 1909–12. Profitability was reduced by the construction of four competing North–South lines rather than two, and by the lack of spurs into mining districts.

The promoters' assumptions about population movements were also not gratified. '"Thousands of Americans will rush into Mexico as soon as railroad facilities are furnished," predicted a Coloradoan. It turned out that they preferred California and Arizona.' The American states possessed such competitive advantages as education systems and the rule of law. The lines finally came into their own at the beginning of the twenty-first century, with the increased traffic to the United States arising from the North American Free Trade Agreement and their linkages with the one-time Southern Pacific line in the United States, now part of the Union Pacific. Collis Huntington would have been gratified by this development.

During the period 1900–13, the United States began for the first time to export capital, about $1 billion in all in 250 separate foreign loans, the major recipients being European (particularly German) municipalities, the London tube and the Mexican railways. These were glory days for the Speyer firm: 'The position of the investment banks strengthened above all in the national context, due to their financing the railroads during the 1870s and 1880s and the large limited liability manufacturing companies in the 1890s as well as to their role in the sweeping trend toward mergers at the turn of the twentieth century.' In 1904, James Speyer participated in an inspection of Mexican railroads on a special train, setting a new speed record. It was reported in New York that 'James Speyer who left on a train through Mexico last week with Mrs. Speyer and a party of friends is travelling in one of the finest special trains that ever went out of New York. It is composed of five private cars and there is not an ordinary sleeping car on the train. The party will take on board six Mexican railroad officials with their secretaries and stenographers. Mr. Speyer intends to remain away for about a month.'

Six months later, James went on another railway tour of Mexico and while attempting to set a new speed record his train was derailed 25 miles south of Laredo while travelling at 75 miles per hour. The conductor and one passenger, J. F. Davis, suffered facial cuts; two cars but not the engine were derailed. In that year, Mexican railroads are said to have absorbed $50 million in American capital, a financial newspaper noting the 'pronounced decrease in new railroad construction in the U.S. during the same period'. In 1909, James made a contribution of $5,000 (about $100,000 now) for Mexican earthquake relief.

However, in 1908, Morgan refused to permit Speyer's inclusion in a group managing a new Mexican issue and Speyer attempted to assemble a competing group, which did not prevail. In order to preserve its syndicate, Morgan had to concede 42.5 per cent of the offering to Noetzlin, a French bank, and 15 per cent to the National Bank of Mexico. In 1910, £22 million in bonds were sold in Paris.

The British Speyer firm had participated in several flotations on behalf of Mexican Railways, including one of £1.2 million in 1897, one of £2.8 million in 1908, one of £4.9 million in 1909, and another in 1913.

In another important respect, the explosion of Mexican railroads did not have all the effects that were desired:

> The capital and technology with which Limantour [the Mexican Finance Minister] planned to modernize Mexico for the upper and middle classes also released the Indians and the lower-class mestizos from the medieval matrix of isolation ... An atavistic violence lay under the surface of the Mexican Indian and the 'progressivism' of the Cientificos and the American promoters helped to bring it out ... [There was] failure to recognize the raw materials of a great social revolution. No country has passed through the Industrial Revolution without great social upheavals: even stable Britain had suffered her Luddite riots and her Peterloos. But American capitalists apparently expected Mexico, with her shallow Republican institutions and enormous social imbalance, to modernize her economy along American lines within a few decades without revolution ... they were strengthening a dictator who refused to spread the benefits of the capital evenly among his people and thereby made violent revolution inevitable.

American railroad investments in Mexico were followed by American mining investments, in which the Speyer firm played little part.

> The most frequently cited estimate of investments in Mexican mining is the 'Letcher report' of 1912. William H. Seamon who had long experience in Mexico as a mining engineer, drew up the report in 1911 from government and company reports, directories, periodicals, reviews and encyclopedias. Consul Marion Letcher forwarded it to Washington and it has since appeared under

his name. The report placed the wealth of Mexico at $2,434,241,422 with Americans owning $1,057,730,000, or approximately half. Seamon estimated American railway holdings in 1911 at $644.3 million and mining holdings at $249.5 million. During the decade 1900–1910, Mexican mines held an understandable fascination for American investors. The *Wall Street Summary* described the situation by commenting that three-fourths of the dividend-paying mines in Mexico were held by Americans and they paid a sum 24 percent in excess of the aggregate net earnings of all the National Banks in the United States, or about $95 million. While bank stock paid an average of 5.45 per cent, 'sixth rate mines in Mexico are paying ten to fifteen percent per annum.' With all due respect for the Summary's optimism, Diaz was in his heaven, all was right with the world.

During the revolution in 1920 that overthrew President Madero, Elias de Lema, the President of Speyer's Mexican affiliate, the Mexican Bank of Commerce and Industry, 'hid the overthrown President in the cellar of his house for two weeks. Later his house was bombed by revolutionists'. The first post-revolutionary government received a Speyer loan of $10 million at 4.5 per cent; Mexico's credit deteriorated rapidly thereafter.

In December 1920 in an article in *The Chronicle*, James Speyer urged the prompt settlement of claims by the new Obregon government. He thought that Mexico had a good future: 'She has practically no paper money outstanding, is very rich in natural resources and with her climactic and other attractions should become a pleasure resort for Americans.' Prompt settlement of American claims would forestall aggressive moves by Europeans, and adventurers should be discouraged from obtaining one-sided concessions.

Speyer is said to have lost much of its interest in Mexican loans in 1921, and Deutsche Bank liquidated its Mexican holdings through a third party. It is said that it also had some interests in Mexican petroleum and other resources. Par value of British investments in Mexican railways was estimated at £51.1 million in 1924. Important railroad interests were sold to the Mexican government in 1945–6 for £3 million, as against original capitalization of £25 million. The British investors enjoyed income of 3.2 per cent in 1910 and less than 2 per cent in the years 1914 to 1934. In short, 'In Mexico, the British railway investment yielded almost nothing.'

In 1922, an International League of Bankers on Mexico under the chairmanship of Thomas Lamont of the Morgan firm undertook to renegotiate the Mexican debt. It had been established in October 1918 before the end of World War I. The Speyer firm was initially not a member

– 'because of his connections with German banking firms, Speyer had not been invited to participate' – but was invited to join it in November 1921 after making a competing offer to the Mexican government. The vice-chairman was Mortimer Schiff of Kuhn Loeb. Other members included Jesse Hirschman of the Speyer firm, George Davison, R. G. Hutchins, Jr, Charles F. Mitchell, John J. Mitchell, Walter Rosen, Charles Sabin, Albert Wiggin and Robert Winsor. The agreement provided for amortization of the Mexican debt over 40 years, with reduced payments over the first five years, financed by a tax on oil exports. The agreement was signed in September 1922 and the first payment of $3.4 million was made by the Obregon government in January 1923. There was a new pact in 1925 after a Mexican default, deferring interest on railway bonds until 1928 and providing for payments of $2.5 million for 39 years; under the bond covenants, the railroads reverted to private management, desired by the bankers, in 1929. There were new negotiations in 1929, which foundered; because of the Depression there was no further agreement on debt payments until a wartime agreement in 1942.

The historian T. R. Fehrenbach has observed that

> Obregon walked his tightrope brilliantly. He refused to nationalize the oil fields, which Mexican opinion demanded, and his Supreme Court upheld the continuation of contracts granted before 1917, but he placed a small tax on oil extraction. The oil companies immediately protested this to Washington, where the State Department took their side. Obregon's finance minister, however, had meanwhile made a deal with United States banking interests by which the oil taxes were assigned to pay off the Mexican debt. He was able to divide, and if he did not quite conquer, he survived because he blunted Washington's pressures in a North American conflict of interest.

Although the post-World War II period has seen much mining investment in Third World countries, it has characteristically taken the form of direct corporate investment from retained earnings, not bond flotations or stock issues. The international flotation of railroad bonds is now also largely a thing of the past for reasons suggested in advice given by Hjalmar Schacht to the Indonesian government in 1952:

> [N]ot merely as private transport but especially in the transport of goods, it is safe to say that the railway era is past. The countries now in process of development have this advantage over the old industrial states: that they are able to by-pass costly rail construction and concentrate instead on the building of long-distance

roads. Road construction and road transport are both cheaper than the railway with its complicated service. Apart from the import of some not too expensive machinery, road construction can be carried out with native material and native labour, whereas everything for the railways – from the actual track, and including locomotives and coaches, to the complicated signalling system – has to be imported from abroad against payment of expensive foreign exchange. There is no need for the government to worry about providing vehicles for road traffic. The provision of delivery vans, trucks and omnibuses can safely be left to private enterprise, which will gladly seize such new business opportunities.

While Schacht's obituary on the railroad age may in some respects be premature, given the development of intermodal transport, in nations not of continental expanse, it embodies an important truth.

CHAPTER 15

Brazilian Loans

'Brazil always will have a great future'

Both the British and American Speyer houses were heavily involved in Brazil. In 1911–13 the London office floated issues in various Brazilian railways (the Sorocabana Railway, the Brazil Railway (ultimately the parent of many others) and the Madeira-Mamore Railway) totalling about £9 million, selling in 1915 at prices from 29 to 63. The Madeira-Mamore Railway, designed to bypass various rapids on the Amazon, has been called 'probably the most isolated railway in the world'. Some 3,600 workers, including ten Americans, are said to have died during the course of its construction. Theodore Roosevelt's journey down a river in its vicinity, with inadequate food and the local malarial infection, is thought to have shortened his life by ten years.

In 1916, there was a $5.5 million loan to the City of Sao Paulo, followed by $3.5 million in October 1919, $10 million in March 1921, $4 million in February 1922 and a $4 million railway loan in April 1922. The municipal loans were sound by Latin American standards: 'few countries had a better record than Brazil's for servicing their sterling government bonds until that record was marred, perhaps mainly because of the world depression during the decade starting in 1932'. Sao Paulo's bonds were redeemed on schedule. However only fractional payments on coupons were made by its water company.

By the end of 1935, there were $359 million in defaulted Brazilian bonds out of a total of $1.9 billion in defaulted foreign bonds. Some of the early railroad loans were in large measure a reflection of the Speyers' involvement with an extraordinary and all-but-forgotten American railway promoter, Percival Farquhar. Farquhar had started as a Tammany ward-heeler, 'one of Hugh Grant's young men who went into the [New York] Assembly at a time [1891–2] when Tammany was encouraging a modicum of social talent in the organization, one of the first of legislators to bring a valet to the capital'. He had graduated from the Sheffield Scientific School at Yale in 1883, and thereafter from the Columbia Law School. One of his business associates said of Farquhar, 'I have seldom met a man like him. He has remarkable powers of impressing his ideas. What might seem extravagant in a less forceful man becomes reasonable and convincing when he tells it.' His grand design was to establish a transcontinental railroad network in Latin America. By 1912, he was well on the way to realizing this objective.

The Brazil Railway, which Farquhar controlled, along with the two other railways receiving prewar Speyer loans, was 'the nucleus of the newly conceived transcontinental system, have nearly 7,000 miles of rights of way … and earn[ed] some $25 million gross. He also controlled the Antofagasta and Bolivia Railway through the Andes, one of the wonders of the railway world – [the] main line is carried through the Andes at a height of 13,000 feet above sea level, one of its branches [later abandoned] reaches the altitude of 15,809 feet.' Lines through Paraguay and Bolivia to Lake Titicaca connected to Peruvian railways by steamer; a director of the Peruvian railways was a member of Farquhar's board, though it was unclear whether he controlled them. The Brazil Railway controlled 560,000 acres of timberland and, through a subsidiary, 6 million acres of grazing land in Paraguay.

Farquhar was said to be 'hungrier for land than anyone in Latin American history since the time of the Incas'. His view was the proof of Georges Clemenceau's proposition that 'Brazil always will have a great future.' In his heyday before World War I, Farquhar had a mansion in Paris and briefly, in 1910, another at 1080 Fifth Avenue in New York. On the latter he spent $350,000 for the house and $350,000 on furnishings, but he never occupied it. In 1910, he controlled a fifth of the Rock Island Railroad. Farquhar's house of cards, based in part on the pyramiding of debt, came crashing to the ground with the curtailment of European credits in 1914, when the Brazil Railway fell into receivership. On the eve of the war he was negotiating with British, French and German bankers for a rescue, and was assured by Edgar Speyer that there would be no war.

'[O]ver-crowding, industrialism, and legality made England seem dull to adventurous dispositions … [Foreign railroads were] a welcome outlet to capital which could no longer be invested in home industries with the same profit as in the days when factories were new or when railroads were being introduced in Europe.'

'Rightly or wrongly, the Brazil Railway Company had attained a reputation in Brazil for reckless financing and poor business judgment.' It was bought by the state of Sao Paulo in 1918, the state paying $7.1 million for rescission of the Brazil Railway's contract and $5.4 million for its invested capital. 'The Brazil Railway doubtless was glad to be rid of a contractual obligation which was probably more favourable to the state than to it.' The state borrowed £3.8 million from the Dresdner Bank to buy the railroad. The Sorocabana, though less successful than some of the 'coffee railroads', enjoyed a 95 per cent increase in freight traffic between 1907 and 1917, though its track was poorly maintained, it operated at less than 40 per cent of capacity and its safety record compared unfavourably with that of other Brazilian railroads. 'Between 1910 and 1913 … Englishmen imprudently invested in some of the pyramided Percival Farquhar railroad enterprises so that the average nominal yield on their capital began to fall off. The nominal rate of return was only 4.7 per cent in 1913, and it dropped to 2.5 per cent in 1923 … In spite of the depression the average nominal yield was better than 1.5 per cent for the years following 1931 until the Sao Paolo, the most profitable of the British railways in Brazil, was sold in 1946.'

Farquhar was said to have assigned arbitrary values to new acquisitions and to have 'raised 420 million francs in France in just 4 ½ years – 181 millions of which were channelled into its founders' pockets as "special payments"'. Fear was expressed that Farquhar was building lines faster than the market could make them pay. 'Some sections of the Brazilian public have become alarmed at the rate Mr. Farquhar's control in Brazil is extending.' By October 1913, *The Economist* viewed the Brazil Railway as 'a very dark horse'. The item 'discount and commission on bond issues' enlarged its fraction of the total assets from 7 per cent in 1910 to 12 per cent in 1912. However, the Sorocabana Railway continued to service its first mortgage bonds after the start of World War I since it 'wished maximum credit-worthiness in order to raise further capital.'

Whatever their defects and initial profitability, Farquhar's railroads did get built and not all of them were failures, though he took full advantage of the 'very low or no legal protection for non-controlling stockholders and bondholders and trifling disclosure requirements of companies' financial information'. 'Farquhar's Brazil Railway was the largest U.S. holding company before the "dance of the utility millions" in the late 1920s.' In 1926, a writer on Brazil's mixed bag of railroads noted that 'When I was in Manaus in 1920, the English manager [of the Madeira-Mamore] told me he was running only one train a week, and losing money steadily on that. The English line that connects the Sao Paulo network with Santos is one of the most difficult feats of railroad engineering in the world executed with absolute perfection.'

Farquhar thought of 'Amazonia as a home for millions of Europe's surplus peasants plus thousands of Japanese. Instead of becoming an Eldorado for Farquhar, Amazonia became a Helldorado, collapsing into total poverty. After 1913, progress in Brazil seemed largely confined to the southernmost 15 per cent of the country.' There were 140,000 migrants to Brazil in 1896, but only 12,000 in 1904. Argentina and the US offered more attractions. In 1912, because of imports from South East Asia, the wild rubber boom collapsed. Farquhar 'failed to realize that the Congo Basin because of its minerals, great waterpower and large areas of good plateau soil and climate was potentially far more important and prosperous than Amazonia'. Panama was said to be 'a resort by contrast'. The Madeira Railway cost $145,000 a mile to construct, a total of $33 million. The poor to modest soils and lack of schools and doctors held no attraction for immigrants, though the promoters 'thought "the tropics" meant only prodigal largesse of fruits and sun and a wide latitude of life'. 'That virulent form of malaria peculiar to some tropical localities is a phenomenon which medical research has not yet explained,' H. M. Tomlinson wrote in his classic *The Sea and the Jungle*. 'In the almost unexplored region of the Rio Madeira the fever is certain to every traveller, though the land is largely without inhabitants; and it is almost equally certain that it will be of the malignant type.' The earlier 1876 attempt to build the railroad cost the lives of 221 of the initial contingent of 941 workers, 'far higher a mortality rate than that of, say, the South African or the American Civil War'.

The fallacy behind the Amazon railway, that *grands projets* such as railroads, dams and hydroelectric developments are sufficient to produce prosperity, persisted well into our own time. Most of the World Bank's lending after World War II, including that conducted in the reign of that master of 'failing upward', Robert McNamara, was conducted on this premise. It is only more recently, partially under the impact of two Peruvian economists, Alvaro Vargas Llosa and Hernando De Soto, as well as Americans like Kenneth Dam, that there has been greater emphasis on other requisites of development. These include education (particularly female education, since mothers as much as schools are the educators of the young), public health services and legal structure (including land recording systems, impartial tribunals and swift remedies for creditors, particularly secured creditors). As we have seen, Mexican railroad promoters entertained the same illusions as their counterparts in Brazil.

'The first to see cracks in Farquhar's empire as a result of the First Balkan War and to sense that he was approaching the beginning of the end was Sir Edgar Speyer, often his dinner guest in Paris and in London. Sir Edgar was quoted in *The Times* (London) on November 12 [1912] as believing that Farquhar's program of railway construction was almost over. Speyer added that "public opinion in Brazil is undergoing rapid change." Late in 1912, Brazil's Congress and press became alarmed at Farquhar's seemingly limitless power and ambition.'

In November 1912, Speyer issued a statement declaring that:

> The Brazil Railway stock has had a big rise, and in times like the present it is not unnatural that stocks which have shown rapid appreciation should be the first to be affected by general depression in the stock markets ... The policy of the Brazil Railway Company, which is largely controlled by the houses which have issued its securities ... will be cautious and conservative, for with the exception of the outlet to Santos, which it is essential the Brazil Railway should obtain, the policy of expansion has now practically come to an end.

Shortly thereafter in 1913 'a Carnival group made a hit as it capered down Avenida Rio Branco in Rio de Janeiro singing a song in samba rhythm and Anglicized Portuguese about the Sindicate Farquhar distributing pots of gold to buy up Brazil'. Some £500,000 of a last £2 million Speyer loan was used to buy the Uruguay Central Railway linking Montevideo to towns on the frontier. An effort by Farquhar to acquire a parallel line was rejected by the Uruguayan Congress. In 1912, Farquhar also acquired an interest in the Antofogasta and Bolivia Railway; he was said to have invested $40 million in 'his hobby of collecting railways', whose books showed a paper investment of $215 million.

Only a third of the Madeira Railway cost was ever recovered; it was doomed by collapse of the rubber boom and the opening of the Panama Canal, but was not abandoned until 1972. As the end neared, Farquhar sold his Cuban and Guatemalan interests in a vain effort to prop up the Brazil Railway, which was further undermined when the Brazilian government defaulted on a $10 million debt due to Farquhar. On the eve of World War I, Farquhar was very nearly successful in borrowing £30 million in equal shares in Paris, London and Frankfurt; Sir Edgar cabled him an assurance that Europe would avoid war. When his last speculations led to disaster, Farquhar fully cooperated with the Brazil Railway's receiver; he was credited with 'accepting things beyond his control, avoiding bitterness or lowered standards'. His later career was devoted to a long and unsuccessful struggle to develop an iron mine in Brazil. His persuasiveness led one banker to exclaim after an interview, 'Thank God I'm not a woman!'

27. Farquhar's Grand Design

Farquhar rehabilitated himself in time to stage a repeat performance, though his new debt pyramids were exposed by the crash in 1929. He was credited with 'the resilience of a rubber ball'. At that point, the Vargas government secured legislation constraining further financial activities by him in Brazil. He was accused by left-wing critics of the 'deaths of thousands of native people, ecological destruction of entire states, abandoned railways, bankruptcies, and even civil wars'. Nonetheless, he was decorated by Brazil with the Order of the Southern Cross in 1949.

28. Percival Farquhar

'The most profitable railroad owned by Englishmen in Latin America was the Sao Paolo. Farquhar had 40 per cent ownership of it. The return on its initial nominal capital of $6 million was 8.3 per cent in 1928; its £3 million in ordinary shares yielded 12 per cent.' From 1876 to 1930 its securities yielded an average of 11.3 per cent, falling thereafter to 3 per cent or a little below until the securities were redeemed at par in 1946. In 1918, it was said that 'The Sao Paulo Railway's main line normally produces more revenue per mile than any railroad in the Western Hemisphere. It annually carries two-thirds of the world's coffee supply.'

By July 1928, there were four more loans to Sao Paulo totalling $39 million. In March 1925, Speyer told the State Department of a proposed loan of $15 million to modernize the Sorocabana Railway. The US Commerce Department under Herbert Hoover agreed not to object to the loan if Speyer gave written assurances that none of the proceeds would be used to maintain coffee prices. It shortly became evident that part of the loan had been so used. Hoover had launched a campaign against high prices fostered by a Brazilian coffee cartel. James Speyer wrote to the Assistant

Secretary of State Leland Harrison to complain of a 'paternal attitude' excluding American bankers from 'safe and profitable transactions', like a new $35 million Sao Paulo loan. 'In the long run, this will help Great Britain and work a disadvantage for the U.S.' The reply declared that 'American credits to foreign combinations engaged in fixing prices to American consumers should be avoided.' Hoover declared at the same time that 'The administration does not believe the New York banking houses will wish to provide loans which might be diverted to support the coffee speculation which has been in progress for the last year at the hands of the coffee combination in Sao Paulo.' To this, Speyer rejoined that 'too close restrictions' would lose for Americans 'the financial leadership and prestige that goes with it', a prophecy realized when Sao Paulo floated a £5 million loan in London.

By the 1930s, 'the era of profitable railroading in Latin America appeared to have ended, to have given way to the era of the omnibus, the truck, and the airplane'. By 1959, '[c]onfronted by the suspicious hostility of nations and governments in need of capital, compelled to compete with cheap loans and benevolent government grants administered by managers and technicians who are the most highly paid "missionaries" that the world has ever seen, private investors in underdeveloped countries seemed to have a hard and treacherous road ahead'.

A sanguine view of Brazilian railroad development was taken by a scholar in 1997:

> Foreign-owned railroad companies earned competitive profits, but rarely more than that. Benefits accrued increasingly to the domestic-use sector of the economy. [There arose] a shrewd and savvy group of regulators and rail experts. Though built using foreign capital to link plantations to ports, the railroads ultimately registered large gains for domestic markets and created new opportunities for immigration and industry. The broader process of railroad development contributed to a bloated government sector and inward-looking policies after World War I.

CHAPTER 16

Bolivian Railroads

'Like bleeding an anaemic body to leave it destroyed'

Speyer, and the National City Bank of New York were also largely responsible for construction of the Bolivian railways, which arose 'from an agreement between the Republic of Bolivia, the National City Bank of New York, and Speyer and Company to build a number of railroads within a period of ten years'. This arrangement, known in Bolivia as the Speyer Contract, was denounced at the time by opponents of President Ismael Montes (1904–9, 1913–17) and his predecessor Jose Prado (1899–1904). These presidents were 'staunch believers in laissez faire, and in the key role of foreign capital in their country's development'. The contract has been criticized ever since as an unsound scheme that was excessively generous to US bankers. Of the 1,000 miles of track envisaged in the Speyer Contract, only 416 were laid, and this at an expense of $22 million to the Bolivian government, the lines including the Oruro–Viacha, Oruro–Cochabamba, Rio Mulato–Potosi and Uyuni–Atocha. Moreover the government's subsequent financial difficulties permitted a British firm, (Farquhar's) Antofagasta, and the Bolivia Railway Company to gain control over the lines constructed by means of the Speyer Contract, and most of the country's other rail facilities as well, a transaction described as a 'master stroke' by that railroad's historian.

The Speyer Contract has been accurately described as 'utterly fantastic' and as a 'transaction which cost the National City Bank and Speyer and Company practically nothing, netted them several millions of dollars on the sale of their share of the Bolivia Railway Company stock, and won for … [a] British company the key to the control of Bolivia's entire railway system'. In addition, the contract provided that rail tariffs could be raised in the event of a fall in the value of Bolivia's currency. When a 27 per cent decline took place in 1921, it triggered a 20 per cent rise in railroad rates, which recouped nearly half the railroad's currency losses. This was described as 'like bleeding an anaemic body to leave it destroyed'. It admittedly left Bolivia 'with a railway system of unquestioned importance in getting her minerals to the coast', but Bolivia had 'no chance short of expropriation of ever owning the roads, as the concession was granted in perpetuity'. It included protection against construction of any parallel road within 40 kilometres, required the use of American materials in construction, a 30-year tax exemption and the right to acquire 1.785 million hectares of contiguous land in the public domain for derisory prices. By 1926, 80 per cent of government revenue and 58 per cent of national income were pledged to debt service, actual payments amounting to 46 per cent of government revenues. 'The bankers sold a large part of the bonds and the stock to the Antofagasta Company and made their principal profit through the construction company.' The contract is not infrequently characterized as the most exploitative feat of 'dollar diplomacy'.

The later extravagances of the Siles government as well as the 1906 Speyer loan were to blame for this, a Bolivian finance minister, Dr J. Santiago Arramago bitterly observing that 'The United States, the richest country the world has ever seen, can also boast like Rome of old of many a citizen with an "itching palm".' Except for mines, there was little economic development due to the 85 per cent illiteracy rate in Bolivia, not conducive to enterprise. The Farquhar-constructed and Speyer-financed Madeira-Mamore Railway, completed in 1912 and reaching Bolivia's north-eastern border, was a consistent loss-maker after the collapse of the wild rubber boom. In 1908, the Bolivia Railway was leased for 99 years to the Antafagosta and Bolivia Railway, thus eliminating any possibility of using other Chilean ports. Nonetheless, the bonds sold at 50 cents on the dollar before World War I.

As late as 1928, on the occasion of a Latin American tour by President-elect Herbert Hoover, 'a sensation had just been caused throughout Latin America by the importation from Europe of several hundred thousand copies of a Spanish translation of Margaret Marsh's recent book *North American Bankers in Bolivia* … Some Bolivian propagandists at Antofagosta made it their business to distribute many copies of the book to the North American newspaper correspondents … an indirect thrust against the autocratic rule of President Siles, which already was tottering to its fall at La Paz.' Bolivia's two railway networks still lack a link between Cochabamba and Santa Cruz.

There were 103 locomotives in 1964, declining to 34 in 1995, but reviving to 55 in 1999, at which time there were still about a million passengers per year, as against about 29 million annually on America's Amtrak.

Speyer was frozen out of some small or abortive flotations in Honduras where the Morgan firm, First National, National City and Kuhn Loeb combined against it. The financial consultant Charles Conant, at the instigation of the Speyer firm, in 1909 put together a plan for promoting monetary reform. In this proposal, refunding loans to underdeveloped countries, including China, Liberia and various Latin American states, were to be linked to currency reforms based on a gold standard. The bankers were to be compensated from half the seigniorage on the new currency. These plans foundered on competition from the Morgan consortium as well as refusal by Congress to ratify treaties with Honduras and Nicaragua. Speyer did make loans to Nicaragua (1905), Costa Rica (1906) and Guatemala (1912) and in 1912 was part of a consortium that settled for $200,000 in a lawsuit arising from construction of the Jamaica Railway. The Bolivian venture may be credited with leaving behind, in the western part of the country, substantial infrastructure that is still in use. Bolivia and Argentina are the only Latin American countries with significant passenger rail systems.

CHAPTER 17

Industrial and Municipal Investments

'A landmark in the history of revenue bond financing'

Speyer continued to be the financial adviser of various American industrial firms during the 1920s and 1930s. These included Allis Chalmers, Pittsburgh and Lackawanna Steel, Sharon Steel, Metal and Thermit Co., Radio Keith Orpheum, Wayne Pump, Corn Products Refining Co., RCA and Victor Talking Machines. The Allis Chalmers company involved a union between a German (Allis) and a Scot (Chalmers); Allis originally brought Speyer the business.

Before World War I, the Morgan firm manifested its continuing hostility toward Speyer by freezing the Lee Higginson company out of an AT&T stock offering because of Lee Higginson's alignment with Speyer.

Speyer represented the Victor Talking Machine Co. before and during its merger with RCA in 1929 before the crash when the resulting company had the huge market valuation of $626 million. In 1926, a group led by Speyer and the Seligman interests obtained an option to acquire Victor stock at $115 a share, Speyer being represented primarily by De Witt Millhauser. It exercised the option in January 1927, paying Victor's founder Eldridge Johnson and other shareholders a total sum variously estimated at $30–$40 million. In ensuing negotiations with David Sarnoff's RCA, Speyer and Seligman are said to have downplayed the extent of Victor's royalty obligations to composers and others, and its relatively high manufacturing costs. Under the merger terms negotiated in 1929, each Victor common share was exchanged for one common and one preferred RCA share, plus $5. Though RCA later prospered mightily with the coming of the television age, the plunge in its share value during the 1929 crash from a high of $549 a share was one of the deepest of all companies.

The American Speyer firm presided over Sharon Steel's merger with Pittsburgh Steel in 1936, and over $8 million in ensuing flotations. James Speyer was one of the defendants in a government antitrust case brought against Corn Products, for whom the firm had sold $5 million in 25-year bonds in 1909, and one of the subjects of an injunction entered by Judge Learned Hand.

Speyer's municipal flotations were limited, although it was the principal banker for the Port of New York Authority, a pioneering bi-state agency. The initial project-specific bonds of the Authority were sold in 1926 by a syndicate headed by the First National Bank; however, the first general refunding bonds of the Authority were underwritten by Speyer in 1935, 'rescu[ing] the Staten Island bridges and the Inland Terminal from financial embarrassment' through a pooling of obligations. 'Almost from its inception, the Port of New York Authority has ranked as the largest issuer of revenue bonds.' 'The Port of New York Authority financing stands out as a landmark in the history of revenue-bond financing for the following reasons: *First*, the issues were very much larger than any previous public offerings of revenue bonds. *Second*, they were for an entirely new type of revenue-bond project, namely, toll bridges. *Third*, they introduced to the public for the first time agency-revenue bonds, issued in this case by a new form of body known as an "authority".'

Speyer also sold bonds for New York City, Los Angeles, and the states of New York, Illinois, Missouri and Maine.

GERMANY

CHAPTER 18

Rehabilitating Central Europe

'We have not simply sold them to the public. We have some ourselves'

The business of the Speyer firm fell off sharply after World War I, partly because there was no European capital to import, partly because of its German associations in the public mind, and partly because of the widening influence of other sources of investment capital. These causes were not peculiar to Speyer. Postwar, 'the great days of Jewish banking fortunes were over'. James Speyer's vanity and prickliness were also a contributing factor. A *New Yorker* profile in 1928 noted that 'he prefers, in business as well as extra-curricular activities to be cock of the walk. In finance, this often takes the form of refusing to allow his firm to take a subordinate position in the floating of loans; thus in the years 1927–30 Speyer and Co. was the tenth private international banking house in the country in point of volume of loans in which it headed the syndicate but in point of gross business transacted it was not among the fifty two private houses which each did a business of four hundred million dollars during those four years.'

The developments unfavourable to Speyer were summarized in a biographical sketch of him:

> With the outbreak of World War I the prestige of Speyer began to decline rapidly. James Speyer was blatantly pro-German and he spent every summer in Germany as a frequent guest of Kaiser Wilhelm. He and the German Ambassador Count Johann von Bernstorff made a futile effort early in the war to enlist funds for a peace drive. Speyer was placed on a British blacklist in 1916 and shortly after the war closed its British branch. A post-war decline in railroad stocks further weakened the company and the shift of the U.S. from a debtor to a creditor nation reduced the importance of foreign capital … The final blow came with

the rise of Nazi anti-Semitism in Germany which in 1934 forced the closing of
the Speyer banks in Berlin and Frankfurt.

Speyer's insistence on first placement was reputedly the reason for Jesse
Hirschman's departure as a Speyer partner in 1924, though he retained
his railroad directorships. Hirschman foresaw that this would exacerbate
relationships with the Morgan firm. The firm made a $6 million loan to
Berne, Switzerland in October 1920; the German house got a $60,000
commission for securing the loan, which was paid off at a premium.

Morgan had declined to lend to postwar Hungary, and the Rothschild
bank in London was not willing to work with Speyer. The problem
originated from J.P. Morgan's dislike of James Speyer. Aside from the fact
that the aristocratic American banker was, in his own words, 'not very
enthusiastic about Jews' and did not want to see business in their hands,
business incidents had burdened their relations. Jeremiah Smith, the League
of Nations financial agent for Hungary, also thought that the Speyer house,
though not insignificant, was speculative and its participation was avoided.

In the final event in 1924, Speyer took $7.5 million of a $60 million
loan, the only American participation; there was a further $1.5 million loan
in September 1924 and a $10 million loan to Hungarian municipalities
in July 1925. In December 1930, Speyer sold $5 million in one-year
Hungarian treasury bills due in November 1931, long-term bond sales then
being impossible. 'The psychological significance of even that smaller [$7.5
million] sum was huge. It was a proof of trust both in the reconstruction
program initiated by the League of Nations and the Hungarian government
but also though not in an official capacity and not always in a tangible
form, between the United States and Hungary.' Speyer had vainly
attempted to get State Department endorsement of the loan, which was
not forthcoming. Although Secretary Hughes supported the Dawes Plan
loans to Germany because of 'chaotic conditions' which would otherwise
ensue, and also endorsed loans to some Latin American countries like Cuba
and the Dominican Republic over which the United States exerted de
facto protectorates, American interests were not seen as vitally involved in
Hungary, and the United States maintained a stand-offish attitude toward
League of Nations projects. There was also fear that the government would
be subject to legal liability if it affirmatively approved issues.

In 1932, Speyer told a congressional committee that the Hungarian issue
'was a most difficult business because a good many people in our country
did not know where Hungary was. We published books with pictures ...
We got some men to write speeches and explain what the purpose of the

loan was. It was quite a campaign. … At least several bankers in this country declined to have anything to do with this matter … The particular loan had a special attraction because it was devoted to a good purpose. We would not have taken it if we had not thought we could make some money. We are business people.'

'Excellent,' exclaimed Senator [Hiram] Johnson. 'We have been hearing a lot of moralists. Your frankness is refreshing.'

The Hungarian government presided over by Admiral Horthy that Speyer supported has been variously characterized. It was installed with at least the passive acquiescence of the Allies, who preferred it to Bela Kun's communists. It practised a confessional (though not racial) anti-Semitism, which did not take a murderous form, and until overthrown by the Arrow Cross with German support in 1944 did not cooperate in Hitler's 'Final Solution'. It became an ally first of Mussolini and then of Hitler. It has also been described as Europe's first fascist government, its accession to power preceding Mussolini's march on Rome. Whether anything better could have been expected given the consequences of Hungary's postwar inflation and its truncated territory is a moot point. 'A policy of strict financial austerity was introduced, and enforced mainly at the expense of the urban middle classes … stabilization and the "loan culture" that it spawned did not yield a permanent solution to the country's economic disabilities.' Speyer is credited with having successfully urged the government to establish a central mortgage bank as a means of regulating foreign borrowing.

The bulk of Western loans to Hungary did not go to productive enterprises; 40 per cent of the long-term loans were used to service and amortize other loans, including prewar debts. 'By limiting the franchise, playing off the many small parliamentary groups, and controlling the press [Count Bethlen] established his domination over parliament. Through a series of measures combining cajolery and coercion, Bethlen weakened the socialists and pacified the far right.'

Although American participation in the initial Hungarian loan was small, $115 million in all was loaned from America by 1928, when the supply of foreign capital dried up because of developments in Hungary. The US share of total flotations was 44.5 per cent. James Speyer did not make these loans from afar. According to his congressional testimony in 1930, he made three visits to Hungary. In 1928, in recognition of Speyer's services, the Horthy government awarded him the Hungarian Order of Merit, 2nd Class, at a ceremony in New York attended by John Dynely Prince, Minister to Yugoslavia and a relative of Mrs Speyer and Henry W. Taft, former President Taft's brother and counsel to the firm.

The Hungarians were credited with good-faith efforts to service their debt during the Depression, making 50 per cent payments on interest coupons until World War II.

The Speyer house was also the first to sell the postwar Greek and Bulgarian bonds floated under League of Nations auspices. The loans were floated at 7 per cent rates, high for the period. The Greek loan was for $7 million in December 1923; the Bulgarian loan for $4.5 million in September 1926. Unlike the Hungarian loans, the loans were for refugee relief. Greek and Bulgarian partial interest payments were sporadic, the Bulgarians having a somewhat better record than the Greeks. The committee handling the then defaulted Hungarian, Greek and Bulgarian loans met with Speyer in December 1932. In defence of Speyer, it has been observed that 'League of Nations loans contained far-reaching provisions to insure their safety: guarantees by several other nations; priority over all other obligations; the obligation of the debtor nation to balance its budget and provisions for financial control to enforce this.' James Speyer made two visits each to Greece and Bulgaria. At the 1930 congressional hearings, Senator King of Utah noted of the Greek loans, made for the benefit of the refugees created by the Treaty of Lausanne: 'I have visited many of the houses built under the guidance of the League of Nations and can say that the work was greatly beneficial.'

There was dissension within the American government as to whether, and to what extent, there should be supervision of foreign lending. Secretary of Commerce Hoover favoured supervision on investor protection grounds; Secretary of the Treasury Mellon sought only to avoid interference with the payment of war debts by the European governments; Secretary of State Hughes sought to avoid interference with foreign relations objectives, as with loans for munitions sales. An initial loose notification and comment system was outlined in a letter from J.P. Morgan to President Harding on 6 June 1921. It was supplanted in March 1922 by a public request to bankers, which in turn was succeeded in 1925 by a circular prompted by correspondence with the Speyer firm asking that bankers recite that approval had been obtained from German authorities. This was followed in 1929 by an elaborate form of words containing various warnings but disclaiming any interest by the Department of State.

In 1925, Speyer had studied a possible Austrian loan but did not make it. It was made by Morgan, motivated less by Austrian credit-worthiness than by fears of an anschluss if the loan was not forthcoming.

James Speyer's obituary credited his firm with being the first to sell German securities after the war, although others appear to have made pre-inflation German mark loans of $52,500 to the city of Frankfurt in February 1920, and $297,200 to the city of Elberfeld and $50,000 to the city of Berlin in April 1922. There were also two loans to German banks totalling $300,000 in April 1922.

German municipalities had sold $30 million in bonds by October 1920 and industries $100 million. However, the greatest boon to pre-inflation Germany was the speculation of American, Dutch and Swedish investors anticipating a rise in the value of the mark due to Germany's industrial prowess. There was an influx of $3.5 billion, representing at one point 36 per cent of German bank deposits, all of which was lost during the inflation. John Maynard Keynes observed that 'the money of the bankers and the servant girls which would have been nearly enough to restore Europe if applied with prudence and wisdom has been wasted and thrown away'. Subsequently, 'massive American loans went to Europe – largely to Germany where they were eventually used to build up the Nazi war machine ... by 1927, American private enterprise had invested more than thirteen billion dollars abroad'.

As early as August 1921 James Speyer was said to be the go-between in negotiations for a credit to Germany of $25–$50 million through the American War Finance Corporation. This fell through when British credits were granted, and because of uncertainty concerning reparations and the unsettled status of Silesia.

According to his 1930 congressional testimony, the first Speyer loan appears to have been a one-year $3 million loan to the city of Berlin in early November 1924, which was fully repaid and which closed before the Dawes Plan loan negotiated in October 1924.

Speyer made numerous additional loans to German municipalities and companies, as follows: Berlin ($15 million in July 1925 at 6.5 per cent); Dresden ($3.75 million in November 1925 at 7 per cent, $2 million of which was redeemed); Frankfurt ($2.8 million in November 1925 at 7 per cent); Leipzig ($3.75 million in September 1926 at 7 per cent, $1.3 million of which was redeemed); Berlin Elevated Railway ($12 million in November 1926 at 6.5 per cent); Westphalian United Electric Power ($7 million in November 1925 at 6.5 per cent and $20 million in January 1928 at 6 per cent); and the Hamburg America Line ($6.5 million, in November 1925 at 6.5 per cent, $3.5 million of which was redeemed).

In addition to these eight publicly-offered post-Dawes German loans totalling $70.8 million, there were also three privately placed loans or lines of credit totalling $16 million: Berlin, $3 million in November 1924 at 7 per cent; German State Railways, $10 million (not drawn down) in

November 1924 to June 1926 at 7 per cent; and United Glanzstoff Mfg. Co., $3 million in May 1927 at 5.5 per cent.

Additional portions of several loans were placed outside of the United States, some with participation of the German branch, totalling $12.2 million: $5 million of the German railway loan; $1.25 million of the Dresden loan; $1.2 million of the Frankfurt loan; $500,000 of the first Westphalian United loan; $1.25 million of the Leipzig loan; and $3 million of the Berlin Elevated loan.

Speyer's total German commitments thus amounted to $99 million; translated into present-day dollars, this amount was equal to at least half of Germany's post-World War II Marshall Aid allocation.

Taken in all, Speyer accounted for about 6 per cent of post-Dawes American loans to Weimar Germany, by both number of loans (there were 135 in all) and amount. All the loans ultimately went into default; Schacht and the Hitler government offered the bondholders either ten-year bonds bearing interest at 3 per cent maturing in 1946 or blocked German marks which could be sold for foreign exchange only at a very heavy discount, all later to prove worthless.

Sinking fund payments on all loans were suspended by late 1935. Speyer, unlike most of the other American banking houses making foreign loans, had 'skin in the game'. 'I myself, and members of my family,' Speyer testified in late 1931, 'have a loss on our books, or depreciation today, on all these securities here [foreign loans issued by Speyer and Co.] of $1,457,692. We have not simply sold them to the public. We have some ourselves.' The exchange with his questioners continued

> Sen. Gore: 'I think that is pretty game. Did you never sell them, or did you buy them back? Did you hold them in the first instance?'
> Mr. Speyer: 'Most of them we bought at the original issue price … I cannot control world conditions … We have depreciation on the very securities you are talking about … We have no secrets. Many were bought back in an effort to sustain the market, but we could not stand against the world.'

Speyer also expressed astonishment at the 'spreads' obtained by some of the late-appearing bankers: 'I do not know of anyone ever getting a spread of 10 per cent, but go ahead … We are always the originators. We never participated under anybody in any public offering.'

Speyer, unlike most of the other bankers, an unhappy lot, appeared to enjoy these hearings. 'Dressed in a black suit, a wing collar, and a black cravat caught at the knot with a gold band, he was the impersonation of the popular conception of an international banker.' He testified that his firm had floated $276 million of foreign bonds in the US, of which $34 million had been taken by European buyers, and $568 million in Europe. Two of five Sao Paulo issues were in default, but none yet in Europe, though there had been much depreciation.

The committee concentrated its fire on recent Colombian, Bolivian and Peruvian issues in which Speyer, Morgan and Kuhn Loeb were not involved, Senator Carter Glass saying of the State Department: 'they had a clerk passing on the loans who didn't know anything more about them than my cat'. Speyer made two short-term fully repaid loans in Havana and to the Dominican Republic. The Colombian loans made by other bankers were notorious, amounting to more than $200 million in 1928. The Colombian Secretary of Finance declared 'quite frankly that the foreign loans contracted in the last three years [before 1928] had reached such a point that the credit, not only of the borrowers, but of the central Government as well, is endangered'.

Speyer emerged unscathed from the most prominent twentieth-century congressional hearings on financial matters. The Pujo hearings of 1912–13 helped give rise to the Federal Reserve System, the Income Tax Amendment and the Clayton Antitrust Act, as well as supplying grist for Louis Brandeis' *Other People's Money*. They were ably conducted by Samuel Untermeyer as counsel, and traumatized the elder Morgan, who died in the following year. There was little mention of the Speyer firm, save in a table of interlocking directorates.

The Pecora hearings of 1932–3, begun under a Republican Senate and ending under a Democratic one, did not call Speyer as a witness but helped produce the 1933 and 1934 Securities Acts and the Glass-Steagall Act separating commercial and investment banking. The younger Morgan was disconcerted when a dwarf girl (later put to death in a Nazi death camp) was deposited on his lap to the accompaniment of flash cameras, but even more traumatic was his need to reveal that he had arranged his affairs so as to pay no income taxes. The Pecora Committee identified six 'agents of concentration' in the economy: Morgan, Kuhn Loeb, National City Bank, First National Bank, Kidder Peabody and Lee Higginson. Since World War I, the Speyer firm was no longer regarded as a giant of finance.

The Nye Committee hearings of 1935, with Alger Hiss as committee counsel, concentrated their fire on so-called 'merchants of death': the Morgan firm during World War I and the financiers of the Chaco War and other Latin-American conflicts. Speyer, as we have seen, was uniquely uninvolved in wartime loans to either the Allies or Central Powers during

World War I as well as in war finance in Latin America. At the 1930 hearings on foreign bond sales, he had said 'I do not think that one ought to help other countries build up their navies or military establishments ... I am a big Navy man.'

Speyer was saved by obscurity from denunciation by the American anti-Semites of the 1930s like Father Coughlin and Gerald L. K. Smith, Kuhn Loeb being their favoured target. Henry Ford's astonishing four-volume screed on *The International Jew: The World's Persistent Problem* struck only a glancing blow: 'The advisors of the Bethmann-Hollweg government were Ballin, Theodore Wolff, Von Gwinner, director of the German Bank who is connected by marriage with the great Jew bankers, the Speyers, and Rathenau.' The Jews were denounced as war-mongers; nothing was said about the Straus-Bernstorff peace initiative fostered by James Speyer.

The same was true of a memorandum including the notorious Protocols of the Elders of Zion circulated by a Russian émigré employed by the US World Trade Board and referred to in a US State Department file which concluded: 'Seems most unwise to give ___ the distinction of publicity.'

Speyer's profits on the eight public and three private post-Dawes German loans were estimated by Robert Kuczynski at about $600,000. The total 'spread' on the $70 million American portion of Speyer's eight publicly offered loans was about $3.8 million. Kuczynski estimated that bankers' total profits and commissions on loans equalled about 70 per cent of the 'spread', which in Speyer's case would compute to about $2.5 million. Speyer's own estimate of his firm's profits was $1.8 million. ('That is why our profit is so small. It is divided up.'). As observed by Kuczynski, 'Some banking houses like J.P. Morgan and Speyer are usually wholesalers.' Since Speyer, though always the manager, was not the sole originator of its larger loans and was not a retail distributor, his estimate appears plausible. Its present-day equivalent is about $27 million.

Between 1925 and 1930, American bankers loaned nearly $3 billion to Germany, a figure that compares with $1.3 billion in shrunken dollars of post-World War II Marshall Aid. The US supplied $1.25 billion in long-term credits of a total of $2.6 billion, about $300 million each being supplied by bankers in Britain and the Netherlands. US banks supplied about $1.4 billion in short-term credit during the later part of this period, about three-eighths of German short-term loans. During the five-year period about 33 per cent of Germany's total investments came from capital imports; German loans accounted for about 20 per cent of US foreign loans. Much of the credit was wasted on uncompetitive German agriculture, textile and iron and steel industries in which there was already overcapacity. However, 'Germany possessed a rationalized industrial plant, a variety of municipal amenities ranging from subsidized workers' housing to swimming pools, and a lavish social welfare provision unequalled anywhere outside Great Britain.'

Robert Kuczynski estimated American bankers' profits at about $50 million on $1.28 billion of long-term loans to Germany. The American journalist Garet Garrett, in a book published in 1932 based on earlier *Saturday Evening Post* articles, summarized the German loan experience as follows:

> That debt need never be paid, that it may be infinitely postponed, that a creditor nation may pay itself by progressively increasing the debts of its debtors – such was the logic of this credit delusion … The fatal weakness of the scheme is that you cannot stop. When new creditors fail to present themselves faster than the old creditors demand to be paid off, the bubble bursts. Then you go to jail, like Ponzi, or commit suicide, like Ivar Krueger.

The Morgan firm had been consistently hostile to loans to Germany, other than the governmentally sponsored Dawes and Young Plan loans. 'Soon after the Dawes Plan had been approved, Morgan informed Germany's ambassador to the U.S. that he believed that leading German businessmen and government officials, especially Foreign Minister Gustav Stresemann, were still monarchists and might recall the Kaiser and promote a war of revenge, if given the chance. Exactly a week after floating the Dawes loan, Morgan publicly announced that, having fulfilled its obligation as fiscal agent for England, France and Belgium, it would take no further part in loans to Germany. This remained the company's policy throughout the twenties.' Theodore Roosevelt before his death in 1918 had expressed the conviction that a second German defeat would be necessary to lay the ghost of German militarism. At the end of World War II, John Foster Dulles, who while at Sullivan and Cromwell had been a leading promoter of loans to Germany, ruefully observed that 'the reparation creditors had built up within Germany a machinery which was intended to enable Germany to pay reparations but which, in fact, enabled Germany to wage the most destructive war of all time'.

Herbert Feis similarly was to observe in 1950 that 'Our financial mechanism was busily creating new targets for our bombers. Some were easier to get up than to knock down,' while the historian Carroll Quigley noted that 'In the period 1924–1929, by means of these funds, the industrial structure of Germany was largely rebuilt. Germany had the most efficient industrial machine in Europe and probably the second most efficient in the world (after the United States).'

The American banking houses in the inter-war period, particularly Morgan and Kuhn Loeb, rendered similar but lesser services to the armament of Japan, American loans to that country approximating $300 million In September 1924, J.P. Morgan Jr and Thomas Lamont set forth the firm's attitude in a cable to Dwight Morrow, who was about to meet with Secretary of State Charles Evans Hughes:

> Whole question turns on the actual desire for peace on the part of Germany. Have been very much disturbed by the attitude of the Nationalists in that country who sold their objections to the carrying out of the Dawes Report for a statement to be made by their government repudiating the war guilt clause in the Treaty of Versailles. So far the German Government has not published this repudiation, but of course we cannot be sure that it will not do so. As against this Montagu Norman is quite certain (and he has seen Schacht quite a little) that apart from the Communists on the one side and the Nationalists on the other, in Germany the great masses of the people want peace and are ready to make the necessary sacrifices to get it ... he believes there is no foreign loan at present in existence which offers as good security as this one. Montagu Norman was perfectly clear that in his opinion unless the loan is made Europe will break. If on the contrary it is made he believes that the results will be as favourable as similar operations for Austria and Hungary have turned out, but on an even larger scale ... What really impresses us favourably in Governor Norman's opinion is not the extent of the foreign control upon Germany but the disposition of the German people at the present time. We have some fear however that that disposition may not continue. However desirous Germany is of getting the loan at the moment in order to free the hold which France has on the industries of the Ruhr, it is almost inevitable that this loan will be unpopular in Germany after a few years. The people of Germany in our opinion are almost certain after sufficient time has elapsed to think not of the release of the Ruhr but of the extent to which what was once a first-class power has been subjected to foreign control.

In October 1925, concern began to be voiced as to the extent of American lending to German municipalities, since Article 248 of the Versailles Treaty gave reparations 'a first charge upon all the assets and revenues of the German Empire and its constituent states'. When Speyer consulted the State Department in routine fashion about a loan for Frankfurt am Main, it got a response from Secretary of State Kellogg declaring that 'the Department is advised that the German Federal authorities themselves are not disposed to view with favour the indiscriminate placing of German loans in the American market, particularly when the borrowers are German municipalities and the loans are not productive'.

Speyer was advised to ascertain whether the Dawes Transfer Committee would interfere with repayment:

'the Department believes that you should consider whether you do not owe a duty to your prospective clients fully to advise them of the situation, … [B]ank head James Speyer and Henry W. Taft ran to see the Secretary of State. Speyer and Taft were in Arthur Young's words 'greatly wrought up' by the Department's letter and insisted that the State Department was 'going outside of its proper field in suggesting what the bankers should tell their clients.' With firm support from Hoover, the State Department refused to back down, 'since the matter is not an ordinary matter of business risk, but is related to negotiations in which the government has had a part.' When James Speyer tried to pin down what the government wanted, he found no room for encouragement. He informed Arthur Young that, as a result of their conversation, his firm had arranged the Frankfurt loan 'subject to the views of' the State Department. As Young reported, 'I stated that the Department did not desire that bankers condition their financing upon its action. Mr. Speyer replied that he had not seen any other way to act in the circumstances.'

The reparations administrator, S. Parker Gilbert, objected to the buck-passing by the State Department which 'raises questions which nobody can answer and suggests doubts which no one can settle, except by the test of actual experience'. He thoroughly agreed with Shepard Morgan's observation that the State Department letter 'ought to be set to music, and it is on such a high moral plane that nothing less than a pipe organ would do for the purpose'. Gilbert declared that the State Department 'proceeds to relieve itself of all responsibility by a closing sentence to the effect that no question of government policy being involved, it raises no objection. What a wonderful little tail for all that dog!'

Gilbert, a 32-year-old former Morgan employee who supervised German finances for five years without learning German, and the mercurial German central banker Hjalmar Schacht were at one in their favouritism toward industrial loans and their stigmatization of loans to municipalities as 'unproductive'. Many of the private loans, however, were to Junker estates and other portions of the economy with over-capacity, while many 'municipal' loans were channelled to industry or devoted to sewer and electric plants necessary to industry. 'Schacht and Gilbert … never mention[ed] the fact disclosed in January 1929 by the German minister of agriculture that three-fourths of the amounts borrowed abroad for agriculture have disappeared never to be seen again, lost through bad crops, large and unfavourable investments, and the excessive interest charges.' Schacht and Gilbert for different reasons viewed the State Department's abdication as a pretext for their own imposition of controls. By early 1927, these had choked off long-term foreign loans. When foreign lending resumed in the second half of the year, it was on a short-term basis. 'Gilbert's ties in New York were to J.P. Morgan and partners and these men had, like Gilbert, no sympathy for the "second-rank" banks that were selling German loans.'

Gilbert let his antagonism toward American bankers show when he told Britain's Ambassador to Berlin, Sir Ronald Lindsay, that he was using the reparations issue as a way to reduce American loans to Germany: 'if he did not, he would merely be clearing the decks for those issuing houses in the U.S. that had to be restrained'.

Gilbert proclaimed in October and December 1927 that 'the accumulating evidence of over-spending and over-borrowing on the part of the German public authorities is almost certain to lead to severe economic reaction and depression'. Anticipating the policies of the Bruning government, he urged 'a regime of strict economy and of ordered public finance'. This led the British Foreign Office to remark that the interests of 'Eastern bankers' were not necessarily the same as those of Morgan, the Federal Reserve Board or the United States Treasury.

The various treasury and reparations agent warnings have been assembled by Robert Kuczynski. The drying up of American loans, the result of both German and reparations agent policy, the attractions of American equity investments before October 1929 and the coming of the American Depression were followed by the severe deflation of the Bruning and Von Papen regimes, illustrating 'the complex and deadly links between international finance and domestic politics' and the incompatibility of 'Germany's failed attempts to stabilize its internal social system through deficit spending and its foreign position through a policy of fulfilment'. In 1927, the Social Democrats in the Muller government had liberalized unemployment benefits, which ultimately claimed 28 per cent of federal and state revenues, and also granted a 25 per cent increase in civil service pay; the Social Democrats were not blameless in the catastrophe that followed, although they were the only political party to vote against Hitler's Enabling Law.

As a result of these factors and the Smoot-Hawley tariff of 1930, the dollars paid out by the United States to foreign countries fell from $7.4 billion in 1929 to $2.4 billion in 1932. In the latter year, debt service payments to the United States amounted to $900 million, an amount somewhat exceeding reparations payments. Between 600,000 and 700,000 American investors held defaulted foreign bonds, their average investment amounting to $3,000. J. Edward Meeker, an economist with the New York Stock Exchange, expressed limited sympathy with them: 'If the Anglo-Saxon race had always waited for a "sure thing," it would still be tending goats on the foothills of the Himalayas, instead of directing the destinies of most of the civilized world today.' William McNeil has observed:

'[I]n the Weimar period, when every tax seemed to be a political assault on private industry, the working classes or other momentarily less powerful groups, relatively modest taxes seemed an unbearable burden. The ability of the state to tax and borrow was limited ... by the political weakness of the Weimar state and system. The state had neither the crude power to compel private banks or the Reichsbank to extend it credit nor the political credibility to convince investors that it could raise taxes to cover its long-term financial obligations.' Moreover, 'the system of cartel prices, administered wages, welfare subsidies, and civil service monopolies had benefitted the special interests at the expense of the consumer and taxpayer for most of Weimar's history.'

Bruning achieved an extraordinary technical success. Through three rigorous wage and price reductions, he brought costs down. He also restricted imports sharply. From 1929 to 1932 he reduced imports from 13.4 billion to 4.7 billion reichsmarks producing a trade surplus of more than a billion reichsmarks in 1932, although as other nations retailiated, German exports fell from 13.5 billion to 5.7 billion reichsmarks between 1929 and 1932. Bruning's plan worked; the Lausanne Conference of June–July 1932 reduced German reparations to a nominal sum. His economic policy had caused an increase in unemployment to one-third of the workforce by February 1932.

Thus the operation was a success but the patient died.

The Hoover Moratorium and Lausanne came too late; Hoover's personal tragedy was that he became President in 1929 and not 1925, by which time the European economy had met its doom from the stubbornness of Coolidge and Mellon over Allied war debts. The debts had been negotiated downward by Mellon in 1923 as to interest but not as to principal, but not sufficiently in the view of many, including John Maynard Keynes and David Lloyd George, the latter of whom later published a vitriolic denunciation of Mellon entitled *The Truth About Reparations and War Debts*, in which he declared: 'A business transaction at that date between Mr. Mellon and Mr. Baldwin was in the nature of a negotiation between a weasel and its quarry.'

Baldwin's companion, Montagu Norman, was described as 'the high priest of the golden calf and his main preoccupation was to keep his idol burnished and supreme in the Pantheon of commerce'.

One historian has observed that

> Secretary Hughes intervened to use American finance instead of French bayonets to maintain the peace of Europe … The whole system of finance – reparations and debts, the ability of American farmers to sell abroad, the economic health of European nations – depended on a continued willingness of the United States to lend money outside its borders. In the middle of 1928, American investment overseas started to fall off, probably because there were better opportunities at home, although partly in recognition of the dubious nature of many of the investments that had been made and were proposed … the underpinnings of the international economy were pulled out and the whole system collapsed.

As observed by the American diplomat Lewis Einstein,

> The American bankers of the twenties served the policies of Secretary Hughes [who] was not unsuccessfully striving to restore a shipwrecked continent with a diplomacy that turned politics into economics and tried to give Europe the respite of a few years' prosperity. The Dawes Plan, which provided for large American loans to the German Government in exchange for a reduced reparations schedule and supervision of reparations payments by a Reparations Administrator was largely Hughes' achievement.

Hughes in 1922 had declared that 'Sooner or later, an international conference must deal with the whole subject of international indebtedness, which includes German reparations and Allied debts to the United States. But at the moment, neither the people of the United States nor France are adequately educated to the facts of the situation. Until this education is achieved, little real good can flow from the conference.'

Coolidge did nothing to educate the American public, nor did Mellon, until his belated support of the Hoover Moratorium and the Treaty of Lausanne forgiveness of reparations in 1930–2. Whether from frustration or a desire to enjoy the rewards of private law practice, Hughes left the Coolidge administration in 1926, making way for the considerably less gifted Frank Kellogg.

It was estimated that Germany paid in all 22.9 billion marks in reparations: 10.5 billion marks before the Dawes Plan, 7.6 billion under the Dawes Plan and 3.7 billion under the Young Plan, plus 1.1 billion as corrections, including deliveries in kind. 'By and large American and Allied creditors and investors paid German reparations. It was only reasonable, Germany did not have the money and they had. The Dawes Plan did not solve the transfer payments, Germany was never permitted to develop trade surpluses that would have given her the excess funds to finance real payments. In fact, Germany's trade balance was passive. She simply lacked the money, but she had to pay it. She solved the problem by paying interest rates of up to 9 per cent, double those of other countries. This solution worked on the principle of the classic swindle, which attracts victims by offering returns greater than those of a sound business. The disproportionate returns bring in new waves of investors whose money and not the profits is used to finance the large payments to the original investors. Eventually something awakens doubt; new investors are frightened away, the old ones try to sell out, and the operation collapses. This is what happened to Germany during the Depression and Bruning's chancellorship.'

This is a slight overstatement, at least as to the interest payments, which almost never exceeded 7.5 per cent.

The younger Morgan's anti-Semitism was certainly robust. '[E]xcept for his attitude toward the Jews, which I consider wholesome, the new Dictator of Germany seems to me very much like the old Kaiser,' he said in 1933. The Morgan bank was instrumental in excluding Speyer from the Dawes Plan loan to the German national government in 1924:

> Morgan drew the line at Speyer and Co. who had been excluded from the Morgan syndicates since 1905 after allegedly violating the boundaries of the gentlemen's code. The partners in New York [Morrow, Leffingwell and others] felt the [Speyer] firm should be included in the German loan. That did not 'mean that we desire or intend to establish personal relationships with Speyers which would be obnoxious to all of us'.

Jack Morgan was reluctantly willing to include Speyer, but took the view that 'our name appearing with Speyers degrades us'. The partners concluded that 'the complete contentment of Morgan is more valuable contribution to the success of the loan than the inclusion of Jimmie [Speyer]'. They cabled to Morgan: 'Jimmie is out.' Morgan replied: 'Quite impossible to express happiness your cable has given me.' Earlier, in 1922, Morgan had said that he would not 'want his name publicly associated with that of Mr. Speyer for any purpose whatsoever'. In 1909, the junior Morgan had said of the Speyers, 'you cannot rely upon them to carry out their agreements if they can at any time break them [to] their advantage'. This hostility appeared to date from the controversy over the London tube and according to Thomas Lamont also to a prewar clash over Mexican government issues. It was manifested also in charitable ventures. Morgan excluded Speyer from the board of the New Theatre, which proved to be a fiasco; in the words of Otto Kahn, 'We enclosed it in a gorgeous abode of brick and mortar, we stifled it with heavy, golden raiment; we fed it on a diet seasoned with "Society" ingredients. We were conscious, and let the public be conscious, of its "high-toned" pedigree. It had been born anemic.'

James Speyer for his part contained his grief at the elder Morgan's death in 1913. His statement on that occasion, in its entirety, declared: 'Mr. Morgan was a very big man and a leading financier. His influence and counsel will be greatly missed, but the welfare and future of the United States cannot be permanently affected by the death of any one man, however prominent.'

One of the cruellest ironies following the war was Germany's dependence on American capital. The two countries had switched their capital market roles. Deutsche Bank's first American transaction after the war was to help float a $50 million US dollar loan for the German government to support the mark, almost an exact mirror image of its role in Morgan's 1896 syndicate to save the US currency, except that the terms were more stringent. In 1924, a syndicate of which Speyer was a member sold an offering of 20 per cent of Deutsche Bank's own shares on the American market. 'Speyer seemed incapable of taking the lead. Although James Speyer entertained Blinzig [of Deutsche Bank] royally during their strenuous visit to New York [in 1927], Blinzig found the [Speyer] bank deeply troubled and feared that it soon would go out of business.'

Most of the funds that were invested in Germany were in the form of foreign-denominated debt rather than direct investment. Although the Morgan firm participated in the Dawes Plan and Young Plan loans to Germany, by 1927 it was choking off credit to Germany. In that year, Thomas Lamont, a Morgan partner, made a speech declaring:

> From the point of view of the American investor it is obviously necessary to scan the situation with increasing circumspection and to avoid rash and excessive lending. I have in mind the reports I have recently heard of American bankers and firms competing on almost a violent scale for the purpose of obtaining loans in various foreign money markets overseas. Naturally it is a tempting thing for certain of the European governments to find a horde of American bankers sitting on their doorsteps offering them money. That sort of competition leads to insecurity and unsound practice.

The British ambassador in Washington in October 1927 similarly noted that except for the Morgan bank, 'an enormous further program of lending is contemplated' notwithstanding the 'broad and sensible view' of the Federal Reserve Board and US Treasury. Hjalmar Schacht at the same time rather flippantly observed that 'whilst Germany was in need of working capital, the flotation of loans in the U.S. merely went to pay reparations'.

The quality of the foreign loans made by American bankers is said to have progressively deteriorated throughout the decade of the 1920s, in which overconfidence resulted from the absence of any loan defaults at all, save in the case of two Brazilian states. Some 6 per cent of 1920 foreign issues later defaulted, as compared with 63 per cent of those issued in 1928. Of the 1920–4 issues, 18 per cent defaulted, as compared with 50 per cent of foreign bonds issued between 1925 and 1929. By 1931, there were no new foreign issues at all except for refunding bonds. During the 1920s, there had been 800 issues of two years or more in length, totalling $7 billion. Speyer's last long-term German loan was in January 1928. In 1932, before any German default, it was written that 'the heavy drop in prices of German bonds following the default of many South American loans has caused a bitter feeling against the "international bankers"'.

The Senate Finance Committee held hearings on foreign loan sales that lasted from 18 December 1931 to 10 February 1932. Generally, when defaults occurred, all the bonds issued within a country defaulted at once, save for those of Argentina and Cuba. In 1931, Brazil defaulted, followed in 1932 by the League loans to Bulgaria, Greece and Hungary, in 1933 by Cuba and Germany (except for the Dawes and Young Plan loans) and in 1934 by the German Dawes and Young Plan bonds. Some of the defaults were partially repaired: in March 1937 the Nazi government issued 3 per cent refunding bonds and paid interest coupons due from June 1934 to December 1936. Brazil in 1937 paid a portion of interest defaults, and Cuba repaired its defaults. Speyer's Cuban loans were among its better ones: British investors enjoyed about a 4.8 per cent return on both railroad and government bonds and the large Cuban government bond issue which Speyer floated in 1915 was redeemed at par in 1940.

The banking houses with the worst records were the three that entered the market after 1925, which had almost 100 per cent defaults. Blair and Co. and Dillon Read plunged into German loans; Dillon Read's German loans were $39 million in 1925 and $117 million in 1926. Morgan and Kuhn Loeb had the second and third best records. Morgan's good fortune was largely due to its almost complete abstention, on political grounds, from German loans; Kuhn Loeb's good fortune was due to the number of

Western European and Dominion loans in its portfolio. The Speyer firm was in the middle of the pack, as a result of James Speyer's interest in the rehabilitation of Germany and Eastern Europe. James Speyer told a Senate committee in 1931: 'our responsibility continues on for twenty or thirty years, the sums of money that we spend on looking after these things, and trying to straighten them out, no one knows anything about ... A pair of shoes lasts for perhaps two years, but for 30 or 40 years our responsibility continues. I think the profit is very small.'

All 23 of the German and Eastern European loans made in 1920 eventually defaulted. There were no such loans in 1921. Half of the 41 loans of 1922 defaulted; none of the 25 made in 1923 did so. From 1924 onward, there were few good loans in the region; 86 in all, as against 970 defaulted loans.

The final collapse of German credit after the drying up of American loans in 1931 was partly due to the French:

> Under M. Laval, French financial jingoism tended to become as aggressive as was Prussian military jingoism before 1914 ... One of the reasons why international bankers had trusted Germany implicitly in the past was that they relied on the sober and realistic mentality of the Germans, politicians and public alike. Nobody believed that a situation might arise when, rather than agree to political concessions, Germany would choose financial default as an alternative. It was the unexpected that happened. Rather than obtain French assistance at the price of abandoning the [Austrian] Customs Union and the cruiser (both of which had to be abandoned eventually in either case), Germany stopped the payment of her external short-term credits. Germany will no longer be in a position to borrow extensively to pay reparations.

The Hoover Moratorium likewise was in part vitiated by Laval's procrastination, which 'robbed Hoover's audacious initiative of its desired psychological effects'. This was not the last instance of over-cleverness by Laval.

The final German default in March 1933, on the eve of the London Economic Conference, has been vividly described by a State Department economic official, Herbert Feis, who characterized Hjalmar Schacht as 'a most skilled banking technician without heart or morals':

> Schacht went on to serve notice, almost as though it were merely incidental, that the German authorities were going to stop all transfers of payment in foreign currencies on all German external obligations ... The German government

apparently intended that the numerous private investors who had bought
German bonds should learn the hard news from the morning newspapers.
But greater consideration was apparently to be shown to the banking group
which had made [Dawes and Young Plan] loans to the Reichsbank and other
German government institutions and banks ... Schacht confided to [Paul]
Warburg (whose long-established and esteemed family bank in Germany would
soon be compelled to close) that the move he had in mind would apply only
to debts outside the standstill agreement, which covered debts mainly due to
foreign banks. ... the President had suggested to Hull that when Schacht came
to see him he should pretend to be deeply engaged in reading documents and
should pay no attention to his visitor while he was left standing for about three
minutes. Hull was then to look up without showing any surprise at Schacht's
presence. He was to find among his papers a note from the President stating
our serious opposition to German default and was to give it to Schacht. [In
further discussions] we pointed out, among other matters, that the failure to
remit dollar payments would injure many thousands of American bond holders;
that the American government had not demanded reparations payments from
Germany ... that American officials and banks had mediated in bringing about
a reduction in the reparations payments from Germany, and had facilitated
the acceptance of reduced schedules by aiding in the flotation of large German
government loans (especially those known as the Dawes and Young Plan loans);
that these and other American investments had enabled Germany to get through
difficult post-war years and to reconstruct its economy; that after the depression
had set in, President Hoover, by trying to bring about a temporary moratorium
on the payment of all intergovernmental debts and reparations, had helped to
preserve the German state at a critical period; and finally that the Reichsbank
would be able to accumulate the means of making substantial payments if
Germany spent less on imports used for rearmament.

Reparations and war debts poisoned Europe's recovery between the wars.
This mistake was avoided after World War II. There were large reparations
in kind from Germany, particularly from the Russian and French zones, in
the year or two following the war, and nominal reparations were paid by
the lesser Axis powers, including Italy, Hungary, Romania and Finland, but
no very large cash reparations. As for war debts, the principal such debts
– those arising from Lend-Lease to Great Britain and the Soviet Union –
were settled for relatively nominal sums after the war. The British deficit of
$21 billion was cancelled in December 1945 in exchange for $650 million,
payable over 50 years; the Soviet deficit of $7.3 billion was settled for $722
million, payable over an extended period, in 1972. In 1953, the London

Debt Agreement provided for the payment of 50 per cent of defaulted German bonds and 90 per cent of defaulted short-term bank loans, without interest. There was a second agreement after German reunification in 1990; the last payments under it were made in 2010.

It was said in retrospect that, by contrast with the investments of modern 'hedge funds', the 'investment pools managed by Deutsche Bank, Speyer and Morgan differed in some respects from their more modern equivalents. They had longer-term horizons and, above all, they actively managed investments on behalf of and sometimes even by the participants themselves. Instead of breaking out and hedging undesired risk, as do their modern counterparts, they attempted to manage it, or perhaps better put, to control specific risk.'

Summarizing the experience of the 1920s with flotation of sovereign loans to private individuals, Gunnar Myrdal was to write in 1956:

> In the twenties, long-term investments on a large scale even started to flow from the United States. America, emerging after the war as a creditor country, opened its banking resources to Weimar Germany. The money was eventually lost to a large extent, and this, coupled with a risky scramble for high-interest earnings in the Balkans and Latin America, had disastrous effects on the willingness of American investors to venture again into foreign lending … the cessation of the capital flow caused a deepening of the depression. The floating in international capital markets of foreign government bonds, once so important in international financing, has almost ceased. Private lending to foreign governments, municipalities and corporations and likewise the acquisition of foreign equities as a regular investment – methods of lending without becoming involved in industry abroad and without holding a controlling interest – are more and more a thing of the past.

A table published in *The New York Times* in early 2013 depicting global capital flows depicts the present situation. Foreign direct investments in developing countries grew from $200 billion in 2000 to $800 billion in 2012. Short-term bank loans, negligible in 2000, rose to $400 billion in 2012. Equity investments reached a peak of about $150 billion in 2009–10, before falling to about $50 billion in 2012. Bond investments of the Speyer type were negligible until about 2004, rising to $200 billion annually in 2010–12; they usually are made by country-specific mutual funds or exchange traded funds; investors typically know little about the merits of the securities held by these entities.

Two contrasting views have been expressed about the same facts concerning foreign bonds issued in the 1920s. One writer notes that 'of the existing foreign bonds that were issued here during the prosperous twenties, around 35 to 40 percent are now [1935] in default'. Another writer celebrated the fact that the glass was still more than half full: 'interest has been paid in full, through the largest and most severe depression of modern times, on almost two-thirds the foreign bonds now [December 1935] outstanding'.

In October 1935, looking back on the German loan experience, Allen Dulles told his colleagues at Sullivan and Cromwell:

> Generally, foreign-held loans [are the first to be defaulted] since maintenance of internal credit [is] essential to continued national economy ... [We] permitted debt to pile up too fast and too high and took moral risk ... default has moral, and not legal consequence as the obligor is without effective remedy ... the foreign bond ... has few of the attributes of a bond ... the bare pledge of revenues should be eliminated [in favour of] the desirability of agreement among lenders for equal treatment.

In November 1937, speaking of Latin American bonds, Dulles said that the 'chief hindsight criticism [places] emphasis on pledges which [are] of little value unless collected by an outside agent'. This continues to be a problem with respect to defaults on government obligations 75 years later, leading some to urge a scheme similar to corporate bankruptcy to be administered by the International Monetary Fund or some other agency. Litigation against Argentina, a perennial scofflaw, in American courts had the result that 'the *pari passu* clause and the fundamental principle of equal payment ... have been reaffirmed again to mean that debtors cannot discriminate in priority of payment to creditors holding comparable classes of debt'. 'From 1924 to 1931 Sullivan and Cromwell handled $1.15 billion in loans to Germany and Europe as well as $250 million to Latin America and $139 million to Japan.'

Speyer shared in Hughes' effort to replace politics with economics. Had the United States come to its senses about war debts by the middle 1920s, this policy might have succeeded. But the combined burden of reparations and ever greater interest payments on mounting foreign debt required a severe domestic deflation that proved to be too much for Germany.

CHAPTER 19

Last Days in Germany

'The Peace Treaty makes no provision for the economic
reconstruction of Europe. The diplomats … have created
no substitute for the old economic units'

A t least until the rise of Hitler and in the summer after it, James
Speyer spent every summer in Germany, and gave press interviews
at the foot of the gangplank on his return to New York. In 1919,
he gave an interview to the *Magazine of Wall Street* in which he approvingly
cited Keynes's *Economic Consequences of the Peace* and declared that 'I do
not believe that the salvation of Europe rests exclusively on an extension
of credit. This seems to be unduly emphasized by many. What Central
Europe needs is raw materials … The Peace Treaty makes no provision for
the economic reconstruction of Europe. The diplomats have been at their
old game of slicing up Europe but they have created no substitute for the
old economic units.' As for American domestic affairs, 'the high cost of
living cannot be overcome by any curtailment of production, be it through
strikes or shortening of work hours. Wrong remedies these and sure to bring
wrong results … It would indeed be a misfortune for the workers themselves
and for our own country if the radical element were to prevail, if only for a
short time.'

Unlike his German and English family members and despite his pro-
Germanism in the early stages of the war, James Speyer shared in the Indian
summer of American investment banking in the 1920s. In Europe, John
Maynard Keynes wrote in 1920:

> [T]he terror and personal timidity of the individuals of this class by now so
> great, their confidence in their place in society and in their necessity to the social
> organism so diminished, that they are the easy victims of intimidation. This was

not so in England twenty-five years ago, any more than it is now in the United States. Then the capitalists believed in themselves, in their value to society, in the propriety of their continued existence in the full enjoyment of their riches and the unbridled exercise of their power. Now they tremble before every insult … Perhaps it is historically true that no order of society perishes save by its own hand.

James Speyer urged improved safety and health conditions for workers:

> When men once find that they can agree on certain measures, it does not take very long to have them discuss other and more difficult points, like hours of work and wages. The relations of capital and labour can never be adjusted by the suppression of the right of free speech on the one side or by the destruction of property on the other. Everyone should be free to work when and as he chooses and the savings and property of every citizen, large or small, shall be protected against attack from whatever source.

His interviewer noted that he 'questions the deportations by the government recently of reds without a fair trial, [and] that he favours parcel posts and postal savings', while remaining a staunch defender of property rights. His was the first Wall Street house to establish a pension plan for its employees. 'You feel his cosmopolitanism as soon as you enter his stately office [he is] not like some prominent New Yorkers who apparently think that the world is bounded on the north by the Polo Grounds and on the south by Coney Island.'

In 1921, he had an interview with President Harding before his departure, and in 1922, he contributed a short article to a symposium on postwar economic problems in the *Annals of the American Academy of Political and Social Science*. He reflected:

> [I]t is just about sixty years since the country engaged in civil war which left the South, particularly, without resources and more prostrate than any part of Europe is today and the whole country with a depreciated currency. British, Dutch and German investors then saw their opportunity and contributed capital to develop our railroads and develop our natural resources. While the situation is, of course, not strictly parallel, we might well profit by their example. European nations too might profit by the example of [what] we did ourselves after our civil war … the determination to forgive and forget.

In 1923, he declared that 'there is no disarmament in Europe except in defeated Germany and dismembered Austria. Politicians over there were swayed by their pre-war prejudices and passions.' In 1925 he noted Hindenburg's commitment to the Dawes Plan and thought that his presidency would resemble the successful seven-year presidency of Marshal MacMahon in France. By 1926, Speyer was confident that the worst effects of the Stinnes collapse were over: 'German securities, carefully selected by a competent people, should afford the American investor an opportunity for safe, profitable investment.' He defended foreign loans, and acclaimed the British central banker Montagu Norman as 'a financial genius', a view not universally shared now.

In August 1927, he observed that the German reparations question needed to be settled, but that 'internal and political conditions are being gradually strengthened due to the sterling qualities of President Hindenburg'. The following year, in a vindication of his firm's wartime conduct, it was awarded $648,039 by the German-American Mixed Claims Commission. In July 1928, Speyer was received by President Hindenburg, whom he acclaimed as a 'masterful personality'. In the same year, he defended foreign loans in an address to the Foreign Policy Association 'to afford members of the FPA an opportunity to look at one of those awful international bankers'. He expressed the view that 'foreign loans probably could not be made if there were a commission with power to prescribe the usage of the funds'.

In January 1931, Speyer delivered a judgement about monetary policy that in the view of most historians could not have been more wrong: 'In this rich country of ours with its stable currency and its efficient Federal Reserve Bank system, there is not real reason for pessimism. On the contrary, prices of good bonds and stocks are sure to improve.' He denounced postwar European nationalism and trade barriers 'cutting up part of Europe into smaller self-governing units, contrary to the economic tendency of modern times, and obstructing century-old free-trade routes through new tariff walls'. In the same month, reversing his earlier position, he publicly urged President Hoover to cancel foreign debts.

In June 1931, he applauded the Hoover Moratorium carrying out this suggestion:

> European nations and we in America have been suffering not so much from the consequences of the war as from the consequences of the peace. It is to be hoped that no narrow local or ultra-nationalistic spirit either here or abroad will delay any carrying out of this first constructive measure, so that before long millions of unemployed everywhere will be able to obtain honest work and an honest living as heretofore … there are certain measures we ought to take at home. Our railroads are entitled to get relief and should be allowed to charge enough to get

a fair return on the enormous amount of capital that millions of our people have directly or indirectly invested in their securities. The Sherman law ought to be revised allowing under proper supervision combinations such as are fostered and encouraged by some foreign governments.

In July 1931 he said that there should be no American debt cancellation 'until [the Europeans] themselves show more good will toward each other … especially by reduced expenditures for land and sea armaments'.

In December 1931, Speyer gave an interview in which he said that the situation in Germany was pitiful, blaming the short-sightedness of the peace settlements, but expressing the hope that the new high British tariffs might benefit its trade. Two months later, he observed with some inconstancy *apropos* of the war debts that 'Great Britain and the United States are the greatest creditor nations; we cannot afford to sanction repudiation.'

Speyer's rather dubious record of political prophecies was preserved intact when in December 1932, after meeting with Luther and Von Krosigk in Germany, he said that the Lausanne Agreement waiving remaining reparations and the disarmament negotiations at Geneva had 'given the German people new hope and confidence in their future'. He lauded the short-lived Schleicher government as 'composed of well-qualified men, each one experienced in his particular field … everybody realizes the importance, and is anxious to have the Republic and the German cities continue, as heretofore, to punctually fulfil their obligations to American bondholders'. He certainly cannot be said to have anticipated the triumph of the Nazis or to have taken alarm at their advances in the polls. Nor was he concerned by the demise of German parliamentary government and the increased reliance on Hindenburg and his presidential powers. Former Ambassador Bernstorff did not wait for the fall of the Schleicher government before fleeing for his life – the accession of Von Papen was enough for him.

Following his visit to Germany at the invitation of Hjalmar Schacht in 1933, Speyer made it plain that he had no illusions about the Hitler government. Speyer was treasurer of the Carl Schurz Memorial Foundation, which continued educational exchange programmes with Germany after the coming to power of the Nazis in January 1933. On 9 September 1933, after Speyer had expressed disquiet over a continuing relationship, the Executive Director of the Foundation, Wilbur K. Thomas wrote:

No further decisions have been made about the future work of the Foundation, and I am waiting until more of our men return from Germany … Mr. Oberlaender returned about two weeks ago. He was in Germany a considerable length of time and among other things, had an interview with Mr. Hitler ... I have been talking with quite a number of our people who have been over there this summer. All of them have many criticisms, but they also have favourable comments; none of them seem to be in favour of isolating Germany, though all emphasize the fact that whatever work is done must be handled in a wise way.

After meeting with Thomas, Speyer conveyed his intention to resign as treasurer, whereupon Thomas, on 11 October, with some insensitivity, asked him to suggest 'some prominent Jewish person who could serve us as Treasurer'. On 20 October, Speyer replied: 'I think that the reasons which compel me to withdraw would very probably apply to others similarly situated, although, of course, as I had the privilege of being a personal friend of Carl Schurz, I may feel more keenly that anybody connected with the Foundation bearing his name should think as I do under the existing circumstances.' Speyer agreed to defer his resignation until the end of the year, while noting that 'under present conditions, I can be of no further service'. On 30 October, after the Executive Committee voted to continue work in Germany, saying 'it is up to the German people to choose their rulers', Speyer replied:

[W]hat I have in mind is that our work is carried on under the name of the 'Carl Schurz Memorial Foundation.' Carl Schurz left Germany because at that time he would not submit to the autocratic regime and the suppression of individual liberties. It seems to me that conditions in Germany in this respect are perhaps worse than they were in 1848, and I am sure that if Carl Schurz were alive today, he would be the first one to speak out loud and protest against the undemocratic suppression of individual liberty of thought and speech and of a free press. I think we owe it to the memory of this great thinker and great liberal to see to it that the Foundation that bears his name does what he would do ... I deeply regret that the majority of the Committee do not share my views, and perhaps I feel more strongly about it because I had the privilege of knowing Carl Schurz, who was very kind to me when I first came back here to my native land.

On 13 December 1933, after the Executive Committee had accepted his resignation on 10 December, Speyer reiterated the grounds for his resignation, noting that Schurz:

upheld in theory and in practice all the ideals which we like to think of as American – enlightened democracy, equal opportunity to all, and justice to everybody, regardless of race, creed, colour, or financial standing. His contribution to American life can be likened to that of Daniel Webster or

Grover Cleveland or Theodore Roosevelt ... I am sure he would not approve of sending young Americans over to Germany, while the present intolerant policies prevail over there ... the Foundation should temporarily suspend its activities over there and keep its funds for a more auspicious period, which, I hope, will soon arrive and once more make me proud of the country of my ancestors, where I received my early education, and for whose people I have been trying in many ways during a long period of years to show my admiration and gratitude.

In September 1936, Speyer declared that the British 'have made real progress for a year or two', while the US had 'a kindly and peace-loving people accustomed to rely on individual work and effort'. People were 'too much alarmed by fear that these deplorable Spanish troubles might lead to some European war ... [The world needs] ordinary trade and intercourse – re-establishment of a fixed money standard.' He had spent the summer in Salzburg, St Moritz and Paris.

In 1938, in an interview given on announcing his retirement, Speyer said that he 'did not think there would be a general war in the near future. He rather discounted his opinion on the subject by smiling and adding 'Neither did I think so in 1914 but I was wrong.'

By the turn of the twentieth century, the Frankfurt house was of diminished importance. In 1901, it floated a Frankfurt city loan which was sold in New York. From then on, its function largely consisted of selling in Germany issues initiated by the London and New York houses.

The Frankfurt Speyer firm struggled after the war, from want of capital, though it opened a Berlin office in 1926. It absorbed C. Schlesinger-Trier and Co. of Berlin in a measure prompted by the increased centralization of the German economy as a result of wartime mobilization. In Germany, the private banks became subordinated to the commercial banks like Deutsche Bank and 'could not undertake by themselves business of the first magnitude'. Speyer Ellissen unsuccessfully promoted American subsidiaries of German artificial silk factories and also unsuccessfully tried to finance the expansion of the French Galeries Lafayette department store into Berlin, though it was credited with making German loans for the New York and Foreign Investment Co., an American Speyer affiliate, and financed expansion of the German rayon industry. A list of securities for which the firm was paying agent issued in February 1929 included those of American Bemberg, American Glanzstoff, Associated Rayon, Galeries Lafayette, Lingner-Werke, Siemens and Halske, Universum-Film and Watauga Development. Numerous German provincial and municipal bonds were on the list, but few foreign securities. The foreign loans included Argentine bonds of 1907 and 1909, New York and Foreign Investing Co. preferred shares, Rock Island railway bonds and two London underground issues. London and New York had to prop up the firm, which was audited by Price Waterhouse and not German accountants. 'After a period of ruinous losses for the bank, [James] Speyer intervened before the great bank crisis of 1931. While the activities of the Lazard Speyer Ellissen bank were paralyzed, the bank was one of the rare German institutions that did not have to call for a moratorium on foreign debts.'

In 1930, there were losses of 4.203 million reichsmarks, of which 3.502 million were attributable to Berlin, 341,000 to Frankfurt and 360,000 to combined operations. Depreciation of securities accounted for 1.26 million of the losses, including 550,000 in Young Plan bonds, 250,000 in American

Frankfurt a. M. / Berlin, im Mai 1928.

Wir beehren uns Ihnen hierdurch mitzuteilen, daß wir unsere Geschäfte und Betriebe in einer neuen Gesellschaft unter dem Namen

Lazard Speyer-Ellissen
Kommanditgesellschaft auf Aktien

vereinigt haben. Die C. Schlesinger-Trier & Co Commanditgesellschaft auf Actien ist laut Beschluss der am 26. April ds. Js. stattgefundenen Generalversammlung in Liquidation getreten.

Wir nehmen noch Bezug auf das beifolgende Rundschreiben der Lazard Speyer-Ellissen Kommanditgesellschaft auf Aktien und empfehlen uns Ihnen

hochachtungsvoll

Lazard Speyer-Ellissen
C. Schlesinger-Trier & Co
Commanditgesellschaft auf Actien

29. Schlesinger-Trier Merger Documents

Glanztoff shares, and 212,000 in Watauga Development Corporation. Write-downs of investments included 877,000 in Galeries Lafayette and 260,000 in Societe Generale de Photomaton. Bad debts included 544,000 for R. Gualino and 250,000 for A. Wollenberg.

The diminution of Lazard Speyer Ellissen is reflected in the assets on its balance sheets from 1928 onwards (in thousands of reichsmarks): 1928 – 104,389; 1929 – 83,472; 1930 – 51,799; 1931 – 32,769; 1932 – 29,320; 1933 – 21,580; 1934 – 6,243 (in liquidation); 1935 – 4,484 (in liquidation).

The German bureaucracy continued to crank away during the Nazi years; as late as the end of 1942, the family members who were shareholders in the German firm and who were citizens of Switzerland or Liechtenstein, both neutral states, were continuing to receive annual statements from the liquidator.

Lucie Speyer, Edgar and James's sister, died in 1918, the last year of the war, and is buried in Frankfurt. When her husband Eduard Beit von Speyer died in 1932, James Speyer was not inclined to help the German firm: 'the choice between renunciation and repeated response was probably not a very hard one'. The German firm had largely devoted itself to placing the issues

30. Eduard Beit von Speyer

of the New York and London houses in Germany. Its last major initiative was the placing of a Frankfurt loan in New York in 1901. Deutsche Bank was increasingly allied with Speyer in American transactions. After Hitler came to power, there was a half-hearted attempt at 'Aryanization' before both the Berlin and Frankfurt banks were closed in 1934, the closing being widely noted in the press.

On 31 March 1933, James Speyer sent a forlorn telegram to vice-chancellor Von Papen, with whom he had been acquainted (and who had been expelled from the United States for complicity in espionage and sabotage during World War I):

> I realize that I have no right to intervene in German internal affairs, but hope you will forgive my cabling you personally. As one who, as you know, before and since the war has always endeavoured [to] strengthen mutual understanding and friendly relations between our two countries, as evidenced by founding Amerikainstitut, exchange professorships, etc, I take the liberty of urging your Government not carry out Nazi pre-election program, but stop and withhold official sanction boycott against German citizens of Jewish descent. Stop. You know such measures against helpless minorities are contrary [to] American custom and humanitarian ideals. Stop. I apprehend they will cause justified criticism here and may also furnish material for renewal anti-German propaganda. Stop. All this also would affect business relations and German credit. Stop. Seriousness [of] situation is my excuse for sending you this personal message. Best regards, James Speyer.

31. Telegram to Von Papen

There was no recorded reply. Von Papen did meet on 28 June 1933 with Max Warburg of the Hamburg firm of M. M. Warburg, and said 'he would do what he could'. Von Papen narrowly escaped assassination two days later in connection with the Night of the Long Knives; thereafter his influence as vice chancellor was at an end.

In April 1933, Herbert advised James 'Dr. Fischer contemplates for political reasons make Moy partner. It must be thoroughly considered before taking this step out of mere opportunism considering experiences … with Moy. Through Moy L.S.E. Berlin will not become a Christian firm.' Count Hugo Moy, a German aristocrat, had married one of Sir Edgar's daughters and was associated with the Berlin firm with which the Frankfurt Speyer firm had merged. On 7 April 1933 James responded: 'I agree with you; anyhow think should not make any changes until see clearer future.'

On 8 May, any optimism having been dispelled, James advised Herbert that 'in view of unsatisfactory German outlooks urges managing partners increase liquidity by realizing security holdings without waiting'. On 17 June, Herbert advised James that 'I intend to vote Moy partner June 21st to be effective only after I have resigned as partner which will do only after I have seen you.' Two days later, James advised Herbert that 'prefer your not voting for Moy or any changes until we have talked matters over'.

In the summer of 1933, after Hitler's accession to power, James Speyer paid his usual summer visit to Germany; it appears to have been his last such visit. The Reichsbank President, Hjalmar Schacht, relates in his memoirs:

> The Jewish question … arose as early as 1933 when James Speyer the New York banker (who has since died) announced his visit. I went to Hitler and told him: 'Mr. James Speyer, one of the most respected of New York bankers and a great benefactor of his former country, is coming to see me and I intend to give a banquet in his honour. I take it you have no objection.' Whereupon he replied in very decided and striking fashion 'Herr Schacht, you may do anything you like.' From this, I gathered that he gave me full liberty to associate with my Jewish friends as hitherto, which I do. And the banquet took place. I mention this only because it was the first time the Jewish question came up between us.

Speyer, notwithstanding this visit, had no sympathy with Nazi Germany. Beginning in September 1933, as previously noted, he sought to have the Board of the American Carl Schurz Memorial Foundation, of which he was Treasurer, formally denounce the Nazi government. The Foundation had continued educational exchange activities with German universities. When the Board declined to do so, Speyer resigned on 12 December 1933; his resignation was followed by those of Oswald Garrison Villard and Edwin R. A. Seligman. The policy he urged – abandonment of exchange programmes in favour of a programme of aid to German refugee scholars – was finally adopted by the Foundation in 1937. This shift enabled it to survive World War II; it finally expired for want of funds in 1977.

On 31 October 1933, James wrote as follows to Herbert

> I do not think that we would be justified in investing a large part of what your father left to you and your sisters in a new firm, because I think the outlook for profitable business in Germany for a Speyer firm is not sufficiently encouraging. I quite agree with you that you ought to resign as Inhaber, but I think you ought to wait until the balance sheet is finally settled and published, when you could resign quietly and become a Mitglied des Aufsichtsrats, without creating too much attention. In other words, hurry the Balance Sheet as much as possible, and, after the Stockholders' Meeting has been held and the Balance Sheet published, resign and take the other position. After you have resigned as Inhaber, there is no reason as far as I can see why you should not in your children's interest and education take up seriously the question of changing your domicile.

In April 1934, James Speyer gave up, noting that 'Dr. Schacht evidently too busy and has shown no sympathy; further delay [in liquidating the German branch] inadvisable.' In the same month he telegraphed to Herbert:

> Evidently Gwinner following egotistic policy of his friend Kurt Meyer is trying by means of threats, etc to effect sale of his shares. Please do not allow yourself to be intimidated and insist on Hans cash payment. You and Executors conserve all your assets in the interest of the Firm and possible repayment of credit. This was my supposition when I guaranteed credit alone.

In May 1934 he prepared a statement explaining the closing of the firm, probably in an effort to stave off any confiscation of assets by the Nazi government:

> The only one of J.S.'s father's children still living (besides himself) is J.S.'s sister, Frau Felix Schwabach [Henrietta Speyer], whose husband (Reregierungarat and a member of the Prussian Abgeordneten-Haus) died many years ago. She had only one son, who was wounded in the war and died as a result thereof. J.S.'s other sister, Lucie died during the war, in 1918. Her husband, Eduard Beit von Speyer died in March 1933. They had two sons, the oldest of whom, Erwin, was killed at the front, in 1914; [he had attended Oxford; despite having fought on the German side, he is memorialized on a plaque in New College Chapel]. The

second son, Herbert Beit von Speyer was wounded in the war and never has been well enough since to take a leading active part in conducting the affairs of the firm ... There is none of the family left to continue the old German banking business, and as J.S. is 73 years old, he thinks it is his duty to proceed with the liquidation of Lazard Speyer Ellissen without delay.

The experience of other firms confirms that there were no opportunities for the firm in Nazi Germany. '[E]arly on, there was an intriguing paradox ... the banks, which were indeed a near personification of the despised bugaboo of "Jewish finance capital," were treated with relative indulgence. The reasons for this lay naturally in the state of foreign cash reserves and the ties between Jewish banks and interests abroad. Dwindling deposits undermined the basis for continued survival. Toward the end of 1935 large old and well-known houses began the process of liquidation or transfer. M. M. Warburg in Hamburg was not Aryanized until 1938.' Arnholds of Berlin and Dresden liquidated in December 1935 and A. Levy of Cologne in February 1936.

M. M. Warburg had lost all of its municipal business and two-thirds of its depositors almost immediately on the accession to power of the Nazis. As of the end of 1934, it retained all but 20 of its 118 corporate directorships. By early 1938, only ten of its directorships, all of Jewish institutions, remained. The process, however, was gradual. Max Warburg and two other Jewish bankers were among the eight directors of the Reichsbank who, along with President Hindenburg and Chancellor Hitler, signed Schacht's appointment as bank president on 17 March 1933, six weeks after the accession to power of the Nazis. It continued to be an authorized issuer of Reich bonds until Schacht's fall from power and effective replacement by Goring in 1938.

Throughout the preceding five years, Warburg's firm had been useful to the government in transferring funds to and from Palestine and elsewhere to assist in the government's policy of encouraging Jewish emigration. In 1938 that policy changed, and Schacht's barter agreements had greatly reduced Germany's need for foreign exchange.

The proceeds of the forced sale of the Warburg firm to its faithful employees and clients were in one way or another confiscated by the government. Warburg was allowed to retain a silent interest, but it too was confiscated after his departure from Germany in 1938. 'Warburg' was eliminated from the firm name in 1941. The remnants of the firm almost miraculously survived the war, and Max Warburg acquired a new interest and had his name restored to the firm in 1948.

In September 1934, James visited Hungary, the site of one of his League of Nations loans, but not Germany.

CHAPTER 20

Philanthropy and Twilight

'The leaden roller that flattens out so many people has not passed over us'

J ames Speyer supported Cleveland for President in 1892 and William Strong for Mayor in 1894, as a member of the Committee of Seventy that defeated Tammany Hall. His German background was reflected in the fact that like most German-Americans, he was a staunch foe of the Prohibition Amendment, leading a rally against it in Madison Square Garden in 1922, and in 1933 presiding over the special New York State convention that ratified its repeal.

In 1912, Speyer along with J.P. Morgan, Seth Low and Jacob Schiff put up $5,000 as capital for the Provident Loan Society, an organization designed to supplant that era's pawnshops and pay-day loan industry by making small loans to workmen at reasonable interest rates; Speyer had been actively promoting this idea since February 1894, when the society had been incorporated. He circulated a broadside concluding as follows:

> We fully agree with Mr. Champion Bissell (see his article in Lippincott's for February) that under our Democratic form of government and under existing political conditions, the state or the city, as such, can, for obvious reasons, not assume the management of establishments for lending money on pledges, nor should they be asked to do so. But why should not a number of public-spirited and philanthropic citizens combine to form a society for that purpose?

The European municipal pawnshops, whose example Speyer declined to follow later gave rise to the Stavisky scandal, centred on the municipal pawnshop at Bayonne, that convulsed French politics in the early 1930s.

Within Speyer's lifetime, the Provident Loan Society was lending $35 million per year on 734,881 loans. It today makes 100,000 loans per year

32. Provident Loan Society

and has five offices, down from a maximum of 17 in 1962. Its board, which includes descendants of some of the founders, has been squeamish about advertising which would encourage debt; its competitors, banks and pay-day lenders, have not been so restrained. Its offices were small temples, buildings of considerable architectural distinction.

Its interest rates are well below those of competing pawnbrokers; its founders would not find edifying the growth of national chains of pay-day lenders charging high and unregulated interest rates. Unlike the other founders, Speyer served for a long time on the Provident board; he retired from it only in March 1941 shortly before his death.

In 1913, James Speyer was one of the 15 founders of the American Society for the Control of Cancer, which has funded more than 40 Nobel prize-winners and is now the American Cancer Society.

In September 1941, shortly before his death, Speyer was commended by the American Social Hygiene Association for having sponsored Dr Paul Ehrlich's work on sulphanilamide as a cure for syphilis. There was more than slight irony here, since Speyer's youthful bout with syphilis had left him sterile and childless; at the time, the cure for syphilis was mercury. Disraeli, who had a similar experience, once observed that Mercury was the consequence of Venus.

The work had originally been fostered in Frankfurt by a foundation established by two German relatives, Georg and Franziska Speyer, who donated a building at the University of Frankfurt (which they helped to found) for Ehrlich in 1906 and provided funding thereafter through the Speyer Stiftung (Foundation). Ehrlich did his most important work after he was 50. And work in Frankfurt became easier as the years passed, for thanks to the interest of the Speyer family in scientific progress, he had almost unlimited funds and laboratories at his disposal. The Georg Speyer Haus for Chemotherapy funded by Frau Franziska Speyer, the widow of Georg Speyer, the banker, became the centre of his personal investigations. It was built for the exclusive purpose of furthering Ehrlich's chemo-therapeutical researches. The Georg Speyer Haus still functions as a centre of research in Frankfurt; it 'was interdisciplinary from the outset and had close ties with industry'.

33. Georg Speyer Haus

Franziska also contributed to a Central Office for Private Care, a German version of the Charitable Organization Society, and to a housing association. On her death in 1909, much of her estate, amounting to several million gold marks, went to the Central Committee for Dental Care in Schools, the Poor Relief Office, the Jewish Hospital, children's convalescent centres and holiday colonies, the Pension Fund of the Frankfurt Theatre Choir and the Friendly Society of the Journalists' Club.

In 1901, James Speyer gave $100,000 (the equivalent of several million today) to the Teachers' College of Columbia University to endow a school for gifted and talented children within the New York public school system, followed by a second gift of $25,000 in 1902. At the same time, he gave a donation to Columbia for the first school of social work in America, founded at the behest of the pioneer social worker Mary Ellen Richmond and initially known as the Speyer School of Social Work.

A seven-storey purpose-built building near Teachers' College, Columbia, at 514 West 126th Street for the gifted and talented school was erected in 1903, in the German Renaissance style with a three-storey-high stepped gable. The school started operations, but these were temporarily discontinued in 1924. The school had many of the attributes of a settlement house, including apartments for staff, showers and a gymnasium for the students, a community library and a roof garden. It initially served 260 pupils in the first eight grades. This included a supervised playroom and classes for young women in cooking, sewing and home nursing. In 1915, it became a secondary school for gifted and talented students, a description of which survives in the memoir of one of them, Michael Lepore, a notable physician. Another notable early graduate was the American composer William Schuman. In 1919, it was leased to the city as an annex to Public School 43 at 129th Street and Amsterdam Avenue. After special classes were given at various schools, the Speyer School was reopened in 1936, but was discontinued in 1941 in part because of the death of its gifted principal, Leta S. Hollingworth, at the early age of 51 in 1939. Special classes at 12 high schools were instituted instead. The closing was also partly due to lack of funds.

34. Speyer School

'With the aid of several large trucks,' Benjamin Fine of *The New York Times* reported, 'the accumulated books, text supplies, papers and other paraphernalia that is found in a modern classroom were carted away. The old weather-beaten doors are to be pad-locked, the windows barred.' Four years later, some enterprising students vainly suggested that the recently closed Townsend Harris high school for gifted students be relocated there. The Speyer School's Final Report discussed its development of new curricula for both slow learners and rapid learners; it found only limited benefit from the new curricula for slow learners, but urged 'continuance of a similar experiment with exceptional children, in cooperation either with one of the local city colleges or with one of our privately endowed colleges'.

Hollingsworth, a pioneer in the education of gifted children, combined a belief in mental measurement through IQ testing and the 1920s interest in eugenics with a commitment to John Dewey's belief in ethnic diversity and progressive education, the curriculum being based on study of the *Evolution of Common Things*, such as transportation by land and by water, shelter, illumination and aviation. A 40-year follow-up of 20 of the students credited the school with 'providing peer interaction, exposing them to competition, causing them to learn and like school for the first time, giving them a strong desire to excel and providing new exposures that were not possible in other schools in New York at that time'.

The Speyer School building was abandoned during World War II and was acquired by the Episcopal Diocese of New York in 1964 and used for civil rights programmes, including the foundation of the 'welfare rights' movement by the Centre for Social Welfare Policy and Law of Frances Piven and Richard Cloward, a development that would have caused James Speyer to turn in his grave. In 1977, the building was given to the Paul Robeson Community Centre, which moved out after several years due to high heating costs. In 1987, it was proposed to be sold as offices for community organizations, 'an empty derelict, its windows broken or blocked up, its elaborate ornament gently decaying'. In 1991, St Mary's Episcopal Church converted it into a 40-room hospice for AIDS victims, a status it retains.

A private school with a similar purpose, the education of gifted students, but with tuition of $28,500 per year, the Speyer Legacy School, was established in 2009.

In 1923, James Speyer, with others, founded the Museum of the City of New York; his initial gift was $250,000 and several valuable paintings. The museum was founded in reaction to the undifferentiated antiquarianism of the New York Historical Society which did not limit itself to city history and which had become an attic for miscellaneous artifacts of the social elite. The director of the new museum in its first few years was Henry Collins Brown. Initially, the museum acquired Gracie Mansion on the East River (now the residence of the Mayor of New York City) and filled it with mediocre period rooms. In 1925, Speyer was instrumental in ousting Brown and replacing him with Hardinge Scholle, a professional curator from the Chicago Art Institute, interested, like Speyer, in following the European models of municipal museums and in public outreach.

35. Museum of the City of New York

In 1926, Speyer had declared that 'London, Paris, Berlin, Stockholm and other European cities have museums to show their development from early days and to perpetuate important events in their history. We have no museum devoted to such a purpose.' The new museum sponsored discussions of New York's future development. Speyer's declared purposes were the same assimilationist aims as those animating the University Settlement: 'There are hundreds of thousands of people living in New York who have come here from other parts of our country and abroad. Such a condition does not exist in European cities. It seems to us particularly important to give to these newcomers and to their children, some knowledge of and pride in the history of New York, to stimulate love for our City and help to make good citizens.'

The new museum put on its first public exhibition at a downtown location on 57th Street in 1926. In 1929, the board undertook to raise $2 million for a new fireproof museum. Speyer offered to donate his Washington Square properties for this purpose, but the City refused to dedicate its own valuable neighbouring properties for this purpose, instead offering a lot adjacent to a high school on Fifth Avenue between 103rd and

104th Street, an offer accepted by the board in late 1927. The colonial-revival building was completed in 1932. Its portico was modelled after the portico of the Federal Building on Wall Street where George Washington had been inaugurated. Speyer ultimately gave to the museum cash gifts amounting in all to half a million dollars.

Sir Edgar Speyer occupied one of the Washington Square houses. James Speyer eventually left his Fifth Avenue house to the museum, which is currently raising $80 million for expansion and renovations. It was the first American museum built entirely through voluntary subscriptions and was the first American municipal museum. When Speyer's house on Fifth Avenue was sold and demolished (it had been appraised for tax purposes at a modest $250,000), a plaque was erected in the lobby of the apartment building that replaced it bearing Speyer's favourite Lincoln quotation: 'I like to see a man proud of the place in which he lives. I like to see a man live so that his place will be proud of him.'

The museum was a reflection of Speyer's belief in local patriotism. Since the time of Baron vom Stein, this was, perhaps, the best part of the German political tradition, revived after World War II under the influence of Helmut von Moltke's Kreisau Manifesto. Under pressure from the centralizers in various 'civil rights' movements and from doctrinaire libertarian sceptics of all government, localism is not today a popular cause in the United States. The Fifth Avenue house had been built by Speyer in 1915; pictures of it appear in a book on *Great Houses of New York*.

36. 1058 Fifth Avenue House

Speyer's 130-acre estate in Westchester County was sold for development in 1946 to David Swope of County Homes, Inc. and eventually became a development of several hundred homes for United Nations personnel. Only the gates survive.

The elegant Pine Street office of the Speyer firm was demolished and replaced in 1957. It had been built in 1902 at a cost of $200,000. It 'attracted more attention than any building of its size and cost in many years'. It had been sold to the Chase National Bank in 1944, at which time its lot was measured at 57' x 71' and was assessed for tax purposes at $640,000.

The Washington Square houses owned by James Speyer – and known as 'Genius Row' after their bohemian tenants – were sold to a developer, Anthony Campagna, in 1945 by James's estate for $2 million and were partially demolished, the facades and Edgar Speyer's home surviving. The surviving building ultimately became the Straus Institute for the Advanced Study of Law and Justice, part of the New York University Law School. James had refused to sell any of the houses during his lifetime for reasons that were not purely commercial: a long-time tenant, Mrs Branchard, ran a rooming-house for artists and writers, many of whom became famous, including Frank Norris, Theodore Dreiser, Stephen Crane, Eugene O'Neill, Willa Cather, Alan Seeger, John Reed, O. Henry, Adelina Patti, Paul Palmer, Arthur Somers Roche, Art Young, Will Irwin, Thompson Buchanan, Maxwell Bodenheim, Gellett Burgess and John Dos Passos.

Swiss in origin, Mrs Branchard was Speyer's tenant at 61 Washington Square for more than 50 years, during which time she appeared in public on only three or four occasions, on the last of which she was quoted as saying: 'Art is great, literature is wonderful. But what a pity it is that it takes so many barrels of liquor to produce them. Why, this is not a house, it's an aquarium.' She was reluctant to appear in public on that occasion, commemorating her 80th birthday: 'The world is going crazy. It will do them no good to stop here. I will be sick. I will go to bed.' She finally consented to be honoured by being driven around Washington Square in a horse and carriage, appearing dressed completely in black, but with a large red rose at the clasp of her cape. She always preferred men guests to women, because the latter 'insisted on washing stockings and cooking in the bathroom'.

Another semi-commercial real estate investment was Speyer's ownership of an apartment house for bachelors inhabited by a number of members of his firm, and others, at 15 East 48th Street in New York, which made news when a number of tenants were subjected to armed robberies in 1914.

In 1941, an interviewer reported:

Access to Mr. Speyer's office is somewhat unique in Wall Street. One's presence is made known by utilizing an ordinary door bell. Tom, faithful employee of the banker, finally cracks the huge bronze door and ushers the visitor into the now-darkened ghost-like rotunda. In due time, there is echoed somewhere from the dimly-lighted balconies or staircases an 'All right, Tom,' and the interview is on, amidst surroundings and in an atmosphere reminding the visitor of Dickens.

Earlier in his career, a financial journalist, B. C. Forbes, further described the Pine Street atmosphere: 'James Speyer goes about his duties more noiselessly than any other leading international banker. And the ways and spirit of the chief permeate the whole establishment of Speyer and Co. Everything runs smoothly and harmoniously.'

Speyer's philanthropic activities did not involve mere cheque-writing, but were of a very 'hands-on' nature. An early secretary, Algernon Blackwood, made the following observation, while Speyer lived on Madison Avenue:

[T]hese establishments for a millionaire bachelor were on a simple scale, though the amount of money necessary for one man's comforts staggered me at first … Mr. Speyer was a generous live-and-let-live type of man who did not want a spirit of haggling over trifles in his home. My employer's zest in the University Settlement movement I found particularly interesting. James Speyer was more than a rich philanthropist; he had a heart. The column for Charities and Presents in the book Mr. Hopf juggled with once a month was a big one while that for Personal Expenditure was rather small.

An appraisal of James's life is not an easy task. He was guilty of a blind Germanophilia which included undue respect for the 'wooden titan', Von Hindenburg, and over optimism about German prospects after World War I. Others, including the Morgan partners and Theodore Roosevelt, did not view Germany as benignly. But he believed also in local patriotism, in settlement houses as educators of the rich as well as of the poor, in the selection and education of the gifted and talented whatever their original station in life, in loans on liberal terms to the hard-pressed, in the life of reason and the value of cultural exchange. His faith in deflationary economics and in the benign effects of rapid Third World development was overdone, and he vacillated on the important question of the Allied war debts, but he leaves as monuments a municipal museum, a school for the gifted, the works of the Port of New York Authority and many still-useful railroads.

His brother Edgar, a less tough character, left a less ambiguous legacy: a musical institution that still endures, a great metropolitan transit system, a concern for the poor manifested in the rescue of a penny savings bank and his weekly visits to the Poplar Hospital accident wards, as well as a major contribution to Britain's foreign investments, the liquidation of which financed Britain's efforts in both wars and sustained Britain's cheap food policy and the social solidarity resulting from it. Foreign investments were not the disaster for Britain that they were for France, where they were lost in the Russian Revolution, or for America, where they were lost in the German inflation and the Great Depression.

Many of the earlier partners in the firm had died or retired; although overshadowed in the public mind by James and Edgar, they were people of substance and substantial means. Carl Bergmann, a partner in the German firm since 1924, had been a close associate of Walther Rathenau and was the author of an history of reparations published in 1928. Harry Oppenheimer, of the American firm, was a noted art collector. Leon Kronthal had been heavily involved with RCA, a major industrial client. Jesse Hirschman, who left the firm in 1924 but continued as a railroad director, was an authority on railroad reorganizations, as was De Witt Millhauser, who stayed until the end in 1939. Gordon Leith of the English firm had a significant subsequent career as a Kuhn Loeb partner after Speyer Brothers' closing in 1922. Martin Erdmann of the American firm retired in 1906 and left a substantial fortune upon his death 30 years later.

George Blumenthal, who left before World War I, was the long-time Head of the Metropolitan Museum of Art. A burglary at the home of George N. Lindsay, a partner when the firm closed, revealed that his Long Island establishment had 25 acres, 16 rooms and at least four servants.

In 1905, James demonstrated his Germanophilia with a gift of $50,000 to Columbia University to establish an exchange professorship with the University of Berlin. In 1910, he made a gift to assist American students at the Amerika Institute in Berlin. In January 1912 he was decorated by the Kaiser with the Order of the Red Eagle, Second Class, a distinction given to only two other Americans: J.P. Morgan and Nicholas Murray Butler. In the previous year, Sir Edgar Speyer had received the Order of the Crown, Second Class from the Kaiser, and earlier, in 1908, Eduard Beit, James Speyer's brother-in-law, had been ennobled by the German emperor.

During the panic of 1907, James was a member of a clearing house committee which issued soothing statements. Many of Speyer's postwar charitable activities also had a German orientation. Like a number of Americans who had attended German gymnasia in their youth before the turn of the century, including the journalist H. L. Mencken and the legal scholar Karl N. Llewellyn, he had a somewhat starry-eyed view of the culture

369

UNITED STATES NAMES

NEW YORK CITY

07706	F U N U K	German Society ~~of New York~~
07707	F U N X N	
07708	F U N Y O	
07709	F U O B P	
07710	F U O D S	Goldman, Sachs & Co.
07711	F U O F U	Goldman, Sachs & Co. and Lehman Brothers
07712	F U O H W	Gould, Edwin
07713	F U O J Y	
07714	F U O L A	*Green, Ellis & Anderson*
07715	F U O M B	
07716	F U O N C	Grace National Bank
07717	F U O P E	Grace & Co., W. R.
07718	F U O R F	Grumbach, Louis J.
07719	F U O S G	Grumbach, Louis J.
07720	F U O T H	Grumbach, Louis J.
07721	F U O V J	
07722	F U O W K	
07723	F U O Y M	
07724	F U O Z N	~~Guaranty Company~~
07725	F U P A M	Guaranty Trust Co.
07726	F U P C O	Guggenheimer, Untermyer ~~& Marshall~~
07727	F U P E R	~~Guinness, B. S.~~
07728	F U P F S	~~Guthrie, William D.~~
07729	F U P G T	Guttag Brothers
07730	F U P H U	
07731	F U P I V	
07732	F U P L Y	
07733	F U P N A	
07734	F U P O B	

37. Speyer Code Book

of Wilhelmine Germany. Unlike Edward Speyer and the writer Thomas
Mann, he did not detect the rot beneath the surface, and particularly the
growth of militarism and nationalism, the latter being described by British
ambassador Horace Rumbold as 'patriotism plus inferiority complex'. In
1919 and again in 1923, he assisted a campaign in aid of German children.
In 1925, he made a gift to Johns Hopkins University to endow an annual

visit by a German scholar. In 1920, he made a large gift of a million marks to the University of Frankfurt in memory of his sister Lucie, followed by a gift to Heidelberg University in 1928. James was made an honorary member of the University of Frankfurt in 1923. The university's Jewish donors caused its statutes to include a provision, unique in Germany, barring all religious discrimination. His brother-in-law Eduard Beit von Speyer gave the University of Frankfurt 250,000 marks in 1911 and again in 1919.

James was Treasurer of the Carl Schurz Memorial Foundation, and for 40 years trustee of a bank that was originally the German Savings Bank. He was a founder of the Ottendorfer Memorial Fellowship Committee at New York University, an organizer and treasurer of an Emergency Society for German and Austrian Science and Art in 1921, and treasurer of an effort to restore the Goethe House in Frankfurt, as well as treasurer of the Germanistic Society of America. He was made an honorary member of the German Red Cross in 1925. The following year, he welcomed a former Hohenzollern prince who was an orchestra conductor.

In 1940, James praised *The New York Times* for endorsing Wendell Willkie in his campaign for the presidency. Though never particularly interested in Jewish causes except as a supporter of Mount Sinai Hospital from 1902 until his death, in 1937 he attended a luncheon for Lord Melchett (son of the industrialist Sir Alfred Mond), who had been an organizer of a British boycott of Hitler's Germany and who appealed for aid to Palestine.

Earlier, in 1934, he clearly proved himself not a favourite of the League of Nations High Commissioner for Refugees, James G. McDonald. Initially, McDonald excluded Speyer from a delegation soliciting contributions for the relief of German refugees from John D. Rockefeller, Jr: 'It was felt that James Speyer should not be included because of his possible expectation of a quid pro quo,' presumably for the Museum of the City of New York, for which Speyer was actively soliciting funds and to which Rockefeller later contributed. A month later, in March 1934, McDonald reported on a lunch with James:

> He annoyed me by inviting his partner [George N.] Lindsay to join us. The latter is a nice fellow but his presence obviously made any talk of finance much more difficult. Moreover Speyer is in some respects very crude talking as he did during all the time we were ordering about the expense of each dish on the menu and trying to be funny on the score of the expense of the order. His sense of humour would do little credit to a Second Avenue pushcart man.

The Speyer that McDonald saw in action was an experienced warder-off of charitable solicitations; at the time he may have shared the view of many German Jews and the Vatican about the Hitler regime: 'this too shall (shortly) pass'.

Two months later, McDonald returned to the attack, recording a meeting 'at Ittleson's office' at which $230,000 was raised, including $50,000 from the Felix Warburgs, but recording his disappointment in 'Morgenthau's paltry $5,000, Arthur Lehman's $7,000 and Speyer's $5,000'. In 1939, James contributed $100,000 through a purchase of debentures to the New York World's Fair; later, he supported an abortive proposal for a pavilion, 'Germany, Yesterday and Tomorrow', which would have depicted pre-Hitler German culture. In May 1941, shortly before his death, by which time the European war was on and Paris had fallen, he joined the interventionist Fight for Freedom committee.

38. James Speyer portrait

The historian Kent Forster wrote in 1941 to 'emphasize the need for controlling and checking the *a outrance* elements in the present conflict ... it should not be forgotten that there is another Germany which cherishes the concepts and methods of decency and peace ... the forces of ultra-

39. James Speyer in old age

nationalism must not be permitted to triumph again, as they did during the years 1914–1918, to create the Versailles of 1919.' Speyer's proposed pavilion can be viewed as a small contribution to the ultimate magnanimous peace.

Speyer's talent for warding off unwanted solicitations had earlier been evidenced by his printing of a supply of correspondence cards reading 'MR. JAMES SPEYER BEGS TO ACKNOWLEDGE RECEIPT OF THE LETTER FROM____DATED___AND SINCERELY REGRETS THAT, IN VIEW OF THE SUPPORT HE IS GIVING TO CERTAIN

CHARITABLE AND EDUCATIONAL WORK, WITH WHICH HE IS
MORE INTIMATELY ASSOCIATED, HE CANNOT COMPLY WITH
THE REQUEST TO CONTRIBUTE AT PRESENT TO THE GOOD
PURPOSE FOR WHICH HIS COOPERATION IS ASKED. 24–25
PINE STREET, NEW YORK.'

James N. Rosenberg, soliciting participation in a Soviet Russian loan,
received one of these cards in April 1928. Rosenberg was the chairman of
an all-but-forgotten charitable endeavour known as the American Society
for Jewish Farm Settlements in Russia, which functioned from the early
1920s until at least 1934 and raised several tens of millions of dollars for the
resettlement of 100,000 Jews in the Soviet Union, which was seen as a place
of refuge from anti-Semitism in Romania and Poland. Its beneficiaries fled
to the East upon the German invasion, settling in Russian cities after the
war; those who did not flee became the victims of Soviet confiscations and
Nazi genocides. Among its supporters in 1934 were at least two Kuhn Loeb
partners, Lewis Strauss and Felix Warburg, as well as Lessing Rosenwald and
New York governor Herbert Lehman. Speyer, so far as can be discerned, had
no involvement at any time with either Soviet or Japanese loans.

In August 1939, James resisted an effort by a German trustee to acquire
a trust fund of which he had been the settler in favour of his niece, Countess
Marie Schwabach Von Kageneck, a daughter of his sister Henrietta, who
had committed suicide in London.

Henry Taft, who ultimately became one of his executors, gave a dinner
for him at the Greenbrier in West Virginia in June 1939. In December 1940
his Canadian niece Ellin visited with him in New York.

James died in October 1941 and is buried in the Sleepy Hollow
Cemetery in Tarrytown. His austere 20-minute funeral service was at his
Fifth Avenue house and was unusual in that it was presided over both by
a rabbi, Jonah Wise, and an Episcopal minister, Charles W. Baldwin, the
rabbi reading the 90th and 91st Psalms and the minister the 23rd Psalm and
lesson. Emanuel List sang Schubert's *The Grave*; there was no eulogy. To the
end, Speyer did not deny his Jewish heritage, but sought to subsume it in
more universal values. It was said of Jacob Schiff's circle that 'More German
than English, a bit like a ghetto of older times, it felt too Jewish and insular
… their entertainments seemed dull. The Schiffs, for example, would stay
home on Friday nights, see the Seligmans on Saturdays, and dine with the
Loebs on Sundays.' This never satisfied Speyer, nor the Kuhn Loeb partner
Otto Kahn.

There were about 200 mourners at Speyer's funeral, but few of great
prominence: these included Henry Taft, his lawyer; Bernard Baruch, his

neighbour on Fifth Avenue; and John D. Rockefeller, Jr, who had joined him in making final gifts of $250,000 each to the museum. Speyer and Rockefeller had made total gifts, not including the bequest of the proceeds of Speyer's Fifth Avenue house, of $450,000 each; Edward Harkness gave $300,000. Speyer also gave the museum the Gilbert Stuart portrait of George Washington.

He had announced his retirement in August 1938. The remaining partners in his firm, essentially a one-man show, were Otto de Neuville, a relative of Herbert's wife; Herbert Beit von Speyer, James's nephew in Switzerland (Eduard Beit's son); Charles Stackelberg; and George N. Lindsay (the father of Mayor John Lindsay of New York). Litigation with the State of New York in the 1920s revealed the partners' shares in the American firm as of 1923: Speyer had a 29.5 per cent share; Jesse Hirschman and Richard Schuster, a German partner who had resigned as a director of the American firm on America's entry into the war and had been reinstated in 1921, 15 per cent each; Eduard Beit von Speyer, a similarly reinstated German partner, 10 per cent; and three partners admitted after the war, Leon Kronthal, Grumbach and Millhauser had 9 per cent, 9 per cent and 12.5 per cent respectively. Hirschman's 15 per cent netted him $107,000 in 1922; Kronthal and Grumbach's 9 per cent about $53,000.

Shortly after James's retirement, Herbert came to the United States, along with Lucie Beit's grandsons, Hugo Beit, who became a successful mechanical engineer with Babcock and Wilcox after graduation from the Sheffield Scientific School at Yale, and Erwin Beit, who also went to Yale and became an electrical engineer. Herbert and Eduard's grandchildren left Switzerland in 1941, bearing Liechtenstein passports, and came to the United States via Vichy France, Spain and Portugal. While the Speyers got some assets out of Germany and were the beneficiaries of trusts set up by James, who had no children of his own, they were able to assert a claim for 61,000 Swiss francs in accounts belonging to Elizabeth de Neuville Beit von Speyer, Herbert's wife, who, though a Gentile by birth, had been found to be a full Jew by the Nazis on account of her marriage, and whose accounts had been first taxed in 1938 and then seized. The children were awarded 774,800 Swiss francs by a claims resolution tribunal in October 2008.

The American firm discontinued operations on 30 June 1939. The obsequies in the press variously attributed its closing to Nazism, the New Deal and the decline of railroads. 'If there is one thing in which President Roosevelt has been consistent since taking office it has been to keep his promise to clip the wings and pull out the tail feathers of Wall Street bankers. That is the real reason,' an editorialist in Springfield, Massachusetts

40. Liechtenstein Passport

proclaimed. *Time* magazine, for its part, emphasized the decline of railroads and Hitler, publishing a cartoon captioned 'His Last Return from Carlsbad', showing Speyer disembarking from a steamer carrying two bags of gold, with a sign in the background reading 'Non-Aryans Verboten', Carlsbad having fallen to the Nazis at Munich.

Earlier, the remaining partners had organized, with the help of $3 million in capital from Credit Suisse, the Swiss American Corporation. This corporation took over the Speyer building at 24 Pine Street, and two years thereafter, swamped with flight capital, expanded into a new building. The Swiss American Corporation survives, as of 2013, with estimated annual volume of $23 million and about 150 employees. The Pine Street building was ultimately sold and demolished in 1957.

41. Departure from Europe

SWISS AMERICAN CORPORATION

announces the opening of offices at

24 & 26 PINE STREET, (SPEYER BUILDING)
NEW YORK CITY

to engage in the investment securities business

DIRECTORS

DANIEL F. NORTON   J. STRAESSLE
GEORGE N. LINDSAY

OFFICERS

GEORGE N. LINDSAY, President
HENRY WEGMANN, Vice-President   CHARLES G. STACHELBERG, Vice-President
OTTO DE NEUFVILLE, Treasurer   CLINTON SHEPPERD, Assistant Secretary

WHitehall 3-7424

July 11, 1939   Cables: SWISSAM

42. Swiss American Corporation

James Speyer's estate amounted to $2,612,000 gross, $2,183,000 net, a minor amount compared to the more than $50 million left by J.P. Morgan on his death in 1913. James Speyer's childlessness made him uncommonly generous during his lifetime, his benefactions as well as *inter vivos* trusts in favour of relatives probably exceeded his estate several-fold, his total wealth being estimated at $20–30 million. The residuary estate was left to a nephew, Herbert Beit von Speyer, who had come to the United States in 1941, and his two sisters Hedwig von Rogues of Zurich and Ellin Beit von Speyer, who resided in Canada, and to three members of the next generation, Hugo, Erwin and Charlotte. There was a $25,000 bequest to the Speyer Animal Hospital, $10,000 each to Mount Sinai Hospital and the Federation of Jewish Philanthropies, $5,000 to the Jewish Child Care Association and $5,000 to the Ossining Hospital, as well as a specific bequest of $25,000 to John Dynely Prince, a diplomat and relative of his late wife. The Fifth Avenue mansion was left to the Museum of the City of New York.

Speyer had long been a supporter of Mount Sinai, one of the few Jewish charities in which he took an interest. In a letter from President Theodore Roosevelt to Nicholas Murray Butler in 1903, Roosevelt declined an invitation to a Mount Sinai benefit, while stating: 'I want to do everything I can for Mr. Speyer ... I should particularly like the chance of speaking at some typical Jewish gathering under Mr. Speyer's auspices, as you know I swear by him.' This, no doubt, had more than a little to do with New York politics.

It has been observed that 'Despite antagonism and conflicts, international banking in the first decade of the twentieth century was conducted in a relatively tight-knit community of men with similar values and educations. Many such as Jacob Schiff and James Speyer travelled together regularly. The success of German-Jewish investment houses rested on their cosmopolitan outlook and international relationships ... Although their approaches to problems and interests reflected national cultures and priorities, the bankers shared a tendency to look beyond national boundaries for opportunities and solutions ... Many shared a common education through international internships within one bank or experiences with related banks. Their partnerships did not require a large preliminary investment, and the reputation for integrity and insight of the individuals composing them was their greatest asset.'

The attributes of the pre-World War I international bankers were summarized by the historian Carroll Quigley:

> They were, especially in later generations, cosmopolitan rather than nationalistic; they were a constant, if weakening, influence for peace, a pattern established in 1830 and 1840 when the Rothschilds threw their whole tremendous influence successfully against European wars. They were usually highly civilized cultured gentlemen, patrons of education and of the arts, so that today colleges, professorships, opera companies, symphonies, libraries, and museum collections still reflect their munificence ... they set a pattern of endowed foundations which still surround us today. The names of some of these banking families are familiar to all of us and should be more so. They include Baring, Lazard, Erlanger, Warburg, Schroder, Seligman, the Speyers, Mirabaud, Mallet, Fould and

above all Rothschild and Morgan. ... [T]hey remained different from ordinary bankers in distinctive ways: 1) they were cosmopolitan and international 2) they were close to governments and were particularly concerned with questions of government debts, including foreign government debts, even in areas which seemed at first glance, poor risks, like Egypt, Persia, Ottoman Turkey, Imperial China and Latin America 3) their interests were almost exclusively in bonds and very rarely in goods, since they admired 'liquidity' and regarded commitments in commodities or even real estate was the first step toward bankruptcy 4) they were, accordingly, fanatical devotees of deflation (which they called 'sound' money from its close associations with high interest rates and a high value of money) and of the gold standard, which in their eyes, symbolized and ensured these values and 5) they were almost equally devoted to secrecy and the secret use of financial influence in political life.

The demise of the Speyer firm may have been due to nationalism, personal prickliness and the brothers' lack of sons, but even if these factors had not been present, the chances are that it would not have long survived World War II. The firm, like all the great investment banking firms, dealt primarily in government and railroad bonds. Fixed income securities were not good investments in a world in which the gold standard had been renounced in favour of the managed currencies of the Bretton Woods system, and in which Keynesianism, counter-cyclical spending and permitted but controlled inflation held sway, as they do still.

James Speyer's original outlook was a conventional deflationary banker's outlook. In the aftermath of the 1893 panic, he was a member of a currency committee of the Reform Club. In 1907, he had celebrated the fact that 'The American people only a few years ago settled the most difficult financial problem by establishing the gold standard.' In the wake of the panic of 1907, he supported the Hepburn Bill, a moderate reform measure that displeased some businessmen by excluding labour from the antitrust laws, while relying primarily on publicity to cure business abuses. He praised the moderation of President Wilson's reform proposals, including that for a Federal Reserve Board. During the Theodore Roosevelt administration, he expressed the view that 'Combinations of capital are just as necessary as combinations of labour ... closer Government supervision of corporations doing interstate business will be to everyone's advantage, if exercised by the right men in the right way.'

By 1932, he was a supporter of Professor Irving Fisher's Stable Money Association, which opposed deflation and urged 'price stability', together with Otto Kahn, Paul Warburg, Owen Young and Henry A. Wallace. But the efforts of Benjamin Strong, Andrew Mellon, Winston Churchill and Montagu Norman had not succeeded in restoring the gold standard on a stable basis between the wars, and the post-World War II dislocations were as profound as those following World War I, even if the gold supply more closely kept pace with economic activity.

The alternative activity of investment bankers – mergers and acquisitions – was not entirely foreign to the experience of the Speyer firm, as the RCA-Victor transaction and some railroad mergers attest. However, nothing in the prior history of Speyer, or for that matter Kuhn Loeb, suggests that the bankers of the pre-World War II era would have been comfortable with transactions like the leveraged buy-outs of RJR Nabisco and the Tribune Company, which unlike Speyer's railroad reorganizations were designed to increase rather than reduce the burden of debt. Speyer's loans, including its railroad loans, were generally productive of massive new infrastructure facilities, not mere changes in corporate management.

As for governmental loans, any investment house pursuing them in the postwar period would have been subjected to massive and repeated 'haircuts' imposed by South East Asian, African and Latin American governments on the commercial banks, governments and international institutions making short-term loans to them.

Speyer's closing was positively dignified by comparison with the fate of its rival Kuhn Loeb. Kuhn Loeb suffered an unhappy merger with Lehman Brothers in 1977. Lehman was later absorbed into Sandy Weill's Shearson American Express in 1984. Weill was the most vehement and successful advocate of financial deregulation. The subsequent divestiture of Lehman by Shearson, and the firm's enforced bankruptcy in 2008, scattering toxic junior mortgage waste all over the world, precipitated a depression that is still with us today.

In writing of the world before 1914, John Maynard Keynes observed:

> [T]he principle of accumulation based on inequality was a vital part of the pre-war order of Society and of progress as we then understood it … this principle depended on unstable psychological conditions, which it may be impossible to re-create. It was not natural for a population, of whom so few enjoyed the comforts of life, to accumulate so hugely. The war has disclosed the possibility of consumption to all and the vanity of abstinence to many. Thus the bluff is discovered; the labouring classes may be no longer willing to forego so largely, and the capitalist classes, no longer confident of the future, may seek to enjoy more fully their liberties of consumption so long as they last, and thus precipitate the hour of their confiscation.

Some words of Judge Learned Hand written in 1950 provide a suitable epitaph for the world of the Speyers:

> While I look back on my nineteenth-century kit of feelings and beliefs, it is not with any complacent satisfaction about the changed times I have lived into. Quite the contrary; in all that makes for human progress, if there is such a possibility, those days appear to me better than the regnant faiths today. None of us of that time were unaware of the terrible failures of the system as it was – well, no, that's too strong, of course. Better: the wise and imaginative knew the lacks and the woeful callousness all around us ... But the ethos of those days forbad so ready a resort to violence: violence of feeling, violence of expression, violence of suppression, violence in action of every kind.

Jacob Burckhardt had taken a more jaundiced view of the successful men of the Victorian age in 1871: '[T]he idea of the natural goodness of man had turned, among the intelligent strata of Europe, into the idea of progress, i.e. undisturbed money-making and modern comforts, with philanthropy as a sop to conscience.' But at the end of his life, in 1889, Burckhardt declared values of behaviour not far from those of the Speyers: '[W]hat we both have in common on our earthly pilgrimage at least since a certain year, has been the need to be satisfied with the moment through one's work, and what is more a varied and stimulating work. The leaden roller that flattens out so many people has not passed over us.'

EPILOGUE

James Speyer Kronthal

'I can't wait till 1984'

The Speyer firm's alleged involvement in the last few years of its life with the ransoming of Nazi-seized art presents interesting questions. James Speyer Kronthal was named after Speyer by Leon Kronthal, a Speyer partner who left the firm at the end of 1933, according to his obituary for reasons of ill-health, and died in October 1935. The younger Kronthal graduated from Yale Phi Beta Kappa in 1934 and became employed by the firm notwithstanding his father's alleged estrangement from Speyer. He was distantly related to the Speyers through his mother Maude, and may well have been treated by James Speyer as the son he never had.

According to a résumé he prepared in 1941, he was employed at Speyer from 1934 to 1938 as a 'financial statistician and security analyst' and was supervised by Charles Stackelburg and De Witt Millhauser. He thereafter spent three years at Harvard, receiving a university fellowship in 1939–40, a Sachs Fellowship in Fine Arts in 1940–1, a Carnegie art scholarship at the University of Paris in the summer of 1939 and a Sheldon Travelling Fellowship for 1941–2, in addition to serving as an assistant to Professor Chandler Post in 1940–1.

It is asserted by several writers, who cite no documents, that while working for Speyer, Kronthal was assigned to assist Jewish refugees from Nazi Germany in ransoming art that they had been obliged to leave behind in Germany: 'He had used the Speyer family connections to sell artworks that the Nazis confiscated from Jews between 1933 and 1940. In addition to becoming the depression go-between for this financial service, he also became personally acquainted with Nazi leaders such as Goering, Himmler, and Goebbels. The emotional cost of profiting from other people's stolen wealth – people who had been sent to death camps – was enormous.'

JAMES S. KRONTHAL

Born August 21, 1912 at Deal, N.J.

Attended Lincoln School of Teachers College, New York City, graduating
    in 1930.

1930-1934:
        Attended Yale University receiving the B.A. Degree with Philo-
        sophical Orations in 1934. Phi Beta Kappa.
        Field of Concentration: European History.

1934-1938:
        Employed by the investment banking firm of Speyer & Co., New York
        City as financial statistician and security analyst.

1938-1941:
        Three years of graduate study at Harvard University in the field
        of History of Art, receiving the degree of M.A. in 1941.

        Awarded a University Fellowship in 1939-40.
        Awarded the Sachs Fellowship in Fine Arts in 1940-41.
        Held position of Assistant to Prof. Chandler Post at Harvard
            and Radcliffe in 1940-41.

        Awarded a Carnegie Art Scholarship in the summer of 1939 for
            study at the University of Paris.

Have travelled and lived abroad at various times covering a total of
        approximately two years, visiting France, Germany, Great Britain,
        Italy, Holland, Belgium, Switzerland, etc.

Languages:
        Have fluent speaking and reading knowledge of French and German,
            also reading knowledge of Italian. Am at present studying
            Spanish in addition.

At present (Winter, 1941-42), holder of a Sheldon Travelling Fellowship
        from Harvard University and engaged in completing thesis for
        the Ph.D. Degree.

Present address:
                138 East 71st St.,
                New York City, N.Y.

43. Kronthal Résumé

It has been said that 'Never have art historians been so useful, their
opinions attended to so seriously, than in Vienna in the spring of 1938
… creating opportunities for the right candidates.' After the extinction
of the Speyer firm in 1939, Kronthal, who was not a lawyer, according
to an edition of Allen Dulles' wartime dispatches from Switzerland, had
known Dulles from working together on matters handled by the law firm of
Sullivan and Cromwell. The Dulles brothers were criticized for performing
legal work in Germany after Hitler's acquisition of power until American
entry into World War II in December 1941. Sullivan and Cromwell, at
the urging of Allen Dulles and over the dissent of his brother, John Foster
Dulles, had closed its Berlin office in June 1935. However, as late as 1938

the firm was involved in an abortive attempt by the Nazi government to float a refunding bond in the United States, thwarted by demands for details of German government and Nazi party finances by the Securities Exchange Commission, and thereafter represented some neutral agents of German interests throughout the war.

In 1941, Kronthal received his graduate degree in art history from Harvard. Thirteen days after Pearl Harbor he spoke with David K. E. Bruce, then American coordinator for information, to whom he had been introduced by Major Lucas Ordway. In April 1942, he became a civilian employee of that office in the Index and Reference Unit of the Foreign Nationalities Branch. He was inducted as a private in the Signal Corps in October 1942, and after six weeks' basic training at Camp Upton in upstate New York was assigned to the Office of Strategic Services (OSS) Headquarters in Washington. Kronthal's superior, De Witt Poole, asked to assess his character in January 1943 declared: 'I can give you something pretty close to a perfect guarantee.' His fitness ratings from Poole ranged from 'Superior' in September 1943 to a low of 'Very Satisfactory' in June 1944; he was rated 'Excellent' in December 1943 and October and December 1944.

Because he was underweight, at 5'6' and 128 pounds and had 20/200 eyesight in both eyes, he required and obtained a medical waiver for his commission. In March 1944, Poole opposed Kronthal's transfer to an historical monuments unit: his work was said to be of a 'highly secret' character: 'Further elaboration would endanger the security of his assignment.' He was made a sergeant in April 1943 and was commissioned as a second lieutenant a month later in May 1943. He became Assistant Chief of the Chancery Unit in October 1943 and was commissioned as a captain in April 1945. Kronthal's OSS training included a one-week course in which he achieved a Superior score on 'A material', being rated High Average in Cipher, Mapping and Police Methods and Low Average in Reporting and Demolitions.

His training officer, Lt Compton N. Crook, reported that Kronthal was 'serious, sincere, conscientious and cooperative'. He 'seemed hardly rugged enough for field work', but would be a 'good executive for a desk job'. In October 1944, Kronthal was sent to London as Head of the Documents Section of the Reports Division and, with the extinction of the OSS, was employed by its temporary successor, the Army's Strategic Services Unit, his final station being in Istanbul.

Previously, Kronthal worked for Dulles at the Office of Strategic Services Berne station. The glossary of names in an authorized collection of Allen Dulles' reports from Berne identifies Kronthal as 'Staff Member OSS Berne from mid-1945, involved in recovery of looted art, knew Allen Dulles from Sullivan and Cromwell.' In June 1945 he was made (at least on paper) Deputy Chief of the Steering Division in Wiesbaden. By the fall of 1945, Kronthal was writing reports from Berne. The glossary also indicates that number 706 was assigned to an otherwise unidentified OSS staff officer at Berne, who figures in none of the collected reports.

On 20 October 1946, Kronthal was reassigned from the position of 'Acting Chief of Division C' to 'Intelligence Analyst – Special Operations' at the newly created Central Intelligence Agency at the same salary. On 3 May 1947, his military service came to an end, although on a personnel questionnaire in 1951 Kronthal indicated that it ended on 15 August 1946, and that he joined the CIA on 19 September 1946. On 21 April 1947 he was made head of the Berne station of the CIA, and returned to Washington in May 1952. He was designated Deputy Director of Training (Special) in place of Rolfe Kingsley, effective 2 February 1953.

A fitness report signed by Richard Helms in May 1948 recorded that 'subject is a top-flight intelligence officer who commands regard from his subordinates more through demonstrated knowledge and i.q. than through personal warmth and affability. He is rather retiring as a person but this does not affect his leadership or firmness of purpose.'

In July 1949, Helms signed another report stating:

[F]or the year since the last reporting period subject has improved the quality of intelligence production from the Station. Further, as he has gained confidence in performing his job, so his relations with his colleagues have demonstrably improved. He has shown leadership and imagination in running the Station. The work which he has performed in the last two years of cleaning up the remnants of wartime and immediate post-war operations has been outstanding.

The OSS efforts, in the last days of the war and just after it, to recover looted art have not escaped criticism:

OSS officers, investigating the Swiss–Nazi connection to Europe, also suspected that Safe Haven [the operation to find looted assets] was being sabotaged. The villain, they confided to Drew Pearson, the noted columnist, was Allen Dulles. The OSS wartime chief in Berne, they believed, [was compromised] by his own use of Swiss banks for sensitive transactions, by the potential embarrassment if the Swiss were to release details of his private life in Switzerland and most of all by the Dulles brothers' [prewar] legal work in New York and Washington for Nazi corporations and banks … Inside Switzerland neither MI6 nor the two American intelligence officers Harvey Ginsberg and James Kronthal had replicated the Allied wartime successes by comprehensively penetrating the Swiss banks, the industrialists' boardrooms, the Corporation Office or Stucki's office. Inconsequential intelligence reports to London and Washington mentioned an increase in food parcels sent to Germany, to suspicious activities of a Christian relief organization, and the continued presence of suspected Germans, but in total it amounted to ignorance.

Kronthal was assigned to Berne after Wiesbaden together with another agent, on the recommendation of Frank Wisner in December 1945: 'We feel their desire [to] work elsewhere than Germany be supported as both interested in possibility of making careers in intelligence.' He had been Deputy Chief of Steering in Wiesbaden before being sent to Cairo and Istanbul in January 1946. Kronthal was separated from the army unit that replaced the OSS and assigned to the Central Intelligence Group on 20 September 1946 at which time he was receiving a salary of $7,102 per year, and was promoted to Chief of Station in Berne on 10 April 1947. He was reassigned as an intelligence officer in Washington at the same salary on 23 August 1952, effective 3 April 1952.

Another study of the asset recovery programme refers to a document (not found by this writer at its indicated position in the National Archives) indicating concern by Frank Wisner of the CIA about the possible revelation of Jewish ransom payments to the Nazis. There is no doubt that the Nazis were willing before the war to sell looted art, including so-called 'degenerate art', for foreign exchange: 'It was Hermann Goering who first suggested that these examples of degeneracy be sold for hard foreign currency and a Commission for the Disposal of Products of Degenerate Art was set up under Goebbels.' Goebbels' sales campaign is said to have ended on 30 June 1941. There was an unsuccessful auction, boycotted by most American and Western European museums, at the Galerie Fischer in Lucerne. Goebbels declared on 13 January 1938: 'Some of them we intend to exchange for decent masters abroad' and in May 1938 had received a letter from Goering expressing the wish that 'We hope at least to make some money from this garbage.' A Munch painting was traded to the Norwegian National Gallery in exchange for a Caspar Friedrich depiction of Sudeten mountains, and a Gaughin was traded for a Rubens. Other sales are said to have been made through dealers, and Harold Halvorsen is said to have conducted an auction of Munch paintings in 1939.

Among the dealers mentioned in a study of these transactions are Angever, Bammann, Ferdinand Moller in Berlin, Alex Vomel in Dusseldorf,

Habenstock, Aenne Abels in Cologne, Galerie Zak in Paris, Colnagh Gallery in London, the Zurich Trust Co.-Fides, Wolfgang and Hildebrand Gurlitt (whose stash of unsold paintings was revealed in 2013 to much public excitement), Boehmer, Buchholz Gallery, and two expatriate dealers, Curt Valentin and Karl Nierendorf. 'A relatively large number of works found their way to the U.S. during these years.' After the war, a Swede, Alfred Anderson, also identified the firm of Littman and Rosenthal in The Hague, which had been taken over by the Nazis. How many of these works were repurchased by their original owners is unclear, as well as whether Kronthal or the Speyer firm served as go-betweens.

Postwar interviews with many of these dealers by the OSS Safe-haven Project and the American Commission for the Protection and Salvage of Artistic and Historic Monuments in War Areas (Justice Owen Roberts Commission) contain no references to Speyer or Kronthal. It is clear that 'that which was regarded as degenerate Jewish art was to be sold off to a slate of cooperative German, Swiss, and collaborationist French dealers'.

It seems likely that Speyer's motive for engaging in these transactions, if it did so, was not a mercenary one, and certainly not a pro-Nazi one. It might have been founded on a desire to preserve modern German artworks that would otherwise have been destroyed by the Nazis, and was of a piece with Speyer's sponsorship of a proposed but aborted pavilion on pre-Nazi German culture at the New York World's Fair in 1939. It was noted that 'the material to be displayed is largely in the hands of a group of Germans in exile in the United States and Europe'. Later, in 1942, there was a display in New York of Flemish paintings for the benefit of the Belgian merchant marine which an article noted had been brought to the United States by mysterious and diverse means.

Two books co-authored by William R. Corson, a former high-ranking CIA officer, claim to give an account of James Kronthal's later years. The second incorporates information purportedly received from another CIA officer, Robert T. Crowley. An earlier work by Corson published in 1977 was described by the respected historian Evan Thomas as '[a]n inside account, but not always reliable'.

The first work, published in 1989, alleges that:

Kronthal showed a sexual proclivity for young boys. He was entrapped by the Gestapo, and it took Goering's personal intervention to get him out of trouble … The information on Kronthal later came into the hands of the NKVD through its penetration of General Gehlen's BND by Hans Feife … Moscow Center set two objectives: one was to blackmail him into becoming a Soviet agent, and the second was to make certain that he was promoted up through the ranks … Chinese boys were supplied to Kronthal in Switzerland … by forcing Kronthal to send regular 'packets' of information to Moscow Center, the Soviets made sure that Kronthal committed treason … For Kronthal, his old mentor becoming head of the service was a personal tragedy. He knew the NKVD would pressure him to wangle a top job from Dulles … Dulles so trusted Kronthal that he was prepared to give him any post he wanted … On March 31, 1953, Dulles decided to find out for himself what position Kronthal wanted in the Agency … There is no evidence that Dulles ever discussed his last conversations with Kronthal that night with anyone else … At home, Kronthal wrote two letters. One letter was addressed to Allen Dulles and the other to Richard Helms … [The police] told the press that investigators had found a handwritten letter to a male friend indicating that Kronthal was "mentally upset because of pressures connected with work".

This letter, to Richard Helms, and another to Dulles were delivered to their addressees rather than held as evidence by the police. The death was quickly hushed up. An autopsy placed the time of death around midnight, but a chemical analysis failed to determine the time of death or the contents of the vial found next to Kronthal's body. The cause of the death was listed as 'apparent suicide'. While the notes to Dulles and Helms were found unmailed in Kronthal's house, he did manage to mail one letter before he died. In a letter to his sister, Susan, Kronthal made a clean breast of his homosexual proclivities and made reference to the 'tremendous difficulties' they posed. Susan, already aware of her brother's sexual persuasion, was not alarmed or fretful over these revelations. However, Kronthal's confession that he was not really in the Department of State but, as she had suspected, in the CIA, caused her great concern. The last sentence in James Kronthal's final testament to his sister was 'I can't wait till 1984. Love, Jim.'

A 'Memorandum for the Record', generated in the CIA after publication of the Corson book and a *Newsweek* article about it on 15 May 1989, noted that a redacted person who knew Kronthal very well recalled his suicide and that 'an autopsy was unable to discover what substance was in his system. There was no thought whatsoever given to him being a spy for the Soviets.' The memorandum was over the signature of Gardner R. Hathaway, Associate Deputy Director for Operations for Counterintelligence, who died in November 2013. Another CIA official, Thomas Polgar, 'writing in the periodical *Foreign Intelligence Literary Scene* argues that no evidence supports the charges that Mr. Kronthal was the first Soviet mole; nor is there a citation to back the suggestion that Kronthal met with foul play.

Mr. Polgar enumerates other instances in which "Widows" makes claims for which there is "no sourcing, attribution, elaboration or proof.'"

A later book by one of the same authors purportedly based on new material abandoned the hypothesis that Kronthal had confessed everything at his meeting with Dulles. Instead, it declares, based on information received from a CIA official, Robert T. Crowley, who was purportedly in the next room, that:

> Allen told Jim that he should have come to him with his personal problems, Allen then gave a sad speech about how personal compulsions destroy careers. Allen said that everything he had built could be destroyed. 'James, sometimes there is no way out. Sometimes the right thing to do is step aside. You need to think about that, because if you don't take this opportunity, things could be very ugly.' Allen probably had a special potion prepared that he gave Kronthal should the pressure become too much. Kronthal was the first mole in the CIA. He served the Soviets for more than five years. [James Jesus] Angleton got his job [as head of counterintelligence] in exchange for not investigating Kronthal and Dulles.

In this version, Kronthal's homosexual proclivities were discovered as a result of the 'positive vetting' demanded by the Truman loyalty-security order adopted under congressional pressure and later described by Truman as his worst mistake. A recent study of the so-called 'Lavender Scare' credits a remarkable and all but forgotten journalist, Rosie Goldschmidt Waldeck, with being the 'mother' of it. Waldeck's career, as contrasted with that of the three women previously discussed, followed a fourth model of feminine influence, that of the adventuress. She was born to a Jewish family in Mannheim, married a member of the Ullstein press family and vainly warned him that the sensationalism of his newspapers and their lack of a positive vision were undermining the Weimar Republic. After a divorce, she married a renowned gynaecologist, the discoverer of the female G-Spot, whose theoretical knowledge did not prevent a second divorce. She was then a journalist, associated with ABC News and Dorothy Thompson, and wrote a book, *Athene Palace: The New Order Comes to Romania*, which has, deservedly, been republished twice, most recently by the University of Chicago Press in 2013, 70 years after its initial publication. It includes remarkable passages deriving from her close connections with Nazi officers:

> [O]nly in a world where the values of fatherland and church were not absolute could [Jews] survive – the Jews have succeeded in raising liberalism and the relativity of all truth to a kind of new religion ... Popularized, the [ideas of

Marx, Freud and Einstein] created an awful disorder and alarm in the hearts and minds of the simple human beings [given] man's yearning for an ordered universe ruled by absolute standards where sin was sin and must be expiated, where you must sacrifice to get your reward, where paradise waited for the innocent and the guilty burnt in hell … For a man to look up to a superior, to respect his authority and to believe in him was as rational as sexual love … the status quo could get along on comparatively few ideas while the usurping force had to show something striking.

Thereafter, during the war, she published a second book, *Excellenz X*, recommending to the Allies that they insist that the German military sign any armistice, and that any postwar leader be a conservative and not an exile. Dr Adenauer proved a better choice than her candidates, Karl Meissner and Hjalmar Schacht. She then dropped out of sight, thereafter producing only a vacuous non-fiction book and some historical novels. Her last prominent literary effort was a highly polemical article, 'Homosexual International', which appeared in a right-wing American periodical with which she previously had no known connection. This article does not gain in persuasiveness from its resort to conspiracy theory, but was enthusiastically taken up by Congressman B. Carroll Reece and others in Congress, giving rise to a purge of several hundred government officials. Its central points seem to be that homosexuals are furtive, are not class-conscious and are not subject to the influence of the boudoir and are therefore not future-minded. The source of the author's passion on this subject is not revealed. She died a Roman Catholic.

The Kronthal affair, if he in fact was blackmailed, suggests that in an era when homosexuality was 'closeted', the 'Lavender Scare' may have had a rational basis. Another book touching on Kronthal, Burton Hersh's *The Old Boys: The American Elite and the Origins of the CIA* (1992), suggests that Kronthal's background was disclosed to the McCarthy Committee by critics of the CIA in the US Army Intelligence organization:

His is the sort of tree up which Army intelligence veterans like Frenchy Grombach became especially fond of barking … Grombach became "quite close" to Senator McCarthy when he was running wildest, and passed McCarthy's subcommittee investigators whatever paperwork looked damaging in the hope of undermining the damnable agency.

It has been reported that 'James Jesus Angleton once told a journalist bitterly that the only reason he was named chief of counterintelligence at the CIA

Security Information

31 March 1953

MEMORANDUM FOR THE RECORD

SUBJECT: James Kronthal.

1. Shortly before noon 31 March 1953 the Personnel Director received a call from Colonel Edwards, Security Officer, CIA, advising that subject individual had been found dead at his residence at about 10:30 AM the same day. Colonel Edwards advised that an empty vial had been found by the body and the presumption was that subject had taken poison.

2. Shortly after twelve noon the Personnel Director called ███████ ████████ is subject's brother-in-law and he was called in preference to subject's next of kin, his Mother, since it was understood the Mother ███████ ██████████ was told that subject had committed suicide. The Personnel Director said he did not know the method used, but was sure he had not shot himself. The Personnel Director also indicated that he did not know the details at that time. ████████████ was asked to break the news to the subject's Mother. ██████████ agreed to do this, but wanted his wife, subject's sister, to be present at that time.

3. At 2:15 PM ████████████ called back and talked to ████████████ He said he had not talked with the Mother as yet and asked if there were any other details. ████████████ promised to call him back and after talking with Colonel Edwards he was called back at 2:30 PM. ████████████ was advised that the presumption was that subject had committed suicide by taking poison, since an empty vial had been found by his bed. The coroner must examine to determine cause. The body is in the morgue and after autopsy will be turned over to the undertaker of the family's choice.

4. ████████████ was further advised that Agency officials were working closely with the Metropolitan Police and that as soon as the autopsy was performed and the body released that someone from CIA would again be in touch with him.

5. While Colonel Edwards had indicated that there had been a personal note left for an acquaintance of subject, no mention was made of this to ███ ████████ since it presumably has no bearing on his family relationships.

APPROVED FOR RELEASE
3/00 b3

Security Information

44. 1953 CIA memo

was because he had taken an oath that he would never subject the Dulles brothers to lie detector tests about their collusion with Nazi party bankers in the 1930s.'

The CIA's publicly released records about Kronthal's career are not notably informative. Kronthal was named as Berne Chief of Station by a memorandum dated 17 March 1947 signed by Richard Helms as Chief

8 May 1989

MEMORANDUM FOR THE RECORD

SUBJECT: James Speyer KRONTHAL; *Newsweek* Article of
          15 May 1989, Entitled: "The Soviet's
          First CIA Mole"

1. On 8 May,   told me the following concerning:

                JAMES SPEYER KRONTHAL.

         knew KRONTHAL very well. KRONTHAL was a former
OSS officer.   and, indeed,
committed suicide, probably in 1952. He was a bachelor
                                       One day he did not
show up for work and several employees went to his home and
found him dead in bed. He evidentially had taken something,
but an autopsy was unable to determine what substance was
in his system.

         There was no thought whatsoever given to him being a
spy for the Soviets.

2. All portions of this document are classified SECRET.

                              Gardner R. Hathaway
                         Associate Deputy Director for Operations
                              for Counterintelligence

Attachment:
  Newsweek Article of
  15 May 1989

cc: DC/CIC/AG w/att
ADDO/CI/GRHathaway/mag (8 May 89)
Distribution:
  Orig - File w/att
    1 - DC/CIC/AG w/att
WARNING NOTICE--INTELLIGENCE
SOURCES OR METHODS INVOLVED

APPROVED FOR RELEASE
3/00 b3

SECRET
(9)

CL BY 056204
DECL OADR HUM 4-82
ALL PORTIONS SECRET

44

45. 1989 CIA memo

of Operations. A request for reassignment made on 17 February 1953 and approved on 29 March 1953, two days before Kronthal's death, reassigned him from 'Training Officer' to 'Deputy Director, Office of Training' at the same salary of $10,800.

A 'Memorandum for the Record', with redacted signature and dated 31 March 1953, records that Kronthal had been found dead at his residence at 10.30 a.m. on that day and it was presumed he had taken poison, a vial having been found. The CIA notified Kronthal's brother-in-law and he was told that there had been a suicide, that the method was unknown, but 'he had not shot himself'. 'While Colonel Edwards had indicated that there had been a personal note left for an acquaintance of subject, no mention was made of this to [family] since it presumably has no bearing on his family relationships.'

A sensational book, *Gestapo Chief: The CIA and Heinrich Muller*, in three volumes, asserts that Kronthal interviewed Muller at his then home in Geneva in August 1948, and includes a purported transcript of the interview of more than 900 pages, citing various archival references. It was referred to in a Senate Intelligence Committee hearing in 1986 by Senator Jesse Helms, who also demanded answers to questions about Kronthal's death. These demands contributed to the creation of an Inspector General for the CIA in 1986. The same writer published a fourth volume purporting to be Muller's American diaries from 1948–50. He represents that he got the transcript and diaries from the late Robert T. Crowley, former Deputy Director of Clandestine Operations at the CIA, also an alleged source for the second of the Trento books. Crowley's son has denied cooperation with Douglas, but not with Trento. Douglas is also the author of a book on the Kennedy assassination called *Regicide*. All five books, published by obscure publishers, appear to be inventive and entertaining forgeries. The late Gita Sereny so described them, relating her contact with Douglas, who also has used the pen name Peter Stahl, and the work was similarly described by David Irving, whose well-publicized academic sins include selective quotation but not forgery. It was also referred to by the eminent historian John Lukacs as 'a clever concoction'. It seems implausible, to say the least, that an 900-page transcript, if authentic, would have been published in three parts at two-year intervals.

An explicitly fictional work portraying Kronthal, a novel entitled *The Witness Tree* by Brendan Howley and John Loftus, appeared in 2007. Loftus was the author of two sensationalist works on postwar history. The novel declares that Kronthal was from a Philadelphia rather than New York family and that he had been associated with Sperrlerbank in Frankfurt, purportedly run by Aryan German cousins, and that he auctioned looted Jewish art for Sperrlerbank in 1941. It continued that John Foster Dulles' German municipal and power and water bond placements were sold through Sperrlerbank; places Kronthal at a New York art auction in 1938; erroneously states that he started in October 1941 as the coordinator for information; places him in Berne in November 1942, as a cipher clerk and participant in an homosexual liaison, and in Berlin in September 1945. This is a blend of fact and fiction, since Speyer's Frankfurt branch closed in 1934.

Kronthal had been prevented since 1935 from studying art at Harvard 'due to family obstacles and difficulties.' In relinquishing his long-awaited and hard-won fellowship in 1942, he wrote that 'I feel that all who are able should place themselves at the service of the government ... there are times when each man must make up his own mind. Let us hope that the world will soon return to a state where we can all pursue the course which we desire.'

While suicide can be seen as sinful and in some places is a crime, Kronthal's death, coming as it did at the height of the McCarthy period, was, if the undocumented allegations about him are true, almost certainly a service. It was a service not only to the reputation of the CIA but to American Jews and to democrats, with both a large and small 'd'. Ground between the tectonic plates of competing ideologies and nationalisms, he has been described as one of the first casualties of the Cold War. For this writer, he may have been one of the last casualties of World War I.

NOTES

Introduction

The Times, 25 March 1960.

Prologue – Early Days

J. Camplin, *Rise of the Plutocrats* (London: Constable, 1976).

V. Carosso, 'A Financial Elite: New York's German-Jewish Investment Bankers', *American Jewish Historical Quarterly* 66 (1976): 67.

W. Mosse, *Jews in the German Economy: The German-Jewish Economic Elite, 1820–1935* (Oxford: Clarendon, 1987), 122, 129; D. Augustine, *Patricians and Parvenus: Wealth and High Society in Wilhelmine Germany* (Oxford: Berg Publishers, 1994), 23; O. Rost, *Die 100 Reichsten im Preusen des Jahres 1910* (2006).

G. Aly, *Why the Germans? Why the Jews* (New York: Metropolitan Books, 2014).

J. Lieberman, 'A stark contrast in Frankfurt's Jewish legacy', *Jewish Review*, 15 July 2010.

T. Collins, *Otto Kahn: Art, Money and Modern Times* (Chapel Hill: University of North Carolina Press, 2002), 49, 51.

T. Sherwood, *Charles Tyson Yerkes: The Transit King of London* (London: Tempus, 2008), 40, n. 52.

James Speyer Obituary, *The New York Times*, 1 November 1941.

P. Emden, *Jews of Britain: A Series of Biographies* (London: Sampson, Low, 1943), 344–7.

Ibid.

S. Birmingham, *Our Crowd: The Great Jewish Families of New York* (London: Longmans, 1968), 201.

J. Kobler, *Otto the Magnificent: The Life of Otto Kahn* (New York: Scribners, 1988), 14.

Ibid., 343.

Idem.

'Edgar Speyer Dies at Berlin', *The New York Times*, 18 February 1932.

P. Hinkson, *Seventy Years Young: The Memories of Elizabeth, Countess of Fingall* (London: Collins, 1937), 113, 115.

P. Emden, *Money Powers of Europe in the Nineteenth and Twentieth Centuries* (London: Sampson, Low, 1937), 274–7.

F. Skolnik (ed.), *Encyclopedia Judaica* (2nd edn, Detroit: Thomson Gale, 2007), 102, 111.

I. Singer (ed.), *The Jewish Encyclopedia* (New York: Funk and Wagnalls, 1909), 508.

M. Wilkins, *The History of Foreign Investment in the United States to 1914* (Cambridge, MA: Harvard University Press, 1989), 116.

D. Kynaston, *The City of London* (London: Chatto and Windus, 1995), 352.

Quoted in J. Franch, *Robber Baron: The Life of Charles Tyson Yerkes* (Urbana: University of Illinois Press, 2008), 292.

R. Swaine, *The Cravath Firm and Its Predecessors, 1819–1998* (New York: n.p., 1948), 594–607, 707, cited in T. Collins, *Otto Kahn: Art, Money and Modern Times* (Chapel Hill: University of North Carolina Press, 2002), 316, n. 37.

H. Kroos, 'James Speyer', in *Dictionary of American Biography*, supplement 3, 1941–5 (New York: Scribner, 1973).

A. Dru (ed.), *The Letters of Jacob Burckhardt* (New York: Pantheon, 1955), 169.

Wikipedia, 'Felix Schwabach', see W. Hoff and F. Schwabach, *North American Railroads: Their Administration and Economic Policy* (New York: Germania, 1906).

W. Mosse, *The German-Jewish Economic Elite, 1820–1935: A Socio-Cultural Profile* (Oxford: Clarendon, 1989), 96, 167, 182.

Chapter 1. The London Tube

V. Carosso, *The Morgans: Private International Bankers* (Cambridge, MA: Harvard University Press, 1987), 158.

R. Chernow, *The House of Morgan* (New York: Simon and Schuster, 1990), 86.

T. Sherwood, *Charles Tyson Yerkes: The Traction King of London* (London: Tempus, 2008), 32. Hearings before the Royal Commission on London Traffic, 1905, vol. II, 249. Speyer's testimony is at vol. II, qq. 6881–6885 and 24604–24775; his written evidence is in vol. III, Appx. 81.

US Department of Commerce, *Handbook on American Underwriting of Foreign Securities* (hereafter 'Handbook'), Trade Promotion Series No. 104 (Washington: G.P.O., 1930), 10.

H. Satterlee, *J. Pierpont Morgan* (New York: Macmillan, 1940), 381.

Extracts of correspondence of E. C. Grenfell, Morgan Grenfell mss 21, 799 in S. Chapman, 'Merchants and Bankers', in W. Mosse (ed.), *Second Chance: Two Centuries of German-Speaking Jews in the United Kingdom* (Tubingen: Mohr, 1992), 338.

C. Wolmar, *The Subterranean Railway: How the London Underground Was Built and How It Changed the City Forever* (London: Atlantic Books, 2005), 197.

R. Swaine, supra, 109.

A. Mandeville, *The House of Speyer: A Candid Criticism of Speyer Flotations* (London: Financial Mail, 1915).

J. Franch, supra, 314.

S. Halliday, *Underground to Everywhere: London's Underground Railway in the Life of the Capital* (London: History Press, 2004).

T. Sherwood, supra, 84.

H. Satterfield, *J. Pierpont Morgan: An Intimate Portrait* (New York: Macmillan, 1939), 381, 382.

J. Franch, supra, 294, 297.

The Times, 17 December 1906, cited in A. Lentin, supra, 180, n. 9.

S. Halliday, *Amazing and Extraordinary Underground Facts* (London: David and Charles Ltd, 2009), 51, 99.

The Times, 24 June 1907.

A. Jackson and D. Croome, *Rails Through the Clay* (London: Allen and Unwin, 1962), 127.

'London Traction Merger Arranged', *The New York Times*, 18 January 1912; 'Speyer Unites London Lines', 20 November 1912.

The Times, 5 January 1920; *Tramway and Railway World*, 10 January 1920.

Churchill to Asquith, 5 May 1909, in R. Churchill, *Winston S. Churchill*, vol. 2, companion volume 2 (London: Heinemann, 1969), 890.

G. Searle, *Corruption in British Politics, 1895–1930* (Oxford: Clarendon, 1987), 104.

'Ecuador to Control Only Railway There', *The New York Times*, 19 May 1925, see E. and K. Brainard, *Railroad in the Sky: The Guayaquil-Quito Railway in Ecuador, 1897–1925* (Marion, MA: Atlantis, 2003); M. Meneses-Jurado, 'Tren el sol: Train to the Sea: Journey on Board the Most Difficult Train in the World', *Americas*, 1 March 2009.

Chapter 2. English Philanthropy

The New York Times, 18 March 1934.

The sketch appears in the *Illustrated London News* for 13 November 1909.

Lancet, vol. 1, part 1, p. 813 (1905).

The Barden Fund, *British Medical Journal*, 9 September 1905, 606–7.

C. Snow, 'Emigration from Great Britain', in W. Willcox (ed.), *International Migrations* (New York: National Bureau for Economic Research, 1931), ch. 9, p. 244, Table 92.

Chapter 3. The House of Music

Obituary, *The New York Times*, 9 June 1935.

H. Wood, *My Life of Music* (London: Gollancz, 1938), 187.

B. Hall, *The Proms and the Men Who Made Them* (London: Allen and Unwin, 1981), 52.

E. Speyer, *My Life and Friends* (London: Cobden Sanderson, 1937), 216.

Obituary, 'Edward Speyer, Friend of Brahms and Wagner', *The New York Times*, 9 January 1934.

The New York Times, 27 June 1923, see ibid., 22 April 1923; 19 August 1923.

F. Sheppard, *Survey of London: The Grosvenor Estate In Mayfair* (London: Athlone Press, University of London, 1977), 155–7.

Grosvenor Street is described in F. Sheppard, *The Grosvenor Estate in Mayfair, Part II, The Buildings* (London: Athlone, 1980), 45–7.

P. Turner, 'The House and Collection of Mr. Edgar Speyer', *The Burlington Magazine* 18 (September 1904), 544ff.

V. Seroff, *Debussy: Musician of France* (New York: Putnam, 1956), 278.

E. Lockspeiser, *Debussy: His Life and Mind* (New York: Macmillan, 1965), 117–19, 138, 299.

M. De-La-Noy, *Elgar the Man* (London: Allen Lane, 1983), 101–2.

S. Fuller, 'Elgar and the Salons: The Significance of a Private Musical World', in B. Adams, *Edward Elgar and His World* (Princeton: Princeton University Press, 2007), 223, 231.

J. Moore, *Edward Elgar: A Creative Life* (Oxford: Oxford University Press, 1984), 580.

R. Anderson, *Elgar* (New York: Schirmer, 1993), 94.

M. Kennedy, *Portrait of Elgar* (New York: Oxford, 1968), 224.

A. De Riencourt, *The Coming Caesars* (New York: Coward McCann, 1957).

P. Hoare, *Wilde's Last Stand: Decadence, Conspiracy and the First World War* (London: Duckworth, 1997), see 'Take Off Salome Say Opera House Directors: Miss Morgan Urged Action', *The New York Times*, 27 January 1907.

M. Boyden, *Richard Strauss* (Boston: Northeastern University Press, 1999), 169–70.

B. Tuchman, *The Proud Tower: A Portrait of the World Before the War* (New York: Macmillan, 1966), 315–17.

M. Gillies (ed.), *Self Portrait of Percy Grainger* (Oxford: Oxford University Press, 2006), 49, 64, 133, 135, 190–1, 226, citing C. Mount, *John Singer Sargent: A Biography* (New York: Norton, 1955).

P. Bullock (ed.), *The Correspondence of Jean Sibelius and Rosa Newmarch, 1906–1939* (London: Boydell Press, 2011), 251, see also E. Tawaststjernn, *Sibelius, 1904–1914* (London: Faber and Faber, 1986), 111.

F. Benestad and W. Halvorsen (eds), *E. Grieg, Diaries, Articles, Speeches* (Columbus, Ohio: Peer Gynt Press, 2001), 128, 130–1.

J. Plumb, supra, 261.

H. Wood, supra, 156, 241.

W. Boosey, *Fifty Years of Music* (London: Benn, 1931), 106; R. Newmarch, 'Queen's Hall in 1914–1915', *Monthly Musical Review* 62 (1932), 36–57.

L. Langley, supra, 69, Table 2.

M. Kennedy, *Richard Strauss: Man, Musician, Enigma* (Cambridge: Cambridge University Press, 1999), 208; see also M. Kennedy, *Richard Strauss* (New York: Schirmer, 1958); M. Boyden, *Richard Strauss* (Boston: Northeastern University Press, 1999), 230.

N. Del Mar, *Richard Strauss: A Critical Commentary on His Life and Work* (London: Barrie and Rockcliff, 1969), 219.

Letter, Jacques Renard, *The New York Times*, 22 June 1947.

S. Fuller, 'Elgar and the Salons: The Significance of a Private Musical World', in B. Adams, *Edward Elgar and His World* (Princeton, NJ: Princeton University Press, 2007), 223, 231, citing M. White, *Friends and Memories* (London: Edward Arnold, 1914), 369.

Obituary, *The New York Times*, 11 February 1956.

E. De Waal, *The Hare With Amber Eyes: A Family's Century of Art and Loss* (New York: Farrar Straus, 2010), 211.

J. Caplin, supra, 289.

National Review, October 1914, 582.

A. Lentin, *Banker Traitor Scapegoat Spy? The Troublesome Case of Sir Edgar Speyer* (London: Haus, 2013), 153.

H. Wood, *My Life in Music* (London: Gollancz, 1949), 291ff.

C. Cockburn, *I, Claude* (Harmondsworth: Penguin, 1967).

L. Langley, supra, 86.

Chapter 4. The Scott Expeditions

'Letter of Scott is Given to Byrd; Presented by the Widow of Explorer's Backer and Is Read at Dinner Here', *The New York Times*, 6 December 1935.

E. Huxley, *Scott of the Antarctic* (London: Weidenfeld and Nicolson, 1977), 55, 180, 183, 261.

H. Ludlam, *Captain Scott: The Full Story* (London: W. Foulsham, 1965), 72, 179.

Leonora Speyer to Scott, 4 October 1906; Scott Polar Museum Archives, Leonora Speyer File, 1453/178D.

Chapter 5. Leonora

Illustrated American, 13 February 1892, see http://songofthelark.wordpress.com/tag/von-stosch-leonora (accessed 9 March 2015).

'Bars Apartments in Speyer House', *The New York Times*, 21 May 1936.

The New York Times, 9 February 1952.

G. Wescott, 'A Canopic Jar', *Poetry: A Magazine of Verse* (1924), 47ff.

L. Speyer, 'Birthday Cake: A Refugee's Story', *The New York Times*, 9 January 1944.

L. Speyer, *Slow Wall. Poems, Together with Not Without Music* (New York: Knopf, 1951), 225–35, originally published in the *Saturday Review of Literature*, and in H. Hull (ed.), *The Writer's Book* (New York: Harper, 1950).

A. Commire (ed.), *Women in World History: A Biographical Encyclopedia* (Warerford, CT: Yorkin, 2002).

Obituary, Vivien Claire Speyer, Mother of Gabrielle Thorp of Norwalk, *Norwalk Hour*, 3 August 2001.

L. Blom-Cooper, Preface to A. Lentin, supra, xv.

'Episcopalian Daughter of Jewish Banker Marries French Catholic Count', *Jewish Telegraphic Agency Mail Service*, 30 May 1926.

Holmes to Marchionness of Tweedale, 4 April 1931, in J. Peabody (ed.), *The Holmes–Einstein Letters: Correspondence of Mr. Justice Holmes and Lewis Einstein, 1903–1935* (London: Macmillan, 1964), 322–3.

Chapter 6. Influence on the Liberal Party

M. Soames, *Clementine Churchill: The Biography of a Marriage* (London: Doubleday, 2003), 120–1.

Churchill to Clementine Churchill, 28 July 1914, quoted in D. Stafford, *Churchill and Secret Service* (London: Thistle, 2013).

E. Tupper, *Seaman's Torch* (London: Hutchinson, 1938), 196; S. Roskill, *Admiral of the Fleet Lord Beatty* (London: Collins, 1980), 88.

'British Extravagance Causes Trade Decline: Edgar Speyer', *The New York Times*, 17 June 1905; E. Speyer, 'Some Aspects of National Finance', *J. Institute of Bankers* 26 (1905), 361.

E. Speyer, *The Export of Capital: Its Effect on the Welfare of the Empire* (London: Liberal Colonial Club, 1911).

The New York Times, 9 August 1914. See G. Paish, 'Capital Investment in Other Lands', 72; *J. Royal Institute of Statistics* (1909), 465; G. Paish, 'Capital Investment in Individual Colonial and Foreign Countries', 74, ibid. 167 (1911); G. Searle, 'The Edwardian Liberal Party and Business', *English History Review* 386 (January 1983), 28–60; Obituary, *The Times*, 18 February 1932, 13b.

A. Allfrey, *King Edward VII and His Jewish Court* (London: Weidenfeld and Nicolson, 1991), 248.

'Company Law: Departmental Committee Report', *Manchester Guardian*, 11 July 1906, 10.

J. Bolan, 'Sir George Paish: Ambassador of Free Trade' (Master's Thesis, Liberty University, Lynchburg, VA, 2011), 28, citing G. Paish, *Memoirs*, 16–17, 19, London School of Economics Library, Coll. Misc. 621/1.

F. Oppenheimer, 'James Speyer on Money and Railroad Problems', *Magazine of Wall Street* 435 (1919), 25; Wikipedia, Albert Stanley.

G. Searle, *Corruption in British Politics, 1895–1930* (Oxford: Clarendon, 1987), 292–3.

Kipling to R. Blumenfeld, 11 August 1914, Kipling MSS 14/19; Aitken to Kipling, 17 September 1914, House of Lords Record Office BBK C/198, both cited in M. Brock, 'Outside His Art: Rudyard Kipling in Politics', *Kipling Journal* (March 1988), 9.

M. and E. Brock (eds), *H. Asquith, Letters to Venetia Stanley* (Oxford: Oxford University Press, 1985), 293.

A. Lennox (ed.), *Diary of Lord Bertie of Thane* (London: Hodder and Stoughton, 1924), 80.

A. Mandeville, op. cit., supra, 25.

J. Colvin, *Life of Lord Carson* (London: Gollancz, 1936), 191.

H. Wells, *The Outline of History* (Garden City, NY: Garden City Books, 1961, original publication 1920), 842.

M. Asquith, *Diary*, supra, July 1918, quoted in Lentin, supra, 78ff.

P. Panayi, *The Enemy in Our Midst: Germans in Britain During the First World War* (Providence, RI: Berg, 1991), 188–9, 290, 223, citing Maxse Papers, vol. 469, letter from Max Aitken, 8 December 1914, 189; vol. 470, letter from M. Hicks-Beach, 4 February 1915, 189, West Sussex Record Office.

W. Churchill, *Lord Randolph Churchill* (London: Macmillan, 1907), 268–9, quoted in J. Lukacs, *Churchill: Visionary, Statesman, Historian* (New Haven, CT: Yale University Press, 2002), 111.

H.C. Debates 574, 11 July 1918.

C. Holmes, *Anti-Semitism in British Society, 1876–1939* (London: Edward Arnold, 1979), 83.

Quoted in E. De Waal, *The Hare With Amber Eyes: A Family's Century of Art and Loss* (New York: Farrar Straus, 2010), 120.

W. Rubenstein, *Men of Property* (London: Berg, 1981), 92, 155.

J. Steinberg, *Bismarck* (New York: Oxford, 2012), 392.

B. de Jouvenel, *The Ethics of Redistribution* (Indianapolis: Liberty Fund, 1951, 1978), 78.

E. De Waal, supra, 156.

Quoted in E. De Waal, supra, 129.

The New York Times, 1 November 1903.

L. Stein, *England and Germany: By Leaders of Opinion in Both Empires* (London: Williams and Norgate, 1912), 39.

J. Plumb, 'The Edwardians', in *In the Light of History* (Boston: Houghton Mifflin, 1973), 249, 251–2.

E. De Waal, supra, 131–2, 181.

C. Jordan (ed.), *Reason and Imagination, The Selected Correspondence of Learned Hand* (New York: Oxford, 2013), 179, 90.

C. Hayes, *Nationalism: A Religion* (New York: Macmillan, 1960), 93, 137.

I. Berlin, 'Nationalism', in H. Hardy (ed.), *Against the Current: Essays in the History of Ideas* (Princeton, NJ: Princeton University Press, 2012), 444.

G. Chesterton, *The New Jerusalem* (London: Nelson, 1924), ch. 13.

Encyclopedia Brittanica (New York: Encyclopedia Brittanica, 11th edn, 1910), 134–46.

Quoted in O. Friedrich, *Before the Deluge: A Portrait of Berlin in the 1920s* (London: Michael Joseph, 1974), 324–6.

Encyclopedia Brittanica (New York: Encyclopedia Brittanica, 11th edn, 1911), 986, 989.

E. De Waal, supra, 152

Felix Frankfurter to Learned Hand, 28 June 1920, in C. Jordan (ed.), *Reason and Imagination: The Selected Correspondence of Learned Hand* (New York: Oxford, 2013), 93.

Chapter 7. Anti-Germanism and Its Consequences

A. Allfrey, supra, 272.

A. Fitzroy, *Memoirs* (London: Hutchinson, 1925), 499.

B. Tuchman, *The Proud Tower: A Portrait of the World Before the War* (New York: Macmillan, 1966), 307.

J. Camplin, supra, 288, citing A. Fane, *Chit-Chat* (London: Thornton Butterworth, 1926), 247–9.

P. Panayi, supra, 97, Table 3.1.

J. Camplin, supra, 256.

A. Lentin, supra, 59.

Quoted in A. Lentin, supra, 59.

H. Croft, *My Life of Strife* (London: Hutchinson, 1948).

P. Hoare, *Wilde's Last Stand: Decadence, Conspiracy, and the First World War* (London: Duckworth, 1997), 230–1.

Hansard, 26 June 1918, *H.C. Debates* 107 (5th series), 1031.

The Times, 5 June 1918.

L. Maxse, 'British Contraction, German Expansion', *National Review* (April 1909), reprinted in L. Maxse, *Germany on the Brain* (London: National Review, 1915), 263–4.

A. Wilson, *After the Victorians: The Decline of Britain in the World* (New York: Farrar Straus, 2005), 134, citing M. Jastrow, *The War and the Bagdad Railway* (New York: Lippincott, 1918).

L. Maxse, 'The Baghdad Railroad', *National Review* (April 1911), reprinted in L. Maxse, *Germany on the Brain* (London: National Review, 1915), 294–6.

C. Clark, *The Sleepwalkers: How Europe Went to War in 1914* (New York: Harper, 2013), 338–9.

L. Maxse, 'In the Trough of Marconi', *National Review* (April 1913), in L. Maxse, *Germany on the Brain* (London: National Review, 1915), 341.

L. Maxse, 'A Warning to German Jews', *National Review* (October 1913), in L. Maxse, *Germany on the Brain* (London: National Review, 1915), 350–1.

Rumbold to Simon, 28 March 1933, *Documents on British Foreign Relations, 1919–39*, 2nd Series, vol. V, No. 5, p. 3.

A. Julius, *Trials of the Diaspora: A History of Anti-Semitism* (Oxford: Oxford University Press, 2010).

G. Himmelfarb, *The People of the Book: Philo-Semitism in England from Churchill to Cromwell* (Los Angeles: Encounter, 2011).

Y. Casis and M. Rocques, *City Bankers, 1890–1914* (Cambridge: Cambridge University Press, 1994), 105, n. 31, citing J. Camplin, *Rise of the Plutocrats*.

D. Judd, *Lord Reading* (London: Weidenfeld, 1982), 117.

J. Proskauer, *A Segment of My Times* (New York: Farrar Straus, 1950), 196–9; 'Memorandum of Edwin Montagu on the Anti-Semitism of the Present [British] Government, August 23, 1917', www.jewishvirtuallibrary.org/source/history/Montagumemo.html (accessed 9 March 2015).

D. Wyman, *The Abandonment of the Jews: America and the Holocaust, 1941–1945* (New York: Pantheon, 1984), 175.

See http://www.ajcarchives.org/main.php?GroupingId=1320\ (accessed 9 March 2015); C. Liebman, 'Diaspora Influence on Israel: The Ben-Gurion-Blaustein Exchange and Its Aftermath', *Jewish Social Studies* (October, 1974).

G. B. Shaw Papers, British Library Addl. mss.50527, fols. 256–57, quoted in L. Langley, 'Building an Orchestra', in J. Doctor, *et al.* (eds), *The Proms: A New History* (London: Thames and Hudson, 2007), 293, nn. 72, 77.

See K. Roiphe, *1185 Park Avenue* (Glencoe, IL: Free Press,1999).

P. Emden, supra.

The New York Times, 7 January 1922.

Rodriguez v. Speyer Brothers [1919] A.C.59.

A. Fitzroy, *Memoirs* (London: Hutchinson, 1925), 613–14, 770.

The New York Times, 4 June 1915; 13 June 1915.

A. Allfrey, supra, 278ff.

P. Emden, *Money Powers of Europe in the Nineteenth and Twentieth Centuries* (London: Sampson, Low, 1937).

The Times, 3 August 1918.

A. Lentin, supra, 57–8; *The Times*, 6 December 1918.

A. Fitzroy, *Memoirs*, supra, 770.

Parliamentary Papers, 1922, Cmd. 1569.

Edgar Speyer to James Speyer, 22 October 1914; Transcript of Denaturalization Hearing 1369.

The New York Times, 30 January 1915.

London Gazette, no.32547, p.10123, 13 December 1921, quoted in the Wikipedia sketch on Edgar Speyer.

The Times, 9 January 1922; Parliamentary Papers, 1922, Cmd. 1569, 156. See K. Fewster (ed.), *Gallipoli Correspondent: The Front Line Diary of C.E.W. Bean* (London: Heinemann, 1914, reprinted London: Unwin, 1983), 29, 30, 75, 77.

A. Lentin, supra, 134.

Letter, *The New York Times*, 20 March 1932.

T. Dreiser, *The Stoic* (New York: World Publishing, 1947), 205–6; see also *The Financier* (New York: Harper, 1912); *The Titan* (London: Constable, 1928).

E. De Waal, supra, 132.

'Speyer Persecuted, Says Untermeyer', *The New York Times*, 15 December 1921.

Record on Appeal, *People of the State of New York ex rel James Speyer v. John Gilchrist et al. constituting State Tax Commission*, New York State Supreme Court, Appellate Division, 3rd Department, No. 169 (1925).

The New York Times, 23 January 1934.

M. Formanek-Brunell (ed.), *The Story of Rose O'Neill: A Biography* (Columbia: University of Missouri Press, 1997), 116–19.

Report of the Death of an American Citizen, filed at Berlin on 4 March 1932 by John F. Stone, US Vice Consul [courtesy of Prof. Antony Lentin].

Chapter 8. Mediation Efforts

P. Kennedy, *Rise of Anglo-German Antagonism* (London: Allen and Unwin, 1980), 304; H. Albrecht, *Alfred Beit: The Hamburg Diamond King* (Hamburg: Hamburgische Wissenschaftliche Stiftong, 1967), 87.

German Diplomatic Documents, 1871–1914 (London: Methuen, 1930), 243.

Bethmann-Hollweg to Metternich, 3 February 1911, 3; ibid., 374; Margot Asquith *Diary*, British Library, Ms Eng d.3211 (entry of 12 February 12, 1911).

A. Offer, 'Empire and Social Reform: British Overseas Investments and Domestic Politics, 1908–14', *Historical Journal* 26 (1983), 226.

The New York Times, 19 April 1911.

G. Paish, *Memoirs*, 35–6, London School of Economics Library, Coll. Misc. 621/1.

F. Maurice, *Haldane 1856–1915* (London: Faber and Faber, 1937), 298. See also R. Haldane, *Autobiography* (London: Hodder and Stoughton, 1929), 238.

C. Clark, *The Sleepwalkers: How Europe Went to War in 1914* (New York: Harper, 2013), 318–20.

Quoted in S. Koss, *Lord Haldane: Scapegoat for Liberalism* (New York: Columbia University Press, 1969), 80.

J. Camplin, *Rise of the Plutocrats* (London: Constable, 1976), 58–62, 288–92; P. Thane, 'Financiers and the British State: The Case of Sir Ernest Cassel', *Business History* 28 (1986), 80.

T. Collins, supra, 105; A. Lentin, supra, 39, 107.

Morgan to Edward Grenfell, 20 September 1914, in R. Chernow, *The House of Morgan* (New York: Simon and Schuster, 1990), 86ff.

Ibid., 199.

J. Kobler, *Otto the Magnificent: The Life of Otto Kahn* (New York: Scribners, 1988), 80–5, 87–8.

'Peace Talk in Berlin', *The New York Times*, 28 September 1914.

D. Curtin, 'Men Behind the U.S. Peace Initiative', *The Times*, 29 November 1916.

R. Doerries, *Imperial Challenge: Ambassador Bernstorff and German-American Relations, 1908–17* (Chapel Hill: University of North Carolina Press, 1989); see also James Speyer to Burton Hendrick, 3 February 1922 in the Oscar Straus Papers, Library of Congress; O. Straus, *Under Five Administrations* (Boston: Houghton Mifflin, 1930).

K. Forster, *Failures of Peace: The Search for a Negotiated Peace during the First World War* (Washington: American Council on Public Affairs, 1941), 62–6.

K. Forster, supra, 148.

The New York Times, 15 July 1916; 31 August 1916.

'Bring New York Into Movement to Stop the War', *The New York Times*, 26 November 1916; 'Assail Jacob H. Schiff as Foe of the Allies', *The New York Times*, 30 November 1916.

A. Lentin, *Banker Traitor Scapegoat Spy? The Troublesome Case of Sir Edgar Speyer* (London: Haus, 2013), 36–7.

The New York Times, 1 August 1914.

Ibid., 9 August 1914.

Ibid., 12 August 1914.

Editorial, 'Starving the Quarrelsome', *The New York Times*, 7 May 1911.

Ibid., 7 June 1912.

Ibid., 30 July 1914.

'Condemns Germans Here: Berlin Paper Attacks Those Who Aided the Allies' Loan', *The New York Times*, 9 October 1915.

The New York Times, 23 April 1915.

T. Collins, supra, 114–17, 136–7.

Handbook, supra, 159, 162.

The New York Times, 2 January 1917.

Ibid., 28 April 1917.

Ibid., 19 July 1917.

R. Doerries, *Imperial Challenge: Ambassador Bernstorff and German-American Relations, 1908–17* (Chapel Hill: University of North Carolina Press, 1989), 59, 86.

Ibid., 248, n. 55. See *The New York Times*, 15 March 1914.

'$2 million Spent by Boy-Ed on German Plot', *The New York Times*, 24 November 1915.

Bernstorff to Bethmann-Hollweg, 20 October 1915, referred to in R. Doerries, supra.

Roosevelt to Spring-Rice, 5 February 1915, in S. Morison, *Letters of Theodore Roosevelt* 8 (Cambridge, MA: Harvard University Press, 1965), 888; Spring-Rice to Valentine Chirol, 13 November 1914 in S. S. Gwynne (ed.), *The Letters and Friendships of Cecil Spring-Rice* (London: Constable, 1929).

K. Born, *International Bankers in the 19th and 20th Centuries* (New York: St Martin's Press, 1983), 202–3.

Quoted in A. Field, *The Truth About the Slump* (London: Ovid, 1962).

M. Page, *The Creative Destruction of Manhattan, 1900–1940* (Chicago: University of Chicago Press, 2001).

The New York Times, 14 October 1918.

C. Quigley, *Tragedy and Hope: A History of the World in Our Time* (New York: Macmillan, 1966), 251–2.

Chapter 9. Ellin

M. Adams, *Harbor Hill: The End of the Line of Gilded Age Hauteur and Hurt*, 178, mrmhadams. typepad.com (accessed 9 March 2015).

The New York Times, 12 November 1897.

D. Wecter, *The Saga of American Society: A Record of Social Aspiration, 1607–1937* (London: Scribner, 1937), 155.

E. Hornberger, *Mrs. Astor's New York: Money and Power in the Gilded Age* (New Haven, CT: Yale University Press, 2001).

A. Blackwood, *Episodes Before Thirty* (London: Cassell, 1923, reprinted New York: Bibliobazaar, 2009).

The New York Times, 22 February 1921.

F. Oppenheimer, 'James Speyer on Money and Railroad Problems', *Magazine of Wall Street* 25 (1919), 435n.

The New York Times, 12 June 1899.

Ibid., 19 April 1908.

Portraits of her appear in M. Carlebach, *Bain's New York: The City in News Pictures* (New York: Dover, 2011).

The New York Times, 19 May 1907; 31 May 1913; 31 May 1914.

Ibid., 19 May 1907; 21 and 27 May 1908; 31 May 1911.

Obituaries, *The New York Times*, 23 February and 1 March 1921.

The New York Times, 22 February 1929.

Ibid., 19 April 1908.

Ibid., 23 February 1924.

'Rich Also Need Aid, Says James Speyer', *The New York Times*, 8 December 1911.

'Settlement House Has Fiftieth Birthday', *The New York Times*, 2 May 1937; 'An East Side Oasis Holds Its Jubilee', *The New York Times*, 29 December 1936.

The New York Times, 13 December 1945.

Ibid., 19 April 1908.

Ibid., 5 February 2011.

'Athletics for Girls in Public Schools', *The New York Times*, 29 November 1905.

'25 Years Ago Today', *New York Sun*, 7 February 1940.

Chapter 10. Carlotta

L. Sheaffer, *O'Neill: Son and Artist* (Boston: Little, Brown, 1973), 223.

A. and B. Gelb, *O'Neill* (London: Jonathan Cape, 1962), 635; see L. Sheaffer, *O'Neill: Son and Artist* (London: Paul Elek, 1974), 282, 532, 608.

L. Sheaffer, *O'Neill, Son and Artist* (Boston: Little, Brown, 1973), 360ff.
Ibid., 282.
S. Black, *Eugene O'Neill: Beyond Mourning and Tragedy* (New Haven, CT: Yale University Press, 1999), 471.
Ibid., 478, 532, 60.
R. Swaine, supra, 711.
M. Smith, 'Paramour or Papa?: James Speyer and the Alluring Carlotta', *Proceedings of the Modern Language Association* (2009); R. Eaton, 'Rubbing Shoulders with the Rich and Famous', *Eugene O'Neill Review* 32 (2010), 38.

Chapter 11. US Railway Promotions

C. Kobrak, *Banking on Global Markets: Deutsche Bank and the United States, 1870 to the Present* (Cambridge: Cambridge University Press, 2007), 40, 106, 108.
Economist, 25 June 1898, 938–9, discussed in E. Campbell, *The Reorganization of the American Railroad System, 1893–1900* (New York: Columbia University Press, 1938), 206–14.
S. Daggett, *Railroad Reorganization* (Boston: Houghton Mifflin, 1908), 26ff.
F. Oppenheimer, supra.
E. Campbell, *The Reorganization of the American Railroad System, 1893–1900* (New York: Columbia University Press, 1938), 214.
V. Carosso, supra, 320, 359.
H. Kroos, supra.
W. Hoff and F. Schwabach, *North American Railroads: Their Administration and Economic Policy* (Official German Report on American Railroads) (New York: Germania Press, 1906), 20, 431–2, 435, 438–9.
Young, *Handbook*, 19.
Ibid., 146, citing T. Collins, *Otto Kahn: Art, Money and Modern Times* (Chapel Hill: University of North Carolina Press, 2002), 43–9.
Ibid., 147–8.
Ibid., 150.
The New York Times, 21 November 1903.
E. Kirkland, supra, 72–3.
Ibid., 125ff.
E. Campbell, *The Reorganization of the American Railroad System, 1893–1900* (New York: Columbia University Press, 1938), 120.
E. Kirkland, *Industry Comes of Age: Business, Labor and Public Policy, 1860–1897* (New York: Holt, 1961), 222–3, citing A. Pound and S. Moore, *More They Told Barron* (New York: Harper, 1931), 126–7.
The New York Times, 22 July 1913.
E. Hobsbawm, *The Age of Capital, 1848–1875* (London: Weidenfeld and Nicolson, 1975), 56–7.
Ibid., 65–6.
G. Evans, *Collins Potter Huntington* (Newport News: Mariners' Museum, 1954), vol. I, 215; vol. II, 463; J. Grodinsky, *Transcontinental Railway Strategy, 1869–1893: A Study of Businessmen* (Philadelphia: University of Pennsylvania Press, 1962), 4.
S. Daggett, *Chapters in the History of the Southern Pacific* (New York: Ronald Press, 1922), 418.
T. Tzeng, 'Eastern Promises: the role of Eastern capital in the development of Los Angeles, 1900–1920', *California History* 88:2 (2011), 32, citing F. Dinkelspiel, *Towers of Gold* (New York: St. Martin's, 2008), 171.
E. Campbell, *The Reorganization of the American Railroad System, 1893–1900* (New York: Columbia University Press, 1938), 255.
V. Carosso, op.cit., supra, 846, n. 126.
The New York Times, 7 April 1900.
Ibid., 4 April 1901.

Ibid., 5 April 1906.

'Speyer the Middleman', *The New York Times*, 17 October 1899, see also ibid., 17 November and 5 December 1899.

G. Upshur, *As I Recall Them* (Clinton, MA: Colonial Press, 1936), 132–3.

'Harriman Syndicate Gets Southern Pacific', *The New York Times*, 2 February 1901, cited in T. Tzeng, supra, n. 35.

The New York Times, 6 September 1900, 27 October 1900, cited in T. Tzeng, supra, at nn. 33–4.

A. Chandler, *The Visible Hand: The Managerial Revolution in American Business* (Cambridge, MA: Harvard University Press, 1977), 145–6, 147–8.

Ibid., 491.

B. Russell, *Freedom versus Organization, 1814–1914* (New York: Norton, 1934), 338.

T. McCaw, *Prophets of Regulation* (Cambridge, MA: Harvard University Press, 1984), ch. 1.

T. Tzeng, supra, at 39.

G. Evans, supra, vol. II, 581.

Hearings, supra, 643.

T. Tzeng, supra.

The New York Times, 1 January 1909.

Ibid., 18 November 1915.

Time, 1 February 1926.

A. Mandeville, supra.

S. Daggett, *Railroad Reorganizations* (Boston: Houghton Mifflin, 1908), 333ff.

The New York Times, 18 January 1912.

Obituary, *The New York Times*, 19 June 1939.

The New York Times, 21 April 1926.

Ibid., 16 February 1938.

Ibid., 3 March 1928.

Ibid., 28 May 1935.

'Court Exonerates Frisco's Bankers, Trustees of the Road', *The New York Times*, 14 October 1938; for earlier developments see 'James Speyer Says Losses Offset $1.9 million Stock Profit', *The New York Times*, 30 March 1935; 'Frisco Will Sue for Stock Losses', *The New York Times*, 15 June 1935; 'Frisco Line Denies $11.5 million Fraud', *The New York Times*, 23 October 1935; 'Court Reinstates Two Frisco Suits', *The New York Times*, 28 November 1936; 'Court Denies Motion to Drop Frisco Case', *The New York Times*, 12 February 1938; 'Questioned on Profit in Rock Island Deal', *The New York Times*, 28 August 1938. See the law reports of *Lonsdale v. Speyer* 249 App. Div. 133 (1936); 174 Misc. 532 (1938), affd. 259 App. Div. 802 (1940), rehearing denied 259 App. Div. 863 (1940), affirmed 284 N.Y. 756 (1940); R. Swaine, supra, 339–40; 524 and 186 ICC 137 (1932).

W. Hayes, *Iron Road to Empire* (New York: Simmons-Boardman, 1953), 225.

The New York Times, 4 July 1941.

Ibid., 30 July 1913; 23 May 1916.

A. Martin, *Railroads Triumphant: The Growth, Rejection and Rebirth of a Vital American Force* (New York: Oxford University Press, 1992), 377.

The New York Times, 16 March 1919.

Ibid., 4 June 1937.

'Truman Says U.S. Carriers Need Revision', *New York Herald Tribune*, 21 December 1937.

The New York Times, 5 June 1937 (Speyer), 22 December 1937 (Brown).

Ibid., 19 December 1913.

Chapter 12. Cuban Loans

The New York Times, 13 February 1904; 16 February 1904.

A. Mandeville, supra.

The New York Times, 23 May 1904; 24 July 1904; 19 October 1904.

E. Rosenberg, *Financial Missionaries to the World: The Politics and Culture of Dollar Diplomacy, 1900–1930* (Durham, NC: Duke University Press, 2004), 88.

The New York Times, 30 May 1924.

G. Simons, *Cuba: From Conquistador to Castro* (New York: St. Martin's, 1996), 217.

D. Lockmiller, *Magoon in Cuba: A History of the Second Intervention, 1906–09* (Chapel Hill: University of North Carolina Press, 1938), 203–4.

The New York Times, 13 February 1932; 5 February 1933; 23 August 1933.

Chapter 13. Phillippine Railroads

The New York Times, 20 February 1908.

Ibid., 15 April 1905.

Far Eastern Review, September 1906, 120–4.

The New York Times, 19 December 1915.

G. May, *Social Engineering in the Philippines* (Westport, CT: Praeger, 1980), 160.

Chapter 14. Mexican Railroads

V. Carosso, op. cit., 417.

R. Howes, 'The Development of the Mexican Railway System from Its Early Beginnings Down to 1911' (Master's Thesis, University of British Columbia, 1970), 128.

Ibid., 158, 180–1.

Railway News 90 (21 November 1908), 836; see also F. Powell, *The Railroads of Mexico* (Boston: Stratford, 1924), 175.

D. Pletcher, 'American Railroad Promoters', in C. Gil, *The Age of Porfirio Diaz: Selected Readings* (Albuquerque: University of New Mexico Press, 1977), 90.

Y. Cassis and J. Collier, *Capitals of Capital: The Rise and Fall of International Financial Centres* (Cambridge: Cambridge University Press, 2010), 122.

The New York Times, 19 April 1904.

Ibid., 20 March 1904.

Ibid., 26 October 1904.

'Got Yankee Gold: Mexican Railways Absorbed $50 million of American Capital Last Year', *New York Globe and Commercial Advertiser*, 11 July 1904.

The New York Times, 6 August 1909.

V. Carosso, op. cit., supra, 584–93.

D. Pletcher, supra, 94.

D. Pletcher, *Rails, Mines and Progress: Seven American Promoters in Mexico, 1867–1911* (Ithaca, NY: Cornell University Press, 1958), 313.

M. Bernstein, 'Mexican Mines and U.S. Capital', in C. Gil, supra, 95, 104–5.

Obituary, Elias de Lema, *The New York Times*, 24 November 1928.

T. Fehrenbach, *Fire and Blood: A History of Mexico* (New York: Macmillan, 1973), 551.

C. Kobrak, supra, 211.

J. Hurt, *Empire and Revolution: The Americans in Mexico* (Berkeley: University of California Press, 2002), 100.

J. Rippy, supra, 9, 110.

R. Smith, *The United States and Revolutionary Nationalism in Mexico, 1916–1932* (Chicago: University of Chicago Press, 1972), 208.

The New York Times, 1 December 1921.

Ibid., 5 September 1922; 23 January 1923.

A. Mussachio, *et al.*, *Instability and Credible Commitments: The Case of Post-Revolutionary Mexico*, www. international.ucla.edu/economichistory/summerhill/musacchio.pdf (accessed 9 March 2015).

H. Schacht, *Confessions of the Old Wizard* (Boston: Houghton Mifflin, 1956), 463–4.

A. Martin, *Railroads Triumphant: The Growth, Rejection and Rebirth of a Vital American Force* (New York: Oxford University Press, 1992), ch. 15.

Chapter 15. Brazilian Loans

The New York Times, 13 June 1939.

Ibid.

US Department of Commerce, *Investments in Latin America and the British West Indies* (Washington: G.P.O., 1918), 155.

See I. Bowman, 'Geographic Aspects of the New Madeira-Mamore Railway', *Bulletin of the American Geographic Society* 45 (1913), 275–81.

T. Roosevelt, *Thru the Brazilian Wilderness* (London: John Murray, 1914); C. Gauld, *The Last Titan: Percival Farquhar* (Stanford, CA: Stanford University Press, 1964), 143, 157, n. 37.

'The Fall in Brazil Railway Stock: Statement by Sir Edgar Speyer', *The Times*, 12 November 1912, 19.

J. Rippy, supra, 126ff.

The New York Times, 17 April 1934; 20 June 1934; 1 September 1934; 22 November 1934; 4 September 1935; 17 October 1935; 3 March 1936.

Ibid., 8 November 1935.

'Two New Yorkers Try to Harrimanize South America', *The New York Times*, 22 September 1912. See also 'The Story of the Brazil Railway Co.', *New York Sun*, 8 July 1914; 'A Harriman for South American Railroads', *Journal of Commerce*, 28 August 1912; 'Harriman of South America', *New York Post*, 31 August 1912.

J. Duncan, *Public and Private Operation of Railways in Brazil* (New York: Columbia University Press, 1932), 76, 81, 83.

J. Rippy, *British Investments in Latin America, 1822–1949* (Minneapolis: University of Minnesota Press, 1959), 153.

D. Aldrighi *et al.*, *Financing Pioneering Railways in Sao Paolo: The Idiosyncratic Case of the Estrado de Ferro Sorocabana, 1872–1919*, citing the *Economist*, 31 August 1912; 20 September 1913; 1 October 1913.

C. Gauld, supra, 180, n. 1.

R. Nash, *The Conquest of Brazil* (New York: Harcourt Brace, 1926), 222.

C. Gauld, supra, 113.

Ibid., 129.

H. Tomlinson, *The Sea and the Jungle* (New York: Random House, 1956), 164, 152.

C. Gauld, supra, 236.

Ibid., 239.

C. Gauld, supra, 257, n. 25, 263, 345.

Ibid., 315ff.

B. Russell, *Freedom versus Organization, 1814–1914* (New York: Norton, 1934), 410.

US Department of Commerce, *Investments in Latin America and the British West Indies* (Washington: G.P.O., 1918), 145.

See Speyer to Harrison, 10 and 25 November 1925; Harrison to Speyer, 21 November 1925, National Archives, RG59, DF 1910–29, 832.51 SA 6/47; Hoover to Speyer, 12 November 1925; Speyer to Hoover, 9 December 1925, National Archives, Department of Commerce, Hoover Papers, Box 231, cited in J. Smith, *Unequal Giants: Diplomatic Relations Between the US and Brazil, 1889–1930* (Pittsburgh: University of Pittsburgh Press, 1991).

J. Rippy, supra, 90.

Ibid., 220.

W. Summerhill, 'Railroads and the Brazilian Economy Before 1914', *Business and Economic History* 26:2 (1997), 318ff.

Chapter 16. Bolivian Railroads

F. Pike, *The United States and the Andean Republics: Peru, Bolivia and Ecuador* (Cambridge, MA: Harvard University Press, 1977), 164.

See M. Marsh, *The Bankers in Bolivia: A Study of American Foreign Investment* (New York: Vanguard, 1928), ch. 5 and notes thereto.

H. Blakemore, *From the Pacific to La Paz: The Antofagasta (Chili) and Bolivia Railway Co., 1888–1988* (London: Lester Crook, 1990).

F. Halsey, *Railroads of South and Central America* (New York: Fitch, 1914); C. Tejada, 'The Pan American Railway in Bolivia', *Bulletin of the Pan American Union* 54 (1922), 123–9.

Quoted in M. Winkler, *Foreign Bonds: An Autopsy* (Philadelphia: Ronald Swain, 1933), 57.

E. Emerson, *Hoover and His Times: Looking Back Through the Years* (Garden City, NY: Garden City Publishing Co., 1932), 60–1.

E. Rosenberg, *Financial Missionaries to the World: The Politics and Culture of Dollar Diplomacy, 1900–1930* (Cambridge, MA: Harvard University Press, 1999), 57, 69.

E. Rosenberg, *Financial Missionaries to the World: The Politics and Culture of Dollar Diplomacy, 1900–1930* (Durham, NC: Duke University Press, 2004).

G. Kolko, *The Triumph of Conservatism: A Reinterpretation of American History, 1900–1916* (Glencoe, IL: Free Press, 1977), 144.

R. Swaine, supra, 105.

Ibid., 624, 735; see the opinion at 151 App. Div. 629 (1912); R. Swaine, supra, 107.

Chapter 17. Industrial and Municipal Investments

The New York Times, 5 January 1929; 28 February 1929; R. Swaine, supra, 396–8.

E. Lyons, *David Sarnoff* (New York: Harper, 1966); K. Bilby, *David Sarnoff and the Rise of the Communications Industry* (New York: Harper, 1986); E. Schwartz, *Last Lone Inventor* (New York: Harper, 2003) R. Sanjek, *American Popular Music and Its Business* (New York: Oxford, 1988).

The New York Times, 11 January 1928; 13 June 1939.

Ibid., 24 April 1909.

Ibid., 14 November 1916; *FTC v. Corn Products Refining Co.*, 234 Fed. 964 (S.D.N.Y. 1916).

J. Fowler, *Revenue Bonds* (New York: Harper, 1938), 71. See *The New York Times*, 18, 25 and 26 March 1935, 23 April 1935, 13 March 1936; 19 October 1937.

Ibid., 26.

Chapter 18. Rehabilitating Central Europe

W. Rubinstein, 'Jews Among the Top British Wealth Holders, 1857–1969, Decline of the Golden Age', *Jewish Social Studies* 24 (1972), 73.

G. Hellmann, 'Banker, Old Style', *New Yorker*, 27 February 1932.

The New York Times, 23 July 1916.

Hearings, supra, 610–11; R. Kuczynski, 'Bankers' Profits', supra, 105.

The New York Times, 21 December 1930.

Z. Peterecz, 'Private American Help in the Financial Reconstruction of Central Europe in the 1920s', *Americana* 5:2 (2009), www.americanae.journal.hu/vol.5no.2/peterecz (accessed 9 March 2015). See also Z. Peterecz, 'James Speyer and Hungary: An American Jewish Banker in Anti-Semitic

Hungary in the 1920s', in L. Vadon (ed.), *To the Memory of Sarolta Kreshtol* (Eger: Esterhazy Karoly College, 2009); G. Peteri, *The Role of State and Market in the Regulation of Capital Imports: Hungary, 1924–1932*, Uppsala Papers in Economic History, Research Report No. 14 (Uppsala: Uppsala University, 1987), 15, 22.

Z. Steiner, *The Lights that Failed: European International History, 1919–1933* (New York: Oxford, 2005), 283, 269.

'Proposed Exchange Conference', *The Times*, 16 August 1921.

E. Rosenberg, *Financial Missionaries to the World: The Politics and Culture of Dollar Diplomacy, 1900–1930* (Durham, NC: Duke University Press, 2004), 168.

Sale of Foreign Bonds or Securities in the US, Hearings before the Senate Finance Committee, 72nd Congress,1st Session, Part 2, 616.

Hearings, supra, 610–11; R. Kuczynski, 'Bankers' Profits', supra, 109.

S. Schuler, 'American "Reparations" to Germany, 1919–1933', in G. Feldman (ed.), *Die Nachwirkungen der Inflation auf die Deutsche Geschicte, 1924–1933* (Munchen: Oldenbourg, 1985), 346–8.

The New York Times, 7 January 1932.

'Role of the State and Markets in the Regulation of Capital Imports: Hungary, 1924–31', in G. Peteri, *Revolutionary Twenties: Essays on International Monetary and Financial Relations After World War I* (Trondheim: University of Trondheim, 1995).

The New York Times, 21 December 1928.

Ibid., 22 November 1932; 27 January 1934; 30 June 1934; 26 September 1934; 25 January 1935; 9 July 1935; 19 June 1935; 27 July 1936.

Handbook, supra, 92, 93, 98.

F. Taylor, *The Downfall of Money* (London: Bloomsbury, 2013), 176.

The New York Times, 22 November 1932; 21 April, 5 May, 19 June and 8 December 1934; 19 June, 26 September, 5, 14, 23 and 28 November 1935; 17 July, 24 August, 10 November and 24 December 1936; 6 August 1937; 2 November and 1 December 1938.

Ibid., 7 December 1932.

I. Mintz, *Deterioration in the Quality of Foreign Bonds Issued in the United States, 1920–1930* (New York: National Bureau of Economic Research, 1951), 74–5.

H. Feis, *The Diplomacy of the Dollar: First Era, 1919–1932* (Baltimore: Johns Hopkins University Press Press, 1950), 8, 16.

The New York Times, 23 March 1925.

C. Quigley, *Triumph and Tragedy* (New York: Macmillan, 1966), 608.

The New York Times, 1 November 1941.

Ibid., 20 January 1935; 24 January 1936.

Ibid., 8 September 1934.

Ibid., 2 December 1935.

R. Kaczynski, supra, 150–5.

The New York Times, 14 December 1935, 29 October 1935, 8 March 1937, 1 November 1938.

Hearings, supra, 625; R. Kuczynski, 'Bankers' Profits', supra, 84.

Hearings, supra, 608; R. Kuczynski, 'Bankers' Profits', supra, 103.

'State Department Blamed on Loans to Latin America', *The New York Times*, 7 January 1932.

M. Winkler, *Investments of United States Capital in Latin America* (Fort Washington, NY: Kennikat, 1972, reprint of 1928 edition), 107–8.

US State Department, Decimal File 861.00/5399.

(Dearborn, MI: Dearborn Independent, 1920–1, reprinted by Luke.com, 2012).

Hearings, supra, 626–8; see R. Kuczynski, 'Bankers' Profits', supra, 51, 139, 164–7, 182–203.

Hearings, supra, 623; R. Kuczynski, 'Bankers' Profits', supra, 99.

G. Garrett, 'A Bubble That Broke the World', in R. Formaini (ed.), *The Great Depression and New Deal Monetary Policy* (Washington, DC: Cato Institute, 1980), 22.

W. McNeil, *American Money and the Weimar Republic: Economics and Politics on the Eve of the Great Depression* (New York: Columbia University Press, 1986), 1–2; 17–19.

R. Kuczynski, supra, 140.

Ibid., 82, citing Wiedfeldt to Foreign Ministry, 15 December 1924, in AA, RM/27, vol. 4 and *Journal of Commerce*, 17 October 1924.

John Foster Dulles to Bernard Baruch, 19 March 1945, Dulles Papers, Princeton, quoted in N. Lisagor and S. Lipsius, *A Law Unto Itself: The Untold Story of the Law Firm Sullivan and Cromwell* (New York: Morrow, 1988), 86–7.

H. Feis, supra, 43.

C. Quigley, *Tragedy and Hope: A History of the World in Our Time* (New York: Macmillan, 1966), 534.

Quoted in H. Feis, *The Diplomacy of the Dollar: First Era, 1919–32* (Baltimore: Johns Hopkins University Press, 1950), 41–2.

W. McNeil, supra, 89–90, citing Federal Reserve Bank of New York, Arthur Young Papers, Box 3, Memoranda of 6, 12, and 16 October 1925.

W. McNeil, supra, 91.

R. Kuczynski, 'Bankers' Profits', supra, 29–30.

Ibid., 168.

W. McNeil, supra, citing Lindsay to Austen Chamberlain, 24 October 1927, in *Documents on British Foreign Policy 1919–39*, Series 1A, 4: 57, 59.

I. Mintz, supra, 77, 81ff.

R. Kuczynski, 'Bankers' Profits', supra, 207–24.

W. McNeil, supra, 280, 235.

I. Mintz, supra, 3.

Quoted in R. Kuczynski, 'Bankers' Profits', supra, 31.

W. McNeil, supra, 132.

D. Felix, *Walther Rathenau and the Weimar Republic: The Politics of Reparations* (Baltimore: Johns Hopkins University Press, 1971), 183–4.

(London: Heinemann, 1932), 116.

W. Leuchtenburg, *The Perils of Prosperity, 1914–1932* (Chicago: University of Chicago Press, 1958), 112–13.

L. Einstein, *A Diplomat Looks Back* (New Haven, CT: Yale University Press, 1968), 201. See also K. Jones (ed.), *U.S. Diplomats in Europe, 1919–41* (Santa Barbara: Clio, 1981), ch. 1; P. Cohrs, *The Unfinished Peace After World War I: America, Britain and the Stabilization of Europe, 1919–32* (Cambridge: Cambridge University Press, 2006).

The Times, 2 March 1922, quoted in D. Felix, supra, 127–8.

D. Felix, supra, 184–5.

Morgan to Countess Buxton, 23 March 1933, quoted in R. Chernow, *The House of Morgan* (New York: Simon and Schuster, 1990).

Cables between J.P. Morgan and Co. and Morgan Grenfell, 2, 3, 4 and 6 October 1924, in Thomas W. Lamont Papers, Harvard Business School Library, Box 177, folders 22, 23 and 24, quoted in S. Pak, *Gentlemen Bankers: The World of J.P. Morgan* (Cambridge, MA: Harvard University Press, 2013), at 297, n. 94; see E. Lamont, *The Ambassador from Wall Street: The Story of Thomas W. Lamont* (Lanham, MD: Madison Books, 1994), 210–11.

Morgan to Lamont, 16 August 1922, Lamont Papers, supra, Box 108, folder 13.

Morgan to Grenfell, 5 January 1909, cited in T. Collins, supra, 103, 321, n. 22.

T. Collins, *Otto Kahn: Art, Money, and Modern Times* (Chapel Hill: University of North Carolina Press, 2013), 45–9; O. Kahn, *Of Many Things* (New York: Boni and Liveright, 1926), 89–90.

C. Kobrak, supra, 219.

Ibid., 220.

Quoted in F. Allen, *The Lords of Creation* (New York: Harper, 1935), 316.

Lindsay to Austen Chamberlain, 24 October 1927, *Documents on British Foreign Policy, 1919–1939*, Series 1A, vol. 4, no. 24, p. 57.

Esme Howard to Austen Chamberlain, DBFP, Series 1A, vol. 4, no. 24, p. 43.

R. Kuczynski, 'Bankers' Profits', supra, 1.

The New York Times, 11 April 1934; 29 June, 25 July 1935; 24 May, 23 June 1936.

J. Rippy, supra, 110ff.

R. Perez and E. Wellett, *Clarence Dillon: A Wall Street Enigma* (Lanham, MD: Madison Books, 1995), 28–38, cited in T. Collins, supra, 326, n. 35.

Foreign Bonds or Securities Within the United States, Hearings before the Senate Finance Committee, 72nd Congress, 1st Session (1931), 617.

P. Einzig, *Finance and Politics* (London: Macmillan, 1932), 11.

P. Einzig, *Behind the Scenes in International Finance* (London: Macmillan, 1931), 89–90.

D. Cannadine, *Mellon* (New York: Vintage, 2008), 438.

H. Feis, *1933: Characters in Crisis* (Boston: Little, Brown, 1966), 142, 138–41.

C. Quigley, supra, 370, 891.

Kobrak, supra, 354–5.

G. Myrdal, *An International Economy: Problems and Prospects* (New York: Harper, 1956), 104.

F. Norris, 'Globalization, Measured by Investment, Takes a Step Backward', *The New York Times*, 2 March 2013.

C. Lewis, *America's Stake in International Investments* (Washington: Brookings, 1938), 398.

J. Madden, *et al.*, *America's Experience as a Creditor Nation* (New York: Prentice Hall, 1935), 136.

Sullivan and Cromwell, Office Dinner Notes, 30 October 1935 and 18 November 1937, quoted in N. Lisagor and F. Lipsius, supra, 135ff.

Editorial, 'When Countries Can't Pay Their Debts: A legal battle involving Argentina highlights a growing problem', *The New York Times*, 18 January 2013, A20.

H. Tether, 'Courts Are Right to Hold Argentina to Equal Debt Treatment', *The New York Times*, 18 January 2013.

Ibid., 97.

F. Oppenheimer, 'James Speyer on Money and Railroad Problems', *Magazine of Wall Street* 25 (1919), 435.

Chapter 19. Last Days in Germany

The New York Times, 24 June 1921.

J. Speyer, 'America's Cooperation in European Rehabilitation Primarily Dependent on Europe', *Annals* 102 (1922), 175.

The New York Times, 19 September 1923.

New York Herald Tribune, 29 April 1923.

The New York Times, 28 August 1926.

'Speyer Would Aid Europe With Loans: Says Those Who Talk of War Debt Cancellations Encourage False Hopes', *The New York Times*, 15 September 1926.

The New York Times, 28 August 1927.

Ibid., 7 July 1928.

'More Loans Abroad Urged by Speyer; Against League Control; J.F. Dulles Says We Must Finance Our Exports by Extending Credit to Pay for Them', *The New York Times*, 25 March 1928.

'Extract of 1931 Views by the Nation's Leaders', *New York Evening Post*, 2 January 1931.

'Debt Cancellation Urged on Hoover by James Speyer', *St. Louis Globe Democrat*, 12 January 1930

'State Bankers Hail Moratorium Move', *The New York Times*, 23 June 1931.

The New York Times, 9 September 1931.

Ibid., 15 December 1931.

'Churchill Urges Price Revaluation', *The New York Times*, 9 February 1932.

The New York Times, 23 December 1932.

'James Speyer Hopeful About Conditions in Germany', *German-American Commerce Bulletin*, January 1933.

Speyer to Wilbur K. Thomas, 9 September, 20 October, 30 October 1933; Thomas to Speyer, 11 October 1933; Speyer to Ferdinand Thun, 18 December 1933, George McAneny Papers, Box 135, Seeley Mudd Library, Princeton University.

G. Kupsky, *'The True Spirit of the German People': German-Americans and National Socialism, 1919–1955* (Columbus: Ohio State University Press, 2010), 205, 211.

'Speyer Back: Sees Little War Peril', *The New York Times*, 8 September 1936.

P. Emden, *Money Powers*, supra, 274–7.

H. Feis, *Europe: The World's Banker* (New Haven, CT: Yale University Press, 1930), 65–6.

E. Rosenbaum and A. Sherman, *M.M. Warburg and Co., 1798–1938* (London: Hurst, 1978), 162ff.

'Berlin Speyer Bank Ends "Alger" Romance: Closing of Century-Old Branch Winds Up German Affairs', *New York Post*, 9 August 1934; 'Liquidationsbeschluss Speyer-Ellissen', *Frankfurter Zeitung*, 17 July 1934.

Obituary, *The New York Times*, 9 March 1933.

P. Emden, *Money Powers of Europe*, supra.

Ibid., 398.

A. De Riencourt, *The Coming Caesars* (New York: Coward McCann, 1957), 225.

J. Keynes, *Economic Consequences of the Peace* (New York: Harcourt Brace, 1920), 237–8.

'Speyer Banking Firm to Liquidate', *The New York Times*, 17 July 1934.

A. Barkai, *From Boycott to Annihilation: The Economic Struggle of German Jews, 1933–1943* (Hanover, NH: University Press of New England, 1989), 76.

H. Trefousse, *Carl Schurz: A Biography* (Knoxville: University of Tennessee Press, 1982), 298–9, citing Speyer to Wilbur K. Thomas, 9 September and 20 and 30 October 1933; Thomas to Speyer, 11 October 1933, and Speyer to Ferdinand Thun, 13 December 1933, in George McAneny Papers, Princeton University.

Chapter 20. Philanthropy and Twilight

James Speyer Papers, Chronological Scrapbook, New York Public Library, Manuscripts Division; R. Swaine, supra, 552.

James Speyer to Herbert Beit von Speyer, 31 October 1933; Speyer Papers, New York Public Library.

H. Schacht, *My First Seventy-Six Years* (London: Allan Wingate, 1955), 468. The date is erroneously given as 1930 rather than 1933 in the American edition of Schacht's memoirs, in which the pagination of the reference to Speyer in the index is also in error.

Quoted in a newspaper column by B. Forbes, 'Do Americans Really Want a Dictatorship?', 30 April 1933.

James Speyer to Herbert Beit von Speyer, 3 April 1934.

Speyer Memorandum, 'Facts Relating to Mr. James Speyer's Family', 11 May 1934, Speyer Papers, New York Public Library.

The New York Times, 2 September 1934.

Chronological Scrapbook, James Speyer Papers, Manuscript Division, New York Public Library.

The New York Times, 10 February 1940.

Ibid., 14 March 1941.

F. Stern, *Einstein's German World* (Princeton, NJ: Princeton University Press, 2001), 23, see T. Lenoir, 'A Magic Bullet: Research for Profit and the Growth of Knowledge in Germany Around 1900', *Minerva* 26 (Spring 1988), 66–88.

W. Mosse, *The German-Jewish Economic Elite, 1820–1935* (Oxford: Clarendon, 1989), 319.

M. Goldsmith, 'Paul Ehrlich', in H. Bolitho (ed.), *Twelve Jews* (London: Rich and Cowan, 1934), 63, 78.

M. Marquardt, *Paul Ehrlich* (London: Heinemann, 1949), 127.

E. Baumber, *Paul Ehrlich: Scientist for Life* (New York: Holmes and Meier, 1981), 84, 264.

'James Speyer', *American National Biography* 20 (New York: Oxford University Press, 1999), 471. On the history of the Speyer School, see L. Hollingworth, 'The Founding of Public School 500 (Speyer School)', *Teachers' College Record* 38:2 (November 1936), 119–28; see also 'Fast Learner', *Time* (8 November 1937), 34–5; *Newsweek* (15 February 1936), 30; G. Palmer, 'School for the

Brilliant', *Readers' Digest* 32 (April 1938), 3–4; G. Palmer, 'Junior Brain Trusters', *Literary Digest*, 19 February 1938, 9–11; E. Barnard, 'Learning by Doing Confidently Takes Stock', *The New York Times Magazine*, 27 February 1938; C. Levermore, *Samuel Train Dutton: A Biography* (New York: Macmillan, 1922), 65–70; M. Lehman, 'Miriam Finn Scott', in P. Hyman and D. Moore, *Jewish Women in America* (New York: Routledge, 1997), 222; J. Scheuer, *Legacy of Light: University Settlement's First Century* (New York: University Settlement, 1985). Pictures of the school appear in E. Washington, *Manhattanville: Old Heart of West Harlem* (Charleston, SC: Arcadia, 2002), 58–60.

The New York Times, 24 October 1902.

M. Lepore, *Life of the Clinician* (Rochester, NY: University of Rochester Press, 2001), ch. 3.

S. Swayne, *Orpheus in Manhattan: William Schuman and the Shaping of America's Musical Life* (New York: Oxford, 2011).

'Fast Learners: Speyer School: The Only U.S. Public School for Children Mentally Gifted', *Time* 30:34, 8 November 1937.

'Gifted Children Get Preferences', *The New York Times*, 26 December 1937; T. Harrington, 'He Will Bed Somewhere', *The New York Times*, 30 May 1937; C. Mackenzie, 'The Gifted Child', *The New York Times*, 2 March 1941; Tompkins, 'Schools to Start Two Novel Projects', *The New York Times*, 2 February 1936; E. Barnard, 'Learning by Doing', *The New York Times*, 27 February 1938.

See R. Rudnitski, 'Leta Stetter Hollingsworth and the Speyer School, 1935–1940: Historical Roots of the Contradictions in Progressive Education for Gifted Children', *Education and Culture* 13:2 (Fall 1996), 1–6; H. Hollingsworth, *Leta Stetter Hollingsworth: A Biography* (Lincoln: University of Nebraska Press, 1943); *Notable American Women: 1607–1950: A Biographical Dictionary* (Cambridge, MA: Harvard University Press, 1971), 206ff. See also J. Van-Tassel-Baska, 'The History of Urban Gifted Education', *Gifted Child Today* 33:4 (2010), 18–27; E. Lagemann, *An Elusive Science: The Troubling History of Educational Research* (Chicago: University of Chicago Press, 2002).

The New York Times, 2 February 1941.

Ibid., 2 February 1941; 17 September 1941.

'Youths Search City to Dispute Mayor', *The New York Times*, 11 April 1942.

B. Greenberg and H. Bruner, *Final Report of Public School 500 (Speyer School) to the Board of Education and Board of Superintendents of the City of New York* (New York: Board of Education, 1941), iv, 154.

W. White, 'The Perceived Effects of an Early Enrichment Experience: A Forty-Year Follow-up Study of the Speyer School Experiment for Gifted Students', http://digitalcommons.uconn.edu/dissertations/AA18509511 (accessed 9 March 2015).

C. Gray, 'Streetscapes: The Speyer School; Essentials of Wholesome Living in a "Settlement House" Setting', *The New York Times*, 18 October 1987.

'Postings: Speyer School Building for Homeless AIDS Victims', *The New York Times*, 6 January 1991.

The New York Times, 18 October 2009.

Ibid., 10 and 22 November 1927.

Ibid., 7 November 1941.

Ibid., 25 May 1946.

Ibid., 30 April 1950; 21 January 1951.

M. Kathrens, *Great Houses of New York* (New York: Acanthus Press, 2005).

The New York Times, 5 May 1946.

Ibid., 9 August 1957.

Ibid., 8 December 1944.

Ibid., 4 February 1945; 16 July 1948.

Obituary, Catherine Branchard, *The New York Times*, 10 January 1937; 'Landlord, 80, Feted in House of Genius', *The New York Times*, 16 April 1936.

'Old Speyer Block', *The New York Times*, 4 February 1945.

The New York Times, 12 November 1914.

Ibid., 22 July 1941.

B. Forbes, *Finance, Business, and the Business of Life* (New York: Author, 1915, reprint New York: Kessenger Publishing, 2003), 202.

A. Blackwood, supra.

Obituary, *The New York Times*, 27 September 1935.

Ibid., 11 July 1936.

Ibid., 5 October 1935.

Ibid., 19 June 1939.

Ibid., 15 April 1946.

The New York Times, 28 January 1937; 1 December 1938.

Ibid., 2 September 1935.

H. Friedenwald, *The American Jewish Yearbook* (Philadelphia: Jewish Publication Society, 1911), 144.

The New York Times, 20 January 1912.

Ibid., 16 December 1908.

Ibid., 21 October 1907.

Ibid., 29 December 1919; 26 January 1923.

Ibid., 5 December 1926.

Letter, *The New York Times*, 22 September 1940.

The New York Times, 13 May 1937.

New York Daily Tribune, 5 January 1902.

R. Breitner (ed.), *Advocate for the Damned: The Diaries and Papers of James G. McDonald, 1932–35* (Bloomington: Indiana University Press, 2007), entries of 27 February 1934; 15 March 1934; and 24 May 1934.

P. Roberts, *Jewish Bankers, Russia and the Soviet Union, 1900–1940: The Case of Kuhn* (Loeb and Co.), www.americanjewisharchives.org.publications (accessed 9 March 2015).

J. Dekel-Chen, *Farming the Red Land: Jewish Agricultural Colonization and Local Soviet Power, 1924–1941* (New Haven, CT: Yale University Press, 2005).

TR to Nicholas Murray Butler, 4 June 1903, Library of Congress, Manuscript Division, Theodore Roosevelt Papers, www.theodorerooseveltcenter.org/Research/Digital-Library (accessed 9 March 2015).

The New York Times, 21 December 1936.

'Freedom Pavilion, $250,000 Drive', *The New York Times*, 13 January 1939; see ibid., 'Reich Press Scores Freedom Pavilion', 14 January 1939; 'Pre-Nazi Exhibit at Fair Abandoned', 2 February 1939.

The New York Times, 13 January 1939; 3 May 1941.

'Nazi Denied Right to Collect Speyer Trust Fund Interest', *Tarrytown News*, 29 August 1939; 'Countess a Suicide, Mari Kageneck, Niece of Speyers', *The New York Times*, 24 January 1939.

The New York Times, 1 and 4 November 1941.

'City Museum Nears Completion', *New York Herald Tribune*, 14 December 1930.

M. Page, *The Creative Destruction of Manhattan, 1900–1940* (Chicago: University of Chicago Press, 1990), 175; 'Last of His Line', *Fortune*, August 1931, 80.

The New York Times, 24 December 1931.

Ibid., 21 August 1938.

Obituary, *The New York Times*, 21 December 1961.

The New York Times, 13 June 1939.

R. Barnum, 'Speyer and Cos. Coming Demise Laid to Roosevelt's Program', *Springfield Republican*, 14 June 1939.

Time, 26 June 1939.

The New York Times, 11 and 12 July 1939.

C. Condon, 'U.S. New Haven for Swiss Wealth', *The New York Times*, 5 May 1940, see also ibid., 26 April 1941.

The New York Times, 7 November 1941.

In re Holocaust Victim Assets Litigation, Case No. CV96–4849. In re Accounts of Elisabeth Beit Von Speyer, Claim No. 402250 (S.D.N.Y. 2008).

C. Kobrak, *Banking on Global Markets: Deutsche Bank and the United States, 1870 to the Present* (Cambridge: Cambridge University Press, 2007), 145.

E. Kirkland, *Industry Comes of Age: Business, Labor and Public Policy, 1860–1897* (New York: Holt, 1961), 220.

C. Quigley, *Tragedy and Hope: A History of the World in Our Time* (New York: Macmillan, 1966), 51–2.

M. Rothbard, 'The New Deal and the International Monetary System', in G. Garrett and M. Rothbard, *The Great Depression and New Deal Monetary Policy* (Washington, DC: Cato Institute, 1980), 79, 88–9.

The New York Times, 16 June 1939; 21 December 1940.

J. Livingston, *Origins of the Federal Reserve System: Money, Class, and Corporate Capitalism, 1890–1913* (Ithaca, NY: Cornell University Press, 1989), 88.

The New York Times, 6 September 1907.

G. Kolko, *The Triumph of Conservatism: A Reinterpretation of American History, 1900–1916* (Glencoe, IL: Free Press, 1977), 135, 260ff.

The New York Times, 6 September 1907.

T. Collins, supra, 48.

Learned Hand to Felix Frankfurter, 20 January 1950, in C. Jordan (ed.), *Reason and Imagination: The Selected Correspondence of Learned Hand* (New York: Oxford, 2013), 289–90.

A. Dru, *The Letters of Jacob Burckhardt* (New York: Pantheon, 1955), 147–8, 219.

Epilogue – James Speyer Kronthal

Obituary, *The New York Times*, 5 October 1935.

National Archives, RG 226, Entry 92A, Stack 190, Row 38, Compartment 18, Shelf 5, Box 25.

W. Corson, S. Trento and J. Trento, *Widows* (New York: Crown Publishers, 1999), 11.

E. De Waal, supra, 252.

N. Lisagor, supra, 137.

Kronthal's military record is at the National Archives, RG 226, Entry 224, Box 0422, OSS Personnel Files 1941–45; see also RG 226, Entry 92A, Box 25, Folder 371 (at Stack 190, Row 38, Comp 18, Shelf 5).

N. Petersen (ed.), *From Hitler's Doorstep: The Wartime Intelligence Reports of Allen Dulles, 1942–45* (State College, PA: Penn State University Press, 1996). The Berne mission reports are said to be at the National Archives in RG 226: Entry 88, Bx. 151–52; Entry 90, Bx. 2–7; Entry 108, Bx. 8, 11, 110; Entry 134, Bx. 193, 232; Entry 139, Bx. 60; Entry 99, Bx. 7, 8.

Documents C 00381184 and C 00381186, CIA FOIA Request F-2013–00956.

T. Bower, *Blood Money: The Swiss, the Nazis, and the Looted Billions* (London: Macmillan, 1997), 191, citing National Archives, RG 226, Records of OSS, Entry 90, Box 2, 5/25/45 and RG 260, OMGUS Property Control and External Assets 1945–50 Switzerland, Box 654.

National Archives, RG 226, Entry 88, Box 590, 7 December 1945.

P. Salter, *U.S. Intelligence, the Holocaust and the Nuremberg Trials: Seeking Accountability for Genocide and Cultural Plunder* (Leiden: Martinus Nijhoff, 2009), 134, n. 373, citing S. Aronson, *Hitler, the Allies and the Jews* (Cambridge: Cambridge University Press, 2004), 163, citing Wash-Commo-R&C381–382, National Archives, RG 226, Entry 88, Box 495.

S. West, *The Visual Arts in Germany, 1890–1937* (Manchester: Manchester University Press, 2000), 192.

A. Huneke, 'On the Trail of Missing Masterpieces: Modern Art from German Collections', in S. Barron, *Degenerate Art: The Fate of the Avant Garde in Nazi Germany* (New York: Harry Abrams, 1991).

J. Goebbels, *Die Tagebucher* (Munich: K.G.Saur, 1987), part 1, vol. 3, 325, 401, 403, quoted in Huneke, supra.

Ibid., part 1, vol. 3, 445, 494.

Ibid.

SAINT Stockholm to SAINT London, National Archives, RG 226, Entry 214, Stack 250, Row 64, Compartment 33, Shelf 2, Box 1.

Record Group 226, Entry 190, Box 294, Folder 1366; Detailed Interrogation Reports, 1945–46, Record Group 239, Stack 350, Row 77, Compartment 2, Shelf 07, Boxes 84 and 84A; OSS Subject File, 1940–46, Cabinet 143, M1944, Rolls 93 and 94.

G. Rickman, *Conquest and Redemption: A History of Jewish Assets from the Holocaust* (New Brunswick: Transaction, 2006), 42.

'Freedom Pavilion at Fair Planned to Celebrate Pre-Nazi Culture: Germany Yesterday and Tomorrow, *The New York Times*, 13 January 1939.

'Art Brought to U.S. Despite Nazi Conquest', *The New York Times*, 12 April 1942.

E. Thomas, *The Very Best Men: Four Who Dared: The Early Years of the CIA* (New York: Simon and Schuster-Touchstone, 1995), 352, n. 23.

W. Corson, S. Trento and J. Trento, *Widows* (New York: Crown Publishers, 1989), 11–15. See 'Failings Reported at FBI and CIA', *The New York Times*, 28 May 1989.

Document C 00381221, CIA-FOIA Request F2013–00956.

J. Trento, *The Secret History of the CIA* (Roseville, CA: Forum-Crown Books, 2001), see also H. Albarelli, *A Terrible Mistake* (Waterville, OR: Trine Day, LLC, 2009); *Congressional Record*, US Senate, 7 November 1989 at S.15111 (remarks of Senator Jesse Helms).

B. Hersh, *The Old Boys: The American Elite and the Origins of the CIA* (New York: Scribners, 1992), 476, n. 2, 327.

D. Johnson, *The Lavender Scare: The Cold War Persecution of Gays and Lesbians in the Federal Government* (Chicago: University of Chicago Press, 2006), 34; see also J. Terry, *An American Obsession: Science, Medicine and Homosexuality* (Chicago: University of Chicago Press, 1999), 329, 345–7.

E. Latham, 'Countess Waldeck and Romania', in E. Latham, *Timeless and Transitory: 20th Century Relations Between Romania and the English-Speaking World* (Bucharest: Editura Vremea, 2012), 183ff.

J. Gunther, 'Rosie Knows Everybody', *Saturday Review*, 13 January 1951; M. Cowley, 'Valuta Girl', *New Republic*, 5 December 1934.

R. Waldeck, *Prelude to the Past: The Autobiography of a Woman* (New York: Morrow, 1934).

R. Waldeck, *Athene Palace: The New Order Comes to Romania* (London: McBride, 1942, reprinted Bucharest: Center for Romanian Studies, 1998, Chicago: University of Chicago Press, 2013).

R. Waldeck, *Excellenz X* (London: G. Bles, 1944), also as *Meet Mr. Blank: The Leader of Tomorrow's Germany* (New York: Putnam, 1943).

Human Events, 16 April 1952 and again on 29 September 1960; see *Congressional Record*, 82nd Congress, 2nd Session, vol. 98, part 10, A2654, May 1, 1952.

S. and P. Seagraves, *Gold Warriors: America's Secret Recovery of Yamashita's Gold* (London: Verso, 2005).

www.codoh.com/library/document/764#douglas (accessed 9 March 2015).

Document C 00381172, CIA FOIA Request No. F-2013–000956.

US Army Intelligence File XE 23 55 39 WJ; National Archives, RG263.

G. Douglas, *The CIA and Heinrich Muller*, 3 vols (San Jose: R. James Bender, 1996, 1997, 1998).

G. Sereny, 'Spin Time for Hitler', [London] *Observer*, 21 April 1996.

J. Lukacs, *Churchill: Visionary, Statesman, Historian* (New Haven, CT: Yale University Press, 2002), 60.

J. Loftus, *The Secret War Against the Jews* (New York: St Martin's, 1997); J. Loftus, *Unholy Trinity: How the Vatican's Nazi Networks Betrayed Western Intelligence to the Soviets* (New York: St Martin's, 1998).

B. Howley and J. Loftus, *The Witness Tree* (Toronto: Random House Canada, 2007), 171–80; 256–9; 267–8.

Harvard Art Museum Archives, Paul Sachs Papers, Box 55, Folder 1091, James S. Kronthal.

DRAMATIS PERSONAE

ABBOTT, EDITH (1876–1957): Dean, University of Chicago School of Social Service Administration 1924–57.

ABBOTT, GRACE (1878–1939): Chief of US Children's Bureau, 1921–34, co-draftsman, Social Security Act; see L. Costin, *Two Sisters for Social Justice*.

ADAMS, CHARLES FRANCIS (1835–1915): Descendant of Adams presidents; Chairman, Union Pacific Railroad, 1878–90.

ADDAMS, JANE (1860–1935): Head, Hull House, Chicago 1889–1935; Nobel Peace Prize winner, 1931.

AITKEN, MAX (Lord Beaverbrook) (1879–1964): Proprietor, London *Express*; Minister of Information 1918; Minister of Aircraft Production 1940–1; see A. J.P. Taylor, *Beaverbrook*.

ALEXANDER, FRANZ (1891–1964): Founder, Chicago Institute for Psychoanalysis, 1932.

ALFARO, ELOY (1864–1912): President of Ecuador, 1897–1901, 1907–11.

ANGELL, SIR NORMAN (1872–1967): Author, *The Grand Illusion* (1910); Nobel Peace Prize winner, 1933.

ANGLETON, JAMES JESUS (1917–87): CIA Chief of Counterintelligence 1954–73; see M. Holtzman, *James Jesus Angleton*.

ARENDT, HANNAH (1906–75): Political philosopher; naturalized 1950; see H. Arendt, *The Origins of Totalitarianism*.

ASTOR, CAROLINE (Mrs William) (1830–1908): Arbiter of New York society; see E. Hornberger, *Mrs. Astor's New York*.

AUSLANDER, JOSEPH (1897–1965): Poet, lecturer at Columbia University.

BAKER, GEORGE F (1840–1931): President and Chairman, First National Bank of New York, 1877–1931.

BALLIN, ALBERT (1857–1918): Led Hamburg-American Line, 1886–1918; participant with Sir Ernest Cassel in abortive peace negotiations, 1911–14; a suicide.

BANTOCK, SIR GRANVILLE (1868–1946): English composer.

BARNETT, CANON SAMUEL (1844–1913): Founder of Toynbee Hall settlement house, 1884.

BARUCH, BERNARD (1870–1965): Financier; Chairman US War Industries Board, 1918–19; James Speyer neighbour on Fifth Avenue.

BATTENBURG, PRINCE LOUIS (1854–1921): Naturalized, 1884; First Lord of the Admiralty, 1908–10.

BEATTY, LORD DAVID (1871–1936): First Lord of the Admiralty, 1919–27.

BECKER, HUGO (1864–1941): British composer and violin cellist.

BEIT, SIR ALFRED (1853–1906): Financier, supporter of Joseph Chamberlain, 'King of the Diamond Mines'.

BEIT, ERWIN (1893–1914): Son of Eduard and Lucie Beit von Speyer and nephew of Speyer brothers; died in World War I on German side.

BEIT, HUGO (b. 1930): Grandson of Eduard; came to US 1940; mechanical engineer with Babcock and Wilcox.

BEIT VON SPEYER, EDUARD (1860–1933): Brother-in-law of Speyer brothers and friend of James at Oxford; head of Frankfurt Speyer house.

BEIT VON SPEYER, HERBERT (1889–1961): Son of Eduard; wounded in World War I; came to US 1940.

BEIT VON SPEYER, LUCIE (1870–1918): Sister of Speyer brothers; married Eduard Beit in 1892; her early death attributed to grief at son Erwin's death in war.

BEN GURION, DAVID (1886–1973): Prime Minister of Israel, 1948–53, 1955–63; participant in so-called Blaustein–Ben Gurion agreement with American anti-Zionists.

BENSON, E. F. (1867–1940): English novelist.

BERGMANN, CARL (1874–1935): German Undersecretary of Finance, 1919–1924; Frankfurt Speyer partner from 1924.

BERLIOZ, HECTOR (1803–1869): French composer; pioneer of modern orchestration.

BERNSTORFF, COUNT JOHANN VON (1862–1939): German Ambassador to US, 1908–17; Member of Reichstag, 1921–8; German delegate to preparatory disarmament conference, 1929–31; self-exiled in Switzerland, 1932–39; see R. Doerries, *Imperial Challenge*.

BERTIE OF THANE, VISCOUNT (1844–1919): British Ambassador to Italy, 1903–4; to France, 1905–18; see A. Lennox (ed.), *Diary of Lord Bertie of Thane*.

BETHLEN, COUNT ISTVAN (1874–1947): Hungarian Prime Minister, 1921–31.

BETHMANN-HOLLWEG, THEOBALD (1856–1921): Chancellor of Germany, 1909–17.

BILLEREY, FERNAND (1878–1951): French architect; employed by Grosvenor Estate from 1906.

BILLING, NOEL PENDLETON (1881–1948): Aviation designer; MP, 1916–21; see P. Hoare, *Wilde's Last Stand: Decadence, Conspiracy and the First World War*.

BIZET, GEORGES (1838–75): French composer of, *inter alia, Les Pecheurs de Perles* (1863).

BLACKWOOD, ALGERNON (1869–1951): English novelist, journalist, and traveller; ended career in dried milk business; see A. Blackwood, *Episodes Before Thirty*.

BLAUSTEIN, JACOB (1892–1970): Founder of American Oil Company; anti-Zionist participant in Blaustein–Ben Gurion Agreement; urged creation of UN Commissioner for Human Rights, 1963.

BLINZIG, ALFRED (1869–1945): With Deutsche Bank from 1899; involved in Dawes Plan and settlement of war claims.

BLUMENTHAL, GEORGE (1858–1941): Sent to US by Frankfurt Speyer house; Lazard Freres from 1893; President, Metropolitan Museum of Art, 1934–41.

BODENHEIM, MAXWELL (1893–1954): American poetry, fiction and essay writer.

BONN, LEO (1850–1929): Head of the London Speyer office until 1887.

BONN, WILLIAM (18??–1910): Head of the New York Speyer office, 1865–89.

BOOSEY, WILLIAM (1864–1933): With Chappell and Co., head of Proms after Edgar Speyer; see W. Boosey, *Fifty Years of Music*.

BOUGHTON, Rutland (1878–1960): English composer of ballets and choral dramas.

BOY-ED, CARL VON (1872–1930): German naval attaché and secret agent in US, 1914–17.

BRANCHARD, CATHERINE (1856–1937): Swiss born; Speyer tenant on Washington Square and chateleine of 'House of Genius'.

BRANDEIS, LOUIS D. (1856–1941): Author of *Other People's Money* (1915); Justice, US Supreme Court, 1916–39; see M. Urofsky, *Brandeis*.

BRIDGES, ROBERT (1844–1930): English poet; author *The Testament of Beauty* (1929).

BROWN, HENRY COLLINS (1862–1961): first director, Museum of the City of New York; see H. Brown, *Fifth Avenue Old and New*.

BRUCE, DAVID K. E. (1898–1977): US Coordinator of Information, 1941–2; US Ambassador to France, 1949–52, Germany, 1957–9, Great Britain, 1961–9; see N. Lankford, *The Last American Aristocrat*.

BRYAN, WILLIAM JENNINGS (1860–1925): Democratic presidential candidate, 1896, 1900, 1908; US Secretary of State, 1913–15.

BUCHAN, JOHN, Lord Tweedsmuir (1875–1940): Novelist; MP, 1927–35; Governor-General of Canada, 1935–40; see J. Buchan, *Pilgrim's Way* (1940).

BUCHANAN, THOMPSON (1877–1937): American playwright.

BURCKHARDT, JAKOB (1818–1897): Swiss cultural historian; author of *The Civilization of the Renaissance in Italy* and prescient essays collected as *Force and Freedom*.

BURGESS, FRANK GELLETT (1866–1951): American humourist and illustrator.

BUTLER, JOSEPHINE (1828–1906): English social reformer and advocate of women's higher education.

BUTLER, NICHOLAS MURRAY (1862–1947): President of Columbia University, 1901–45; Nobel Peace Prize winner, 1931.

BYNNER, WITTER (1881–1968): American poet and translator.

BYRD, RICHARD (1888–1957): American polar explorer and aviator; led expeditions to Antarctica, 1928–30, 1933–5.

CARNEGIE, ANDREW (1835–1919): steelmaker, 1865–91; philanthropist noted for endowment of libraries.

CARSON, LORD EDWARD (1854–1935): Barrister; MP, 1892–1921; upheld cause of Ulster; Lord of Appeal, 1921–9; see J. Colvin, *Life of Lord Carson* (3 vols).

CASSEL, SIR ERNEST (1852–1921): Naturalized, 1878; financed enterprises in Egypt, China, Mexico, Turkey and Morocco; named to Privy Council in 1902.

CATHER, WILLA (1876–1947): Author of *My Antonia* among other novels.

CHAMBERLAIN, JOSEPH (1836–1914): Liberal Unionist and advocate of imperial preference, finally adopted as British policy in 1932.

CHANDLER, ALFRED (1918–2007): American business historian; see A. Chandler, *The Visible Hand*.

CHESTERTON, GILBERT KEITH (1874–1936): British writer and Catholic apologist; author, *inter alia*, of *The Napoleon of Notting Hill* and the *Father Brown* mysteries.

CHURCHILL, JENNIE (Lady Randolph) (1854–1921): Mother of Winston Churchill and wife of Randolph Churchill from 1874 to his death in 1895.

COCKBURN, CLAUDE (1904–1981): British journalist; see C. Cockburn, *I, Claude*.

COIT, STANTON (1857–1944): Leader of the Ethical Culture movement in England from 1888.

COLUM, PADRIAC (1881–1972): Irish poet and playwright.

CORSON, WILLIAM R. (1926–2000): Former Marine colonel and critic of Vietnam War; see W. Corson, *The Armies of Ignorance*.

COUGHLIN, CHARLES (1891–1979): American Catholic priest and radio evangelist noted for denunciation of international bankers; silenced by order of the Vatican in 1936.

CRANE, STEPHEN (1871–1900): Author of *The Red Badge of Courage*.

CROCKER, CHARLES (1822–88): President of the Southern Pacific Railroad from 1871.

CROFT, LORD HENRY PAIGE (1881–1947): Leader of the World War I-era National Party, with nine seats in Parliament; junior minister in Churchill government, 1940; see H. Croft, *My Life of Strife*.

CROMER, LORD EVELYN (1841–1917): British proconsul in Egypt, 1883–1907.

CROWLEY, ROBERT T. (1924–2000): Assistant Deputy Director for Operations, CIA.

CURZON OF KEDLESTON (George Nathaniel), MARQUESS (1859–1925): MP, 1885; Viceroy of India 1899–1905; member of War Cabinet, 1915–19; Secretary of State for Foreign Affairs, 1919–24.

DAM, KENNETH (b. 1932): Deputy Secretary of State 1982–5; Deputy Secretary of the Treasury, 2001–3; see K. Dam, *The Law-Growth Nexus*.

DAVIES, SIR HENRY WALFORD (1869–1941): British composer and organist; Master of the King's Music from 1934.

DEBUSSY, CLAUDE (1862–1918): French modernist composer; see V. Seroff, *Debussy: Musician of France*.

DE JOUVENEL, BERNARD (1904–87): French economic historian.

DE LEMA, ELIAS (1863–1928): Head of the Speyer bank in Mexico City at the time of the Mexican Revolution; hid President Madero in his basement prior to his assassination; later economic advisor to the Calles government.

DELIUS, FREDERICK (1862–1934): English composer of German descent.

DE NEUVILLE, OTTO: Partner, Speyer and Co., to 1939.

DE SOTO, HERNANDO (b. 1941): Peruvian development economist.

DEWEY, JOHN (1859–1952): Pragmatist philosopher and advocate of progressive education; professor at Columbia University from 1904.

DIAZ, PORFIRIO (1830–1915): President of Mexico 1876–1911.

DOS PASSOS, JOHN (1896–1970): American writer, best known for his post-World War I US trilogy.

DOUGLAS, LORD ALFRED (1870–1945): Associate of Oscar Wilde; writer and translator.

DOUGLAS, WILLIAM O. (1898–1980): Professor of Law at Yale, 1931–9; Chairman, Securities Exchange Commission, 1936–9; Justice of the US Supreme Court, 1939–75.

DREISER, THEODORE (1871–1945): American realist writer; author of *Sister Carrie* (1900), *An American Tragedy* (1925) and a trilogy of novels based on the life of Charles Yerkes; see W. Swanberg, *Dreiser*.

DREXEL, ANTHONY J. (1826–93): Member of financial house of Drexel and Co. from 1847.

DUKAS, PAUL (1865–1935): French composer of Edwardian era.

DULLES, ALLEN W. (1893–1969): Partner in Sullivan and Cromwell before World War II; headed US Office of Strategic Services in Switzerland until 1945; Director of the Central Intelligence Agency, 1953–62.

DULLES, JOHN FOSTER (1888–1959): Partner in Sullivan and Cromwell; at Versailles peace conference; US Secretary of State, 1953–9.

DVOŘÁK, ANTONÍN (1841–1904): Czech composer of orchestral and operatic works.

EHRLICH, PAUL (1854–1915): German bacteriologist and discoverer of sulfa drugs; Nobel Prize winner in Medicine, 1908; see M. Marquandt, *Paul Ehrlich*.

EINSTEIN, LEWIS (1877–1967): American diplomat; author of *A Prophecy of War* (1913); Minister to Czechoslovakia 1922–32; adviser to Secretary Cordell Hull; see L. Einstein, *A Diplomat Looks Back*.

ELGAR, SIR EDWARD (1857–1934): English composer, best known for *Dream of Gerontius* and *Pomp and Circumstance* march; see R. Anderson, *Elgar*.

ERDMANN, MARTIN (1863–1936): Speyer and Co. partner, retired in 1906.

FARQUHAR, PERCIVAL (1964–53): Latin American railroad promoter; see C. Gauld, *The Last Titan*.

FEIS, HERBERT (1893–1972): Economic adviser to the US State Department, 1931–44; historian; see H. Feis, *Scenes from E.A.: Three International Episodes*.

FISHER, IRVING (1867–1947): Economist; professor at Yale from 1898; known for his work on monetary theory and his sometimes inaccurate economic forecasts.

FISK, JIM (1834–72): American speculator in gold and securities of Erie Railroad; see W. Swanberg, *Jim Fisk*.

FITZROY, SIR ALMERIC (1851–1935): Clerk to the Privy Council; see A. Fitzroy, *Memoirs* (2 vols).

FORBES, BERTIE CHARLES (1880–1954): Journalist and founder of *Forbes' Magazine*; see C. Forbes, *Finance, Business, and the Business of Life*.

FORD, HENRY (1863–1947): Auto manufacturer, sponsor of World War I Peace ship and of books and newspapers attacking Jewry.

FORTAS, ABE (1910–82): Deputy Secretary of the Interior during New Deal; Justice of the Supreme Court, 1965–9, from which he resigned due to financial scandal.

FRANCK, CESAR (1822–90): Belgian-French composer.

FRANKFURTER, FELIX (1882–1965): Professor of Law at Harvard, 1914–39; Justice of the US Supreme Court, 1939–62; unofficial adviser to Franklin Roosevelt.

GARRETT, GARET (1878–1954): American economic journalist; see G. Garrett and M. Rothbard, *The Great Depression and New Deal Monetary Policy*.

GARY, ELBERT H. (1846–1927): Chairman, US Steel Corporation, 1901–27.

GAYNOR, WILLIAM (1849–1913): Mayor of New York City, 1909–13.

GERARD, JAMES W. (1867–1951): US ambassador to Germany, 1913–17.

GIBRAN, KHALIL (1883–1931): Syrian poet resident in the US from 1910.

GILBERT, S. PARKER (1892–1938): Undersecretary of the US Treasury, 1921–3; Agent General for German reparations, 1924–30; partner in J.P. Morgan and Co., 1930–8.

GLASS, CARTER (1858–1946): Congressman, 1902–18; Secretary of the Treasury, 1918–20; Senator, 1920–46; House sponsor of the Federal Reserve Act; Senate sponsor of the Glass-Steagall Act.

GODDARD, HENRY W. (1876–1955): United States District Judge for the Southern District of New York, 1923–54.

GOOSSENS, EUGENE (1893–1962): English conductor and composer, who moved to the US in 1923 and to Australia in 1947.

GOSCHEN, VISCOUNT GEORGE (1831–1907): Chancellor of the Exchequer, 1886–92.

GOUNOD, CHARLES (1818–93): French composer, best known for his *Faust* and *Ave Maria*.

GRAINGER, PERCY (1882–1961): Australian composer; settled in London in 1899 and went to the US in 1914; see M. Gires (ed.), *Self-Portrait of Percy Grainger*.

GRENFELL, LORD EDWARD (1870–1941): Morgan partner in London office from 1904; Director, Bank of England, 1905–40; Conservative MP for City of London, 1922–30.

GRIEG, EDVARD (1843–1907): Norwegian composer best known for his songs and *Peer Gynt*; see F. Benestad (ed.), *Edvard Grieg: Diaries, Articles, Speeches*.

GROMBACH, JOHN V. 'FRENCHY' (1901–82): US Army Intelligence officer.

GRUMBACH, LOUIS (1874–1952): Speyer and Co. partner from 1920.

GURLITT, WOLFGANG (1888–1965): German art dealer whose cache of paintings was discovered in 2013.

GWINNER, ARTHUR VON (1856–1931): Married to Anna Speyer, 1885; with Deutsche Bank from 1893; see C. Kobrak, *Banking on Global Markets*.

HALDANE, VISCOUNT RICHARD (1856–1928): MP, 1885–1911; Secretary of State for War, 1905–12; Lord Chancellor, 1912–15, 1924; Leader of Labour opposition in the House of Lords, 1925–8; see S. Kass, *Lord Haldane: Scapegoat for Liberalism*.

HAND, LEARNED (1872–1961): Judge of the US Second Circuit Court of Appeals, 1921–61; see G. Gunther, *Learned Hand*.

HARKNESS, EDWARD (1874–1940): Oil heir and American philanthropist who gave Harvard University its House buildings.

HARRIMAN, EDWARD H. (1848–1909): President of the Union Pacific Railroad from 1903; involved in struggle with James J. Hill for Northern Pacific.

HARRISON, LELAND (1883–1951): US Assistant Secretary of State, 1922; thereafter minister to Sweden, Uruguay, Romania and Switzerland.

HATHAWAY, GORDON (1925–2013): CIA Deputy Director of Operations for Counterintelligence.

HAYES, CARLTON (1882–1964): Professor of History at Columbia 1919–42; US ambassador to Spain, 1942–5.

HELMS, RICHARD (1913–2002): Chief of Operations, CIA, 1952–8; Director of Central Intelligence, 1966–73; US ambassador to Iran, 1973–7; see T. Powers, *The Man Who Kept the Secrets*.

HENRY, O. (William S. Porter) (1862–1912): Became successful short story writer after jail term for embezzlement during his youth.

HERMANN, FERDINAND (1845–1912): Speyer partner in New York.

HERRICK, MYRON (1854–1929): Governor of Ohio, 1903–5; US ambassador to France, 1912–14, 1921–9.

HERSCHELL, BARON FARRELL (1837–99): Solicitor General, 1880; Lord Chancellor, 1886, 1892–5.

HEWITT, ENID (1896–1978): Daughter of Leonora Speyer by her first marriage, violinist.

HICKS-BEACH, SIR MICHAEL (1837–1916): MP, 1864–1906; Colonial Secretary, 1878–80; Chancellor of the Exchequer, 1885–6.

HILL, JAMES J. (1838–1916): Active in railroads in north-western US and Canada, 1882–1912.

HILL, OCTAVIA (1838–1912): British housing reformer and co-founder of the National Trust.

HIMMELFARB, GERTRUDE (b. 1921): American intellectual historian; see G. Himmelfarb, *The People and the Book*.

HINDENBURG, PAUL VON (1874–1934): Member of General Staff, 1877–1911; Field Marshal, 1914–19; President of Germany, 1925–34.

HIRSCHMAN, JESSE (1876–1939): With Speyer and Co., 1897–1924; railroad director, maternal grandfather of author.

HISS, ALGER (1904–96): Counsel to Nye Committee on Munitions Sales, 1935; Secretary to Dumbarton Oaks Conference and Secretary General, UN Charter Conference; convicted of perjury, 1951; see A. Cooke, *Generation on Trial*.

HOLLINGSWORTH, LETA (1888–1939): Director of the Speyer School; see H. Hollingsworth, *Leta Stetter Hollingsworth*.

HOLST, GUSTAVE VON (1874–1934): English composer of varied works.

HOPKINS, MARK (1813–78): One of four founders of the Central Pacific Railway.

HORTHY, MIKLOS (1868–1957): Austro-Hungarian admiral, 1914–18; Regent of Hungary, 1920–44.

HOUSE, COLONEL EDWARD (1858–1938): Foreign policy adviser to Woodrow Wilson; see E. House, *The Intimate Papers of Colonel House* (4 vols).

HOWLAND, LOUIS (1855–1928): First husband of Leonora Speyer, married in 1894; divorced in Paris in 1902.

HUGHES, CHARLES EVANS (1862–1948): Republican presidential candidate, 1916; US Secretary of State, 1921–6, guided the Washington Naval Conference and the Dawes Plan.

HUNTINGTON, COLLIS P. (1821–1900): Organized Southern Pacific Railroad, 1884; also interested in Central Pacific and Chesapeake and Ohio railroads; see G. Evans, *Collis Potter Huntington*.

HUSSIENI, AMIN AL (1897–1974): Grand Mufti of Jerusalem, 1921–48.

HYDE, JAMES HAZEN (1876–1959): Heir to Equitable Life Assurance Society; subject of financial scandal after costume ball; see P. Beard, *After the Ball*.

IRVING, DAVID (b. 1938): Revisionist historian of World War II; lost libel case in which he was accused of denying the Holocaust.

IRWIN, WILL (1873–1948): American journalist and writer.

ISAACS, RUFUS (Marquis of Reading) (1860–1935): MP, 1904–13; Solicitor General, 1910; Attorney General, 1913; Lord Chief Justice, 1913; special envoy to US, 1918–19; Viceroy of India, 1921–6; Secretary of State for Foreign Affairs, 1931; see D. Judd, *Lord Reading*.

ITTLESON, HENRY (1971–1948): Founder, CIT Financial Corporation.

JABOTINSKY, VLADIMIR (1880–1940): British Zionist leader; founder of Irgun, antecedent of Israeli Likud party; opponent of Peel Commission partition proposal.

JESSEL, SIR GEORGE (1824–83): Solicitor General, 1871–3.

JOHNSON, ELDRIDGE (1867–1948): Founder, Victor Talking Machine Co.

JOHNSON, HIRAM (1866–1945): Governor of California, 1911–17; his failure to support Charles Evans Hughes gave rise to his fateful defeat in 1916 presidential election; progressive and isolationist senator from California, 1917–45.

JULIUS, ANTHONY (b. 1956): British solicitor advocate; see A. Julius, *Trials of the Diaspora*.

JUSSERAND, JULES (1855–1932): French ambassador to Washington, 1902–25; Pulitzer Prize winner for History, 1917.

KAHN, OTTO (1867–1934): Naturalized in US, 1893; with Speyer until 1897, then with Kuhn Loeb; patron of the Broadway stage and president of the Metropolitan Opera to 1931; see T. Collins, *Otto Kahn: Art, Money and Modern Times*.

KELLOGG, FRANK (1856–1937): US Senator, 1917–23; US ambassador to Great Britain, 1924–5; US Secretary of State, 1925–9; Nobel Peace Prize winner, 1929; judge of the Hague Court, 1930–8.

KEYNES, BARON JOHN MAYNARD (1883–1946): Economist, author of *The Economic Consequences of the Peace*; see R. Skidelsky, *John Maynard Keynes* (3 vols).

KING, WILLIAM H. (1863–1949): Democratic Senator from Utah, 1917–41.

KIPLING, RUDYARD (1865–1936): Poet laureate; Nobel Prize winner for Literature, 1907.

KREISLER, FRITZ (1875–1962): American violinist, naturalized in 1943.

KRONTHAL, LEON (1873–1935): Joined Speyer and Co. 1902; partner, 1920–33.

KROSIGK, LUTZ GRAF SCHWERIN VON (1887–1977): German Finance Minister, 1932–45; Chancellor and Foreign Minister under Hitler's Testament, May 1945; sentenced to ten years imprisonment in 1949, amnestied in 1951.

KUN, BELA (1885–1937): Communist Premier of Hungary, March to July 1919; deported to Russia.

LA FOLLETTE, SUZANNE (1894–1983): American libertarian and feminist journalist; art historian.

LAMONT, THOMAS (1870–1948): Member of J.P. Morgan and Co., 1911–48; Chairman of American bankers' committee on Mexico after World War I.

LANDIS, JAMES (1899–1964): Chairman of the Securities Exchange Commission, 1935–7; Dean of Harvard Law School, 1937–46.

LAVAL, PIERRE (1883–1945): French politician; member of Chamber of Deputies from 1914; Minister of Foreign Affairs 1931–2, 1934–6; Premier under Fourth Republic and Vichy, 1931–2, 1935–6, 1942–5; executed for treason; see G.Warner, *Pierre Laval and the Eclipse of France*.

LEFFINGWELL, RUSSELL (1878–1960): Morgan partner; Chairman, Council on Foreign Relations, 1944–53.

LEHMAN, ARTHUR (1873–1936): Senior partner, Lehman Brothers.

LEHMAN, HERBERT H. (1878–1963): Partner in Lehman Brothers from 1908; Lieutenant Governor of New York, 1928–32; Governor of New York, 1932–42; Director of United Nations Relief and Rehabilitation Administration, 1942–6; US Senator, 1946–58; see A. Nevins, *Herbert H. Lehman*.

LEITH, GORDON (1879–1941): In London office of Speyer Brothers, 1900–19; thereafter at Kuhn Loeb London office, 1927–30.

LEPORE, MICHAEL (1910–2000): American physician; see M. Lepore, *Life of the Clinician*.

LIMANTOUR, JOSE (1854–1935): Mexican Minister of Finance under Porfirio Diaz, 1893–1911.

LINDSAY, GEORGE N. (1888–1961): Partner in Speyer and Co., New York, from 1933 until its closing in 1939; father of New York Mayor John Lindsay.

LIST, EMANUEL (1888–1961): Bass with Metropolitan Opera.

LLEWELLYN, KARL (1893–1962): American law professor at Yale, Columbia and Chicago; awarded Iron Cross, Second Class, during World War I; draftsman of the Uniform Commercial Code; see W. Twining, *Karl Llewellyn and the Realist Movement*.

LLOSA, ALVARO VARGAS (b. 1966): Peruvian development economist.

LOW, SETH (1850–1916): Mayor of Brooklyn, 1882–6; President of Columbia University, 1890–1901; Mayor of New York City, 1901–3.

LOWERY, JOHN A. (1833–90): New York lawyer; first husband of Ellin Prince Speyer from 1871.

LUKACS, JOHN (b. 1924): Hungarian-born independent historian; author of, *inter alia, The Great Powers and Eastern Europe* and *A New Republic: A History of the United States in the Twentieth Century*.

LUTHER, HANS (1879–1962): Minister of Finance in Stresemann and Marx governments; Chancellor of Germany, 1926–6; German Ambassador to the United States, 1933–7.

MADERO, FRANCISCO (1873–1913): President of Mexico, 1911–13; shot after being overthrown.

MAGOON, CHARLES E. (1861–1920): Governor of the Canal Zone, 1905–6; Provisional Governor of Cuba, 1906–9; see D. Luckmiller, *Magoon in Cuba*.

MAHLER, GUSTAV (1860–1911): Czech composer and conductor; director, Imperial Opera in Vienna, 1897–1907.

MANDEVILLE, A. MORETON (1880–1952): Editor, *Financial Mail*; author, *The House of Speyer*.

MANN, THOMAS (1875–1955): German novelist; author of *Buddenbrooks* (1901); left Germany, 1933; emigrated to US 1938; naturalized, 1944; Nobel Prize winner for Literature, 1929.

MARSH, MARGARET (1893–1984): Author, *North American Bankers in Bolivia*.

MARSICK, MARTIN (1847–1924): French violinist and composer.

MCCARTHY, JOSEPH R. (1908–57): US Senator from Wisconsin noted for making charges of Communism; censured by US Senate, 1954; see R. Rovere, *Senator Joe McCarthy*.

MCDONALD, JAMES G. (1886–1964): League of Nations Commissioner for Refugees; see R. Breitner, *Advocate for the Damned: The Diaries and Papers of James G. McDonald*.

MCLEOD, Archibald Angus (A. A.) (1848–1902): President, Philadelphia and Reading Railroad, 1890–3; see M. Dion, *The Philadelphia and Reading Railroad: The McLeod Years*.

MEEKER, J. EDWARD (1890–1934): Economist of the New York Stock Exchange.

MEISSNER, OTTO (1880–1953): Chief of Presidential Chancellery under Ebert, Hindenburg and Hitler; acquitted after World War II.

MELLON, ANDREW (1855–1937): Pittsburgh financier interested in steel, oil, aluminum and banking; Secretary of the Treasury, 1921–32; US Ambassador to Great Britain, 1932–3; donor of the National Gallery of Art, Washington; see D. Cannadine, *Mellon*.

MELTCHETT, LORD (1898–1949): Imperial Chemical heir; leader of British boycott of Nazi Germany.

MENCKEN, HENRY L. (1880–1956): American journalist, literary critic and lexicographer; see M. Rodgers, *Mencken*.

MILLHAUSER, DE WITT (1884–1946): Speyer and Co. 1899–1939; Director of Radio Corporation of America.

MITCHEL, JOHN PURROY (1879–1918): Reform Mayor of New York, 1914–18.

MITCHELL, CHARLES E. (1877–1955): President, National City Bank, 1921–33; indicted and acquitted for trading irregularities, 1933, but suffered large civil judgement.

MOLTKE, HELMUT VON (1907–45): Convener of the Kreisau Group planning for post-Hitler German government; see H. Moltke, *Letters to Freya*.

MONTAGU, EDWIN (1879–1924): Undersecretary of State for India, 1910–14; Financial Secretary to the Treasury, 1914–16; Minister of Munitions, 1916; Secretary of State for India, 1917–22.

MONTEREY, CARLOTTA (Hazel Taasinge) (1888–1970): Actress; James Speyer's mistress until 1927; third wife of Eugene O'Neill, 1927–53.

MONTES, ISMAEL (1861–1933): President of Bolivia, 1904–9, 1913–17; Minister to Great Britain, 1911, and France, 1917; exiled, 1920; returned to Bolivia as leader of the Liberal party, 1928.

MORGAN, JOHN PIERPONT (1837–1913): Most prominent US investment banker; joined father's firm, 1856; established J.P. Morgan and Co., 1895; see R. Chernow, *House of Morgan*.

MORGAN JR, JOHN PIERPONT ('Jack') (1867–1943): Head of J.P. Morgan and Co. after 1913; instrumental in floating Allied loans during World War I.

MORGAN, JUNIUS S. (1813–90): With George Peabody, 1854; organized J.S. Morgan and Co., Lindon, 1864, and served as president to 1890.

MORGENTHAU JR, HENRY (1891–1967): US Secretary of the Treasury, 1934–45; sponsor of the abortive and severe Morgenthau Plan for Germany.

MORROW, DWIGHT (1873–1941): Morgan partner from 1914; US ambassador to Mexico, 1927–30; US Senator from New Jersey, 1930–1; father of Anne Morrow Lindbergh.

MOUSSORGSKY, MODEST (1835–81): Russian composer of, *inter alia, Boris Gudunov.*

MOY, COUNT HUGO (1900–38): Partner in Berlin Schlesinger firm which merged with Speyer; married to Pamela Speyer in St Patrick's Cathedral, New York, in 1926 after annulment of prior marriage to cabaret artist Lina Ansels; died in riding accident.

MULLER, HERMANN (1876–1931): German Minister of Foreign Affairs, 1919–20; signed Treaty of Versailles; Social Democratic Chancellor of Germany, 1920, 1928–9.

MUNCH, EDVARD (1863–1944): Norwegian painter.

NEWMAN, ROBERT (1858–1926): Manager of the Queen's Hall and Proms.

NEWMARCH, ROSA (1857–1940): British patron of music and friend of Sibelius; see P. Bullock, *The Correspondence of Jean Sibelius and Rosa Newmarch, 1906–39.*

NICOLSON, SIR ARTHUR (Lord Carnock) (1849–1928): Ambassador to Spain, 1904–6, and Russia, 1906–10; prepared ground for Triple Entente.

NIERENDORF, KARL (1889–1947): Art dealer in Cologne; in Berlin, 1926–33; and in New York, 1936–47, when his collection escheated to the state of New York on his death and was bought by the Guggenheim Museum.

NORMAN, MONTAGU (1871–1950): Governor of the Bank of England, 1920–44.

NORRIS, FRANK (1870–1902): American realist novelist, known for *The Pit* (1903).

NORTHCLIFFE, VISCOUNT (Alfred Harmsworth) (1865–1922): Newspaper publisher, noted for anti-Germanism in years prior to World War I.

OBREGON, ALVARO (1880–1928): Mexican general, 1910–20; President of Mexico, 1920–4.

O'NEILL, EUGENE (1888–1953): American playwright, Nobel Prize winner for posthumously published autobiographical play *Long Day's Journey Into Night*; see L. Sheaffer, *O'Neill: Son and Artist.*

O'NEILL, ROSE (1874–1944): American illustrator and author.

OPPENHEIMER, HENRY (1860–1932): Affiliated with Speyer in New York; later became noted British art collector.

ORPEN, SIR WILLIAM (1878–1931): British painter; appointed official artist during World War I.

PAGE, WALTER HINES (1855–1918): Journalist; Editor of *The World's Work 1900–13*; US Ambassador to Britain, 1913–18.

PAISH, SIR GEORGE (1867–1957): British free trade economist; adviser to Chancellor of the Exchequer Lloyd-George 1914–15; see J. Bolan, *Sir George Paish: Ambassador of Free Trade.*

PAPEN, FRANZ VON (1879–1969): German military attaché in Washington, expelled in 1915; Chancellor of Germany, 1932; Premier of Prussia, 1932–3; Vice Chancellor under Hitler, 1933–4; envoy to Austria, 1936–8, and Turkey, 1939–44; acquitted at Nuremberg largely by reason of a speech he gave at Marburg in 1934 and convicted by German court.

PATTI, ADELINA (1843–1919): Operatic soprano, thrice married.

PECORA, FERDINAND (1882–1971): Naturalized, 1887; New York County District Attorney, 1918–30; counsel to US Senate financial investigation, 1933–4; member of Securities Exchange Commission, 1934–5; Justice of New York Supreme (trial) Court from 1935; author of *Wall Street Under Oath* (1939).

PINERO, SIR ARTHUR (1855–1934): Playwright of comedies; knighted, 1909.

POLGAR, THOMAS (1923–2014): CIA Station Chief, Frankfurt, 1949; Saigon, 1972–5.

POOLE, DE WITT (1885–1952): With Foreign Nationalities Branch of OSS, 1942–5, then with State Department.

POST, CHANDLER (1881–1959): Professor of Art History at Harvard, 1923–50.

PRADO, JOSE (1849–1917): President of Bolivia, 1899–1904.

PRINCE, JOHN DYNELY (1868–1945): Nephew of Ellin Prince Speyer; Minister to Denmark, 1921–6, Yugoslavia, 1926–334; Professor of Semitic Languages, New York University, 1892–1902; of Slavonic Languages, Columbia University, 1915–21, 1933–7.

PROSKAUER, JOSEPH (1877–1971): Noted trial lawyer; adviser to Governor Alfred E. Smith; Judge, New York Supreme (trial) Court, 1927–30; anti-Zionist Jewish leader; see J. Proskauer, *A Segment of My Times.*

PUJO, ARSENE (1861–1939): Congressman from Louisiana, 1903–13; Chairman of House Banking and Currency Committee conducting 'money trust' investigation, 1911–13.

QUIGLEY, CARROLL (1910–77): Professor of History at Georgetown, 1941–76; see C. Quigley, *Tragedy and Hope*.

RATHENAU, WALTHER (1867–1922): Director of electrical companies and of raw materials in Prussian war ministry, 1914–15; Minister of Reconstruction and Foreign Minister, 1921–2; signed Rapallo Treaty with Soviet Union, 1922; assassinated, 1922; subject of the novel *The Man Without Qualities* by Robert Musil; see D. Felix, *Walther Rathenau and the Weimar Republic*.

RAVEL, MAURICE (1875–1937): French composer.

REECE, BRAZILLA CARROLL (1889–1961): Republican Congressman from Tennessee, 1920–30, 1932–47; Chairman, Republican National Committee, 1950–5; critic of private foundations; see F. Bowers, *Republican: First, Last and Always*.

REED, JOHN (1887–1920): American journalist; author of *Ten Days that Shook the World* (1919); buried in the wall of the Kremlin.

RICHMOND, MARY ELLEN (1861–1928): American social worker; founder of Columbia School of Social Work.

ROCHE, ARTHUR SOMERS (1883–1935): American fiction writer.

ROQUES, HEDWIG VON (1896–1973): Daughter of Edward Beit von Speyer; writer on the symbolism of fairy tales.

ROSENBERG, JAMES N. (1874–1970): Chairman of committee to resettle Jews as agriculturalists in the Crimea; later sponsor of the UN Genocide Convention and painter.

ROSENMAN, SAMUEL I. (1896–1973): Judge, Supreme (trial) Court of New York, 1932–43; counsel to Presidents Roosevelt and Truman, 1943–5; see S. Rosenman, *Working With Roosevelt*.

ROSENWALD, LESSING (1891–1979): Sears Roebuck heir; book and art collector.

ROSSINI, GIOACCHINO (1792–1868): Italian operatic composer of *The Barber of Seville* and 38 other operas.

ROTH, JOSEPH (1894–1939): Austro-Hungarian and inter-war novelist and journalist, best known for *The Radetzky March* and *Hotel Savoy*.

ROTHSCHILD, BARON NATHAN (1840–1915): MP, 1865–85; first Jewish member of the House of Lords, 1885–1915; helped finance British acquisition of Suez Canal shares.

RUHLENDER, HENRY (1867–1944): Speyer partner to 1916; director of various railroads to 1935.

RUMBOLD, SIR HORACE (1869–1941): 'The greatest of Britain's ambassadors', per Anthony Eden; head of legations in Switzerland, Poland, Turkey, Spain and Germany; Vice-chairman of Peel Commission on Palestine; see M. Gilbert, *Sir Horace Rumbold*.

RUNCIMAN, VISCOUNT WALTER (1870–1949): MP intermittently from 1899 to 1937; President of the Board of Trade, 1914–16, 1931–7; head of British mission to Czechoslovakia laying foundation for Munich Agreement, 1938.

RUSSELL, EARL BERTRAND (1872–1970): Mathematician, philosopher and political writer; his books in the last category include *Freedom versus Organization, 1815–1915* and *Power: A New Social Analysis*; Nobel Prize winner for Literature, 1950; imprisoned for opposition to World War I.

SAINT-SAENS, CAMILLE (1835–1921): French pianist, organist and composer best known for *Samson and Delilah*.

SALOMON, WILLIAM (1852–1919): With Speyer to 1917; founded Salomon Brothers.

SAMUEL, VISCOUNT HERBERT (1870–1963): Various Cabinet offices in Liberal governments, 1909–16; Home Secretary, 1931–2; High Commissioner to Palestine, 1920–5; leader of Liberal party, 1931–5.

SARGENT, JOHN SINGER (1856–1925): Portrait artist; refused knighthood, 1907, on grounds of his American citizenship; see C. Mount, *John Singer Sargent*.

SARNOFF, DAVID (1891–1971): President and chairman of Radio Corporation of America and affiliates, 1930–70; see E. Lyons, *David Sarnoff*.

SATTERLEE, HERBERT (1863–1947): Morgan son-in-law and biographer; see H. Satterfield, *J. Pierpont Morgan.*

SCHACHT, HJALMAR (1877–1970): President of the Reichsbank, 1923–29, 1933–9; Acting Minister of National Economy, 1934–7; acquitted at Nuremberg.

SCHIFF, JACOB (1847–1920): With Speyer, 1865; joined Kuhn Loeb 1875 and rose to head of firm; active in railroad flotations and loans to Japanese government before and after World War I; declined to make loans to Allies while Czarist Russia was their co-belligerent.

SCHIFF, MORTIMER (1877–1931): Succeeded his father as head of Kuhn Loeb and was in turn succeeded by Otto Kahn.

SCHONBERG, ARNOLD (1874–1951): Austrian modernist composer; naturalized in the United States in 1940.

SCHRODER, JOHN HENRY (1825–1910): Head of banking firm in London bearing his name.

SCHUMAN, WILLIAM (1910–92): American composer; President, Julliard School of Music, 1945–62; Lincoln Center for the Performing Arts, 1962–9.

SCHURZ, CARL (1829–1906): German-American political leader; US Secretary of the Interior, 1877–81; see H. Trefousse, *Carl Schurz.*

SCHUSTER, SIR FELIX (1854–1936): Banker, Union of London and Smith's Bank, 1895–1918; member of Council of India, 1906–16.

SCHUSTER, RICHARD (1879–1950): German Speyer partner, 1906–17, 1921–9; organized Mexican Speyer bank.

SCHWABACH, FELIX (1855–1928): Husband of Henrietta Speyer; National Liberal member of the Reichstag, 1907–18, and of the Prussian Diet, 1908–13; privy councillor; co-author, *North American Railroads* (1906).

SCOTT, ROBERT FALCON (1868–1912): British Antarctic explorer, 1901–4, 1910–12, members of his expedition perishing after having reached the South Pole shortly after Roald Amundsen's expedition; Edgar Speyer founded the Scott Polar Institute at Cambridge in his honour; see H. Ludlam, *Captain Scott: The Full Story.*

SEEGER, ALAN (1888–1916): American poet; enlisted in French Foreign Legion in World War I; author of *I Have a Rendezvous with Death.*

SELIGMAN, EDWIN R. A. (1861–1939): Member of the Seligman banking family; taught at Columbia, 1885–1931, chiefly on public finance.

SERENY, GITTA (1921–2012): Historian and journalist; see G. Sereny, *Albert Speer: His Battle with Truth.*

SHAW, GEORGE BERNARD (1856–1950): Irish playwright and author of books on Socialism; Nobel Prize winner for Literature, 1925.

SIBELIUS, JEAN (1865–1957): Finnish composer, best known for his tone poem *Finlandia*; see E. Jawastjerna, *Sibelius 1904–1924.*

SOKOLSKY, GEORGE (1893–1962): American journalist; supporter of Senator Joseph McCarthy.

SPEYER, EDGAR (1862–1932): London Speyer partner, chairman to 1915 of London Underground Railway; Richard Strauss's opera *Salome* is dedicated to him; see A. Lentin, *Banker Traitor Scapegoat Spy?.*

SPEYER, EDWARD (1840–1934): The 'Elstree Speyer', patron of classical music; came to Britain, 1859.

SPEYER, ELLIN PRINCE (1853–1923): Widow of James Lowery prior to her marriage to James Speyer, she being eight years his senior; co-founder of the University Settlement; founder of the Speyer Animal Hospital.

SPEYER, GEORG (1835–1902): Husband of Franciska Speyer; head of the Frankfurt office.

SPEYER, GUSTAVUS (1825–83): Speyer partner in New York 1845–63.

SPEYER, ISAAC (1748–1807): Head of German Speyer firm; Imperial Court banker.

SPEYER, JAMES (1861–1941): New York Speyer partner and railroad banker, associated with Collis Huntington; co-founder, Museum of the City of New York.

SPEYER, JOSEPH (1783–1846): Head of Lazard Speyer Ellisen, Frankfurt.

SPEYER, LEONORA (nee von Stosch) (1872–1956): Married Edgar Speyer, 1902, after divorce from Louis Howland in Paris; violinist; Pulizer Prize winner for Poetry, 1927.

SPEYER, LEONORA ('Baba') (von Wolff) (1905–87): Daughter of Edgar Speyer.

SPEYER, MICHAEL (1644–92): Banker in Frankfurt.

SPEYER, PAMELA (Moy) (1903–85): Rally car driver; daughter of Edgar Speyer.

SPEYER, PHILIP (1815–76): Founded American Speyer office, 1837.

SPEYER, VIVIEN (1907–2001): Daughter of Edgar Speyer.

SPRING-RICE, CECIL (1859–1918): British Minister to Persia, 1906–8; to Sweden, 1908–13; Ambassador to the United States, 1913–18; see S. Gwynne, *The Letters and Friendships of Cecil Spring-Rice*.

STACKELBERG, CHARLES (1900–83): Speyer partner from 1933 to end of firm in 1939.

STANFORD, LELAND (1824–93): Governor of California, 1861–3; founder of Stanford University.

STANLEY, ALBERT (b. Knattriess) (Lord Ashfield) (1874–1948): MP, 1916; President of the Board of Trade, 1916–19; raised to peerage, 1920; manager of the London tube until 1949.

STAVISKY, SERGE (1886–1934): Naturalized in France, 1914; fraud involving bonds sold by municipal pawn shop of Bayonne discovered 1933, resulting in scandals ending with convictions of nine persons in 1936.

STEED, HENRY WICKHAM (1871–1956): British journalist; foreign editor of *The Times*, 1914–19, and its editor, 1919–22.

STINNES, HUGO (1870–1924): Trained as mining engineer; head of industrial production in Germany during World War I; acquired numerous businesses during period of German inflation; member of the Reichstag, 1920–4.

STRAUS, OSCAR (1850–1926): Member of department store family; US envoy to Turkey, 1887–9, 1898–1900, 1909–10; member of Permanent Court of Arbitration at The Hague, 1902–6; US Secretary of Commerce and Labor, 1906–9; see O. Straus, *Under Five Administrations*.

STRAUSS, LEWIS (1896–1979): Kuhn Loeb partner; Chairman, US Atomic Energy Commission; see L. Strauss, *Men and Decisions*.

STRAUSS, RICHARD (1864–1949): German composer of, *inter alia, Salome, Elektra* and *Der Rosenkavalier*; see M. Boyden, *Richard Strauss*.

STRAVINSKY, IGOR (1882–1971): Russian composer; lived in France from 1910; naturalized in US in 1946.

STRESEMANN, GUSTAVE (1878–1929): Member of Reichstag from 1907; Chancellor of Germany, 1923; Minister of Foreign Affairs, 1923–9; shared Nobel Peace Prize, 1926.

SULLIVAN, SIR ARTHUR (1842–1900): British composer best known for operettas for which W. S. Gilbert wrote the lyrics, and as the composer of *Onward, Christian Soldiers*.

SWAYTHLING, BARON SAMUEL MONTAGU (1832–1911): Financier; MP, 1885; supporter of bi-metallism as member of gold and silver commission, 1887–90.

TAFT, HENRY W. (1859–1945): New York lawyer and counsel to Speyer and Co.; author of books on varied subjects.

TCHAIKOVSKY, PETER (1840–93): Russian composer, especially known for ballet music.

THOMAS, WILBUR (1882–1953): Chairman of the Carl Schurz Memorial Foundation; Secretary, American Friends' Service Committee, 1918–29.

THORP, GABRIELLE (b. 1928): Granddaughter of Edgar and Leonora Speyer; a retired realtor in Norwalk, Connecticut.

TIRPITZ, ALFRED VON (1849–1930): German admiral; State Secretary of Navy, 1898–1916; advocate of unrestricted submarine warfare; fled to Switzerland and published memoirs, 1918; returned to Germany as member of the Reichstag, 1924–8.

TOMLINSON, HENRY M. (1873–1958): English journalist, novelist and essayist.

UNTERMEYER, SAMUEL (1858–1940): Counsel to mining interests and to the Pujo investigation of the 'money trust'; American counsel for Edgar Speyer in his de-naturalization proceeding; Chairman of board framing World War I income tax law.

VALENTIN, CURT (1902–54): German art dealer; naturalized in US, 1937; associated with Alfred Barr of Museum of Modern Art; authorized by Nazi government to sell art for foreign exchange in the US; see Cohan, 'MoMA's Problematic Provenances', *Art News*, 17 November 2011.

VERDI, GIUSEPPE (1813–1901): Italian opera composer, including *Rigoletto*, *La Traviata* and *Aida*.

VILLARD, OSWALD GARRISON (1872–1949): American journalist and author of books on Germany; Editor and owner of *The Nation*, 1918–32.

WAGNER, COSIMA (1837–1930): Daughter of Franz Liszt; developed and was art director of Bayreuth Festival until 1908.

WAGNER, RICHARD (1813–83): German operatic composer and writer on music.

WALD, LILLIAN (1867–1940): Founder of Henry Street Settlement and successfully proposed creation of US Children's Bureau, 1908.

WALDECK, ROSIE (nee Goldschmidt) (1898–1982): Naturalized in the US, 1939; journalist; see R. Waldeck, *Prelude to the Past*.

WALLACE, HENRY A. (1888–1965): Secretary of Agriculture, 1933–40; Secretary of Commerce, 1945–6; Vice President of the United States, 1941–5; Progressive Party candidate for president, 1948; Editor, *New Republic*, from 1946; researcher and writer on agriculture.

WARBURG, FELIX (1871–1937): Banker with Kuhn Loeb; naturalized in US, 1900; philanthropy was his primary interest.

WARBURG, MAX (1867–1946): Head of M. M. Warburg in Hamburg; adviser to the Reichsbank, from 1924; last Jewish banker to leave Germany, 1938; recovered interest in bank after World War II.

WARBURG, PAUL (1868–1932): Naturalized in US, 1911; joined Kuhn Loeb, 1902; helped plan Federal Reserve Board, 1907–14, and was a member of it, 1914–18; warned against speculative dangers in 1929; see R. Chernow, *The Warburgs*.

WASSERMANN, JAKOB (1873–1934): Married Julie Speyer, 1901.

WEILL, SANFORD (b. 1933): Chairman Shearson Loeb Rhoades, 1965–84; Chairman Citigroup, 1998–2003; Advocate of repeal of Glass-Steagall Act.

WEINMAN, ADOLPH (1870–1952): Sculptor; designed 1916 dime and half dollar; monument to Mayor Gaynor in Brooklyn; facade of Post Office Building in Washington, DC; Lincoln Memorial in Madison, Wisconsin.

WELLS, H. G. (1866–1946): British novelist and historian; his *Outline of History* (1920) was hostile to nationalism.

WESCOTT, GLENWAY (1901–87): American fiction writer.

WHITE, MAUDE (1855–1937): English composer; Victorian songwriter; see M. White, *Friends and Memories*; *My Indian Summer*.

WIGGIN, ALBERT (1868–1951): President of Chase Bank; involved in short-selling scandal.

WILDE, OSCAR (1854–1900): Anglo-Irish poet and dramatist; champion of art for art's sake; imprisoned for sodomy, 1895–97, giving rise to *The Ballad of Reading Gaol*.

WILLIAMS, RALPH VAUGHAN (1872–1958): British composer.

WINSOR, ROBERT (1858–1930): Banker with Kidder Peabody.

WISE, JONAH (1881–1959): Leader of American Reformed Jewry; delegate to Evian Conference.

WISE, STEPHEN (1874–1949): Founder of Zionist Organization of America; President of American Jewish Congress; rabbi from 1907 of Free Synagogue, New York.

WISNER, FRANK (1909–65): CIA official; suicide; see E. Thomas, *The Very Best Men*, chs 1–2.

WOLF, LUCIEN (1857–1930): English journalist and historian; involved in drafting of League of Nations minority treaties.

WOLFF, THEODORE (1868–1943): Editor, *Berliner Tageblatt*, to 1933; see W. Kohler, *A Life in Europe, 1868–1943*.

WOOD, SIR HENRY (1869–1944): British orchestra conductor and composer; conductor of promenade concerts at Queen's Hall, London, from 1907; see H. Wood, *My Life of Music*.

YERKES, CHARLES (1837–1905): American financier; imprisoned in Pennsylvania in youth; secured Chicago transit franchises including Loop railway, 1882–99; led syndicate promoting London tube from 1900; subject of trilogy by Theodore Dreiser (*The Financier, The Titan, The Stoic*); Yerkes Observatory in Wisconsin is named in his honour; see T. Sherwood, *Charles Tyson Yerkes*.

YOUNG, OWEN D. (1874–1962): Chairman of the Board, General Electric Corp., 1922–39, 1942–44; Chairman of the 1929 Reparations Conference giving rise to the Young Plan and loan to Germany.

INDEX

de Jouvenel, Bernard 56
De Lima, Elias 114
De Neuville, Otto 181
De Soto, Hernando 120
Debussy, Claude 24, 26
Denaturalization 67
Deutsche Bank 96, 114, 140, 148, 152, 162
Diaz, Porfirio 111
Dillon Read and Co. 149
Disraeli, Benjamin (Lord Beaconsfield) 57,
    63, 167
Dominican Republic 133, 139
Donska, Maria 44
Dos Passos, John 173
Douglas, Alfred, Lord 68
Douglas, Gregory 199
Douglas, William O. 106
Dreiser, Theodore 18, 70, 173
Dresden 137
Dresdner Bank 97, 119
Dulles, Allen 2, 153, 189, 194
Dulles, John Foster 2, 141, 189, 199

Ecuador 20
Edward VII, King 56, 64
Ehrlich, Paul 2, 167
Einstein, Lewis 48, 146
Elgar, Edward 25, 26, 27, 62
Emigration 22
Enabling Law 144
Ephrussi Family 70
Erdmann, Martin 175

Farquhar, Percival 117
Federal Reserve System 139, 144, 185
Fehrenbach, T. R. 115
Feis, Herbert 141, 150
Ferrocaril International 111
Ferrocaril Interoceanic 111
Ferrocaril National 111
Fifteen East Forty-Eighth Street 173
Fight for Freedom 178
Finland 151
First National Bank 127, 139
Fisher, Irving 185
Fitzroy, Almeric 8, 60, 66
Forbes, B. C. 101, 174
Ford, Henry 140
Forster, Kent 78, 178
Fortas, Abe 106
Frankfurt 137, 159
Frankfurt Theatre Choir 168

Frankfurter, Felix 59
Franz Joseph, Emperor 57
Furst, Hans Heinrich 9

Galerie Fischer 192
Galerie Zak 193
Galeries Lafayette 159
Garrett, Garet 141
Gary, Elbert H. 75
Gaynor, William 75
Geneva Convention 60
Genius Row 173
George V, King 54, 63, 68
Gerard, James 76
German High Seas Fleet 2
German Red Cross 177
German Savings Bank 177
German State Railways 13
Germanistic Society of America 177
Gibb, George 17, 50
Gibran, Khalil 70
Gilbert, S.Parker 143
Glass-Steagall Act 139
Goddard, Henry W. 70
Goebbels, Josef 2, 188, 192
Goering, Hermann 2, 188, 192
Goethe House 177
Goldschmidt-Rothschild, Max 9
Goschen, Sir Edward 76
Gracie Mansion 171
Grainger, Percy 27, 29
Great Britain 140, 151, 157, 159
Greece 135, 149
Grenfell, E. C. 19, 76
Grey, Sir Edward 55, 75
Grieg, Edvard 1, 25, 27
Grosvenor Street 24, 47
Grombach, John V. 196
Grumbach, Louis 81, 181
Gualino, R. 161
Guatemala 121, 127
Guayaquil-Quito Railway 20
Gurlitt, Wolfgang 193
Gwinner, Arthur 9, 64, 96, 140

Habenstock 193
Haldane, Lord Richard 57, 75
Halvorsen, Harold 192
Hamburg-America Line 75, 137
Hand, Learned 59, 129, 187
Harding, Warren 136, 155
Harkness, Edward 181

Runciman, Lord Walter 50
Russell, Bertrand 103

St. Louis San Francisco (Frisco) Railway 96, 105
St. Mary's Episcopal Church 179
St. Mary's Free Hospital for Children 86
Salome (Strauss) 26
Salomon, William 8
Samuel, Lord Herbert 50, 59
San Francisco 105
Santa Fe Railroad 99
Sao Paulo 117, 123, 139
Sargent, John Singer 27, 29, 37
Sarnoff, David 128
Satterfield, Herbert 17
Schacht, Hjalmar 115, 138, 143, 149, 150, 157, 163, 165, 196
Schaffgotsch, Hans Ulrich 9
Schiff, Jacob 6, 8, 76, 78, 100, 180, 184
Schiff, Mortimer 76, 115
Schleicher, Kurt 157
Schlesinger-Trier 159
Schoenberg, Arnold 27
Schroder, Lord Bruno 75
Schuman, William 169
Schuster, Richard 81
Schwabach, Felix 11, 97
Scott, Robert 1, Ch. 4, 40
Scott Polar Institute 33
Sea Marge 2, 46, 61
Securities Acts 139
Seeger, Alan 173
Seligman, Edwin R. A. 109, 164
Seligman and Co. 128
Sereny, Gita 199
Sharon Steel 128
Shaw, George Bernard 62
Shearson American Express 186
Sibelius, Jean 29, 31
Siemens and Halske 159
Siles, Hernando 126
Sleepy Hollow Cemetery 87
Smith, Gerald L. K. 140
Smith, Jeremiah 133
Smoot-Hawley Tariff 144
Social Democrats 144
Societe Generale de Photomaton 161
Sokolsky, George 65
Sorocabana Railway 117, 123
Southern Pacific Railroad 99, 104, 107
Soviet Union 151, 180

Speyer, Anna 9, 96
Speyer, Edward 23, 31, 55, 176
Speyer, Ellin Prince 2, Ch. 9, 112
Speyer, Franciske 9, 167
Speyer, Georg 9, 167
Speyer, Gustavus 6
Speyer, Henrietta 11, 97, 164
Speyer, Isaak 5
Speyer, Joseph 5, 6
Speyer, Leonora (von Stosch) 7, 24, Ch. 5, 62, 72, 81
Speyer, Leonora ('Baba') 44, 72
Speyer, Lucie 8, 10, 69, 161, 164, 177
Speyer, Michael 5
Speyer, Pamela 44, 72, 163
Speyer, Philip 6
Speyer, Vivien 44
Speyer Animal Hospital 184
Speyer Code Book 176
Speyer Contract (Bolivia) 125
Speyer Ellisen 6, 23, 159, 161
Speyer Legacy School 170
Speyer School 1, 169
Speyer School of Social Work 168
Speyer Stiftung, Isaac 5
Speyer Taxes (Cuba) 108
Spring-Rice, Cecil 76
Stable Money Association 185
Stackelberg, Charles 181, 188
Staggers Act 107
Stahl, Peter 199
Stanford, Leland 101
Stanley, Venetia 53
Stavisky Scandal 166
Steed, Wickham 56
Stein, Heinrich vom, Baron 172
Steinhart, Franklin 109
Strategic Services Unit 190
Straus, Oscar 76, 140
Strauss, Lewis 180
Strauss, Richard 1, 25, 31
Stresemann, Gustav 141
Strong, Benjamin 186
Strong, William 166
Sullivan and Cromwell 2, 141, 153, 189
Swaythling, Lord Samuel 50
Swiss American Corporation 181

Taasinge, Hazel Neilson (Carlotta Monterey) Ch. 10
Taft, Henry W. 109, 135, 189
Taft, William Howard 75, 108, 110